ARKOGRAPHY

Cultural Geographies + Rewriting the Earth

Series Editors
Paul Kingsbury, Simon Fraser University
Arun Saldanha, University of Minnesota

ARKOGRAPHY

A Grand Tour through the Taken-for-Granted

Gunnar Olsson

University of Nebraska Press | Lincoln

Portions of this book have previously appeared
in *Abysmal: A Critique of Cartographic Reason*
(Chicago: University of Chicago Press, 2007) and
in "Skinning the Skinning," in *Spaces of Danger*,
ed. Heather Merrill and Lisa M. Hoffman (Athens:
University of Georgia Press, 2013), 44–47.

Credit lines and copyright notices for illustrations
without captions appear on pages 194–95.
All illustrations without credit lines were
created by the author.

Library of Congress Control Number: 2019053512

Designed and set in Minion Pro by L. Auten.

Contents

Preface: Who Is Who and What Is What   vii

I

Red River Wake   3

    Enuma elish   3

    Gilgamesh   6

    Genesis   10

    Exodus   23

    Platopolis   35

II

Imaginare Necesse Est   41

    Saussurean Bar   44

    The Republic   48

    Edging   67

    Island of Truth   75

MAPPA MUNDI UNIVERSALIS   87

III

Crystal Palace   111

    Inside   113

    Basement   115

    Prophets' Hall   117

    Ball Room   128

    Attic   135

    Penthouse   144

IV

Archives   163

    Travelogue   163

    Notes   167

    Hidden references   169

    Alpha and Omega   194

    Given   195

Index   199

Preface
Who Is Who and What Is What

Of many guises is the present author, occasionally of two bodies as well. The many in me are nevertheless one, and that explains why the present text might alternatively be read as a *Reader's Digest* equally intended for the neophytes who missed the originals and for the cognoscenti who might wish to be reminded; an orgy of self-plagiarism; an encyclopedia of quotations without quotation marks; plays of oblique references and esoteric combinations; a retrospective exhibition; a fairy-tale for grown-ups; a potpourri of fragrant flowers and popular tunes. More than anything else, though, an impromptu farewell party, Frank Sinatra opening the gates to the *comme d'habitude* of doing it my way.

*

But where does this odyssey take us? To yet another struggle with the relations between individual difference and collective identity, ambiguity and certainty, the one and the many. Most likely a last attempt to understand how we are made so obedient and so predictable, the once promising freshman now an aging emeritus doing his best to keep a battered skiff on course, long-term memories crystal clear, recent events fading away. By all accounts a dangerous genre prone to self-deception, the old man not always aware of his own odor.

The roots reach deeply into the sculptured catechesis of *Mappa Mundi Universalis* (2000) and the book *Abysmal: A Critique of Cartographic Reason* (2007). The differences are nevertheless crucial, for while a decade ago it was the scholar who interpreted the artist, here the perspective is reversed. The hope is in fact that the offered house-tour through the Crystal Palace will cast light on what in *Abysmal* had been too close to be noticed. Here, as elsewhere, the ambitious goal is to weave together what I am writing *about* and the language I am writing *in*.

And so it is that what follows comes in four parts, a text which takes the explorer from the oldest creation epics extant to the power struggles of today; a minimalist attempt to codify the taken-for-granted; a search for the present-day counterparts to the biblical ark, the container that held the commandments and the social relations that came with them. Hence the book's title, a freshly minted word hinting at an as yet unrecognized discipline. Hence also this unusual preface, an anamorphic peek into the *Étant donnés*, a visitor's guide to uncharted territory.

Part I—Red River Wake—tells about a journey down an imagined river, initially on a float tossed around by swift currents, eventually on a slowly drifting ark with an upper deck arranged for learned seminars. Throughout, a search for knowledge with visits first to a ruined library that holds the manuscript of *Enuma elish*, the beginning of everything that was to follow, then to the city of Uruk, home of Gilgamesh, the king who suffered all and accomplished all. Then, finally, some close readings of Genesis and Exodus, formative tales about the relations between mortal people and immortal gods; who is actually who, God an image of Man, Man an image of God? "Will I too die?" asked Gilgamesh after the death of Enkidu. "Here I am," said Abraham on his way to Mount Moriah. "Thou shall have no other gods before me," declared the LORD, Moses's first stone tablet the prototype of every constitutional law, a brilliant blend of political philosophy and social psychology. A chiastic Möbius band is the telling epigram of this first part, the closing emblem a beautiful ark—not, however, the classic box made of acacia wood dressed in gold and with the Testimony inside it, but a shrine of gilded silver with the battered crown and skeleton of King Erik, the latter killed on the doorsteps of the Uppsala Church, sanctified by the locals, ignored by the pope.

No wonder the arkographers wish to pursue their newfound insights, to somehow grasp what it means to be human. And when they are looking out over the widening river they see in the distance the contours of a city and a ship heading their direction. And then with the Athenians' help they find themselves moored to the quay of Platopolis, home of learned academies and schools of navigation. An invitation impossible to refuse.

Part II—Imaginare Necesse Est—reports from a tour de force arranged by owl-eyed Pallas Athene, long ago sprung from Zeus's head, millennia later from my own, Odysseus her favorite among men. Disguised as a seaman she declares that the arkographer must now be turned into an arkologist prepared to learn the laws of logic and geometry, his teachers a triumvirate of mind-surveyors who spent their lives measuring in and marking out the limits of imagination. Much to master, of course, and after many visits to Saussure's Bar and Plato's Republic the explorer finally finds himself in the chapel of the Kantian Island of Truth. Once there he gets so enchanted by its *Mappa Mundi Universalis* that he risks his life to get inside it. While the epigram of this second part pictures Janus, my own favorite among gods, the closing emblem is a stylized map of the Human Territory, the silent Mindscape on one side, the mute Rockscape on the other. An up-to-date merger of the philosopher's good life in the good city and the prophet's design of the sacred tent and whatever might transpire within it.

But what does the arkologist see when he looks out over the foggy ocean? An ontological transformation of the art-work that had so excited him: a crystal palace on a faraway shore. "I'll help you get there," says friendly Athene. A touch of her wand and the arkographer/arkologist is turned into a recreated Icaros who halfway to the other side plunges into the sea.

The god Poseidon quakes a tsunami and the unconscious arkonaut is cast ashore, by no coincidence just outside the Crystal Palace. And who is there to carry him inside and bring him back to life? Grey-eyed Athene, of course.

Part III—The Crystal Palace—a house-tour for which the arkographer, now turned arkotect, had almost drowned, a structure marvelous in its geometric simplicity: a square base of dark granite with a glass tetrahedron growing out of it; from each of the bottom corners a projection-ray that hits the opposite wall at a right angle; a red ruby at the Basement center. Close your eyes and you will see it, some viewers bursting into tears at the sight. Wondrous experience.

Viewed from the inside, however, that same creation becomes the stage of a struggle over who is who and what is what, a throat-slashing war of identity and difference, the rhetoric of the first stone tablet decomposed, a rendering of the original sacrifice, the victim not a bewildered Isaac or a bleating ram but the concept of difference in and of itself. Most remarkably, the corner stones of this magic structure are one with Charles Sanders Peirce's concepts of symbol, icon, and index, customarily turned into the signs of /, — , and = . It is the force of these variously mixed connectives that holds every imagination together, the fix-points of what might one day be recognized as the social scientist's counterpart to the biologist's DNA.

No small order given to an octogenarian. But who else would dare accept it, four floors and a scary Attic to visit: 1/ the Basement with its three corners and a well of blood at the center; 2/ the Sharing Cross Station and the Prophets' Hall with a ceiling à la the Sistine Chapel; 3/ above it a Ball Room full of people conversing about the prepositions *of*, *at*, and *in*, Titian's painting *The Flaying of Marsyas* a crucial example; 4/ an Attic with the three signs gone berserk; 5/ finally a Penthouse as power-filled as the Nicaea palace, the perfect setting for a secular communion, a novel confession and a thank-you speech to Pallas Athene, the goddess who saw it all through. Hence she forms the epigram of this third part, the closing emblem a stylized version of her self-portrait, my own signature as well.

Part IV—Archives—a condensed travelogue hung on the epigrams and emblems previously shown but not discussed. In addition, a list of exhibited pictures and hidden references, virtually all of them in my private library; a piece of erasure poetry; an autopoietic measure of how I myself became whatever I became; the master key to the labyrinth of my own taken-for-granted, Ariadne's thread a total of five-hundred-and-thirty titles long. Easy to get so taken by a particular thought-position (*tankegemak*) that one would rather stay than move on.

Some grateful acknowledgments and a security exit as well. The epigram is Marcel Duchamp's *Fountain*, the best known of his readymades, the emblem a potpourri vase originally owned by Madame de Pompadour, its lid pierced with small holes to let the fragrance out.

∗ ∗ ∗ ∗ ∗

Breathe normally. And you too might experience how the prow shears through the night and into the dawn.

April 1, 2019

— —

/

=

ARKOGRAPHY

I

Red River Wake

The Red River runs, on the right the Rocky Mountain ravines, on the left the misty hills of Mindscape. Near its source—actually a well of sacrificial blood—the stream is wild and narrow, our raft tossed around by swift currents, our bodies soaked, our minds unformed. Echoes from afar: What does it mean to be human? Who are you and who am I, and how do we approach the identity/ difference between us? Whence did we come and whither are we bound?

Godly questions impossible not to pose, the archive of creation epics an obvious place to search for answers, most of them variations on the theme of chaos turned into cosmic order, each and every one a time-bound palimpsest of layered meanings. Glimpses of the past cast onto the future.

Enuma elish

And when the rafters let their eyes wander from the river to the Left Bank what they see is the ruins of what once was a library. Anchors dropped, footprints showing the way to *Enuma elish*, the Akkadian original written sometime between 1700 and 1100 BCE. The prototype of everything that has followed, the *topos* of *topoi*, the germ of cartographic reason. To be precise:

When on high the heaven had not (yet) been named
(And) below the earth had not (yet) been called by a name.

When none of the (other) gods had been brought into being
(When) they had not (yet) been called by (their) name(s), and their
   destinies had not (yet) been fixed.[1]

Nothing but the two coordinates of *above* and *below*, cardinal points waiting
to be inundated by the waters of the abysmal Apsu and the chaotic Tiamat,
the former sweet, the latter bitter. And out of that fetal fluid emerged in
rapid succession a series of deities, the storm-god Ea the most outstanding
among them.

Through a magic spell that same figure puts Apsu to sleep, removes his
crown, and puts it on himself. Thus, having established his position, he
first kills his father and then, on top of the corpse—i.e. *across the abyss*—he
builds a splendid house for himself and his wife Damkina. There, in the
Chamber of Destinies, their son Marduk is conceived, an offspring so
perfectly made that his godhead was doubled, a creation impossible to
understand and too difficult to perceive. Four were his eyes, four his ears.
And when his lips moved, fire blazed forth.

Not merely a coup d'état but a patricide as well, a crime so serious that
Tiamat has no choice but to respond, her army a terrifying force of snakes
with venom instead of blood in their veins, a phalanx of dragons, a sphinx,
a horned serpent, a rabid dog, a scorpion man, a fish-man, a bull-man, and
eleven more of the same kind. As commander in chief she appoints Kingu,
an upstart in whom she invests absolute power and whom she forces to
share her bed lest he run out of control.

As things are rapidly getting out of hand, Ea asks Marduk to be equal
to himself and vanish the chaos-god. The son agrees but only on one
condition: **Through the utterance of my mouth shall I determine your
destinies!** When the other gods hear these words they rejoice; they bless
their Lord, bestow on him the scepter, the throne, and the royal robe,
and send him off to do his duty. Kingu runs away in panic, Tiamat loses
her mind. Face-to-face they come, they close for battle, the Lord spreads
his net and blows a wind that makes the grandmother explode. From the
blood-drenched body parts he then builds the world; out of her eyes well

the Euphrates and Tigris, her nipples become mountains, her crotch the fulcrum of the sky.

The creation of the world thus completed, Marduk reenters the stage in new clothes, the warrior's coat of mail changed to the land surveyor's uniform, his fix-point of fix-points most carefully chosen; as reported, "He crossed the sky to survey the infinite distance; he stationed himself above apsu, that apsu built by [Ea] over the old abyss which now he surveyed, measuring in and marking out." As a result, the Earth was made as the mirror of Heaven, just as Babylon—that most marvelous of cities—was built in the shape of a net.

In honor of himself Marduk, now addressed as OUR KING, then builds himself yet another palace, hosts yet another banquet, delivers yet another speech. To placate his followers, he declares that they will never need to work again, that after next election leisure will be their blessed lot. And to that end he (or is it his father) swiftly creates primeval man, the prototype of you and me, by definition slaves of the gods. Not, however, an invention formed in his own image (for how could anyone be like him), but a savage concoction stirred together from the blood of the slaughtered Kingu, mankind nothing but a black sausage, a *Boudin à la Méseopotamie*; a deed appropriately described as a deed impossible to describe. And at the next celebration the vassals—now totaling six hundred, half of them stationed as watchers of Heaven, the other as guardians of the Earth—were served by black-headed waiters. White ties! Hail to the Chief!

Finally, the seventh and last tablet, which tells how the Absolute gave himself fifty names, so numerous that if attacked he could always hide behind another alias. Not yet a full-fledged tautology, but a step in the same direction. Never catchable as the specific this *or* that, always on the move as an ambiguous this *and* that. Never a logical either-or, always a dialectical both/and—the void-in-between a secluded place reserved for the Ruler.

*

And thus it is that the Babylonians were well aware not only that naming is the name of the game but that the universe of human relations is created in the mirror image of the Court of Power, the king the gods' representative. In addition, they knew that geometry is the instrument with which both land and mind are surveyed, measured, and marked, the rulers the world's best astronomers, the priests masters of the horoscope. Constellations in the sky showing the way on the ground.

Gilgamesh

With that insight forever etched into our minds, we are returning to the raft. Anchors aweigh, the Red River now both wider and calmer than before.

Two days later—or rather a millennium earlier—there it lies before us, the city of Uruk and the *Epic of Gilgamesh*, the so-called standard version poetically rendered by the priest Sîn-lēqi-unninni and in 1845 CE partly recovered from the ruins of ransacked Nineveh, later deciphered by a galaxy of scholars; the oldest masterpiece of world literature, an outstanding study of power, fame, friendship, and the fear of death.

Moored to the quay, the first thing the rafters see is a welcoming sign, an invitation impossible to resist:

He had seen everything, experienced all emotions,
from exaltation to despair, had been granted a vision
into the great mystery, the secret places,
the primeval days before the Flood. He had journeyed
to the edge of the world and made his way back, exhausted
but whole. He had carved his trials on stone tablets,
had restored the holy Eanna Temple and the massive
wall of Uruk, which no city can equal.
See how its ramparts gleam like copper in the sun.
Climb the stone staircase, more ancient than the mind can imagine,
walk on the wall of Uruk, follow its course
around the city, inspect its mighty foundations,
examine its brickwork, how masterfully it is built,
observe the land it encloses.
Find the cornerstone and under it the copper box
that is marked with his name. Unlock it. Open the lid.

Take out the tablet of lapis lazuli. Read
how Gilgamesh suffered all and accomplished all.[2]

Much to admire and much to scorn, for as a young man Gilgamesh behaved
as an arrogant bastard, an absolute monarch beyond reach, one of his duties
to break the hymen of every newly wed bride. People complained and the
gods sensed that his problems were somehow related to the loneliness
that came with his superiority. Hence they asked the mother goddess to
create yet another hero that in everything should be Gilgamesh's opposite
and double image, the only difference being that the former was born as a
two-thirds god, the latter as a two-thirds animal. Made from clay, Enkidu
was the newcomer's name.

It is this savage that Gilgamesh orders Shamhat—prostitute and priestess
in the same threshold-crossing figure—to bring from the wilderness into
the city, the sharing of bodily pleasures the means for doing so. Therefore,
when the two finally meet, she holds nothing back, spreads her legs, puts
him inside her and shows what a woman is. For seven days he stays erect,
and when he wants a break, the animals run away. Shunning the loneliness
he returns to Shamhat certain that his mind has somehow grown larger,
that he now knows something no animal could ever know. Meanwhile
she tells him that in a dream, King Gilgamesh has not only met him but
embraced and caressed him like a wife. In his heart Enkidu too felt the
longing for a true friend.

After this the harlot takes the wild-man's hand and they begin their walk
to Uruk, breaking bread and drinking beer along the way. Once inside
the walls Enkidu finds himself outside one of the wedding houses that
Gilgamesh is about to enter. The two face each other and join for combat.
They wrestle, and bending their backs as bulls, they smash the door-jambs
and shake the walls. A fight of equals, yet at the end Enkidu submits, not,
however, to Gilgamesh's physical strength but to his social authority. They
kiss and they form a friendship that shall last forever.

Enkidu's eyes are filled with tears, and to distract him Gilgamesh suggests
they go on a joint expedition to the Cedar Forest, an area reserved for the

gods, a faraway place guarded by Humbaba, a most fearsome ogre. Ignoring the elders' warnings that the king is too young for the task, indeed that he does not know what he is talking about, they take off. And after a long and dream-filled march they are finally standing face-to-face with the monster. No mercy, for even though the brute pleads for its life and offers to be their slave, it is swiftly slaughtered. High on testosterone Enkidu pulls out its lungs and Gilgamesh cuts off its tusks, trophies to be taken home and hung over the royal bed. In triumph they return to Uruk, the walled-in center of human power, perhaps the first city in human history.

Watching from a distance is Ishtar, in the same figure the goddess of sex and the deity of the city. Her loins on fire she asks Gilgamesh to be her husband, a proposal the latter scornfully rejects; in very plain words he tells her both that she cannot be trusted and that she is not as attractive as she thinks. This in turn makes her so furious that in tears she begs her father Anu to let her borrow the Bull of Heaven, a force fierce enough to do away with Gilgamesh once and for all. First Anu rejects the request (like most fathers he knows his daughter), then, shocked by her earth-shattering threats, he has no choice but to hand over the nose-rope of the frightening creature, an animal known for snorting so forcefully that pits open in the ground, one of them actually swallowing none less than Enkidu, albeit only to the waist. Stirred into action the reformed savage springs up, seizes the bull by its horns, puts his foot on its back, and calls for Gilgamesh. Like a skilled matador the latter presses his dirk between the yoke of the horns and the slaughter spot. The brute falls to the ground, and that is the end of the famous Bull of Heaven.

The following night there is singing and feasting in the palace, the king praising himself as the finest among men, the people greeting him as their savior. Yet he himself is well aware that by killing Humbaba and the Bull of Heaven he has penetrated deeply into the forbidden realm of the gods, violations of holy territory that will not go unnoticed. Indeed they do not, and when the two comrades are asleep, the great gods meet in council, deciding that one of the intruders must die. Given that Enkidu had been created as a two-thirds animal, the choice was easy.

At this stage Enkidu has yet another dream, a nightmare in which he is taken to the Dantesque Netherworld where he can see for himself the kind of existence that awaits him. His arms bound like the wings of a bird, he is led to the house of darkness, a house of dust that those who enter can never leave, rooms of crowned heads with open mouths and empty eye sockets. Drowning in despair he watches himself fade away and finally die. Yet it is not until maggots creep out of the corpse's nose that Gilgamesh accepts what has happened, lays his comrade to rest, and finally understands that death is not an abstract idea but a concrete reality, his friend returned to the clay he had been made from. And when the funeral is over he lets his hair grow, takes off his royal garment and dresses in a lion's skin, and leaves the city to roam the world, his heart full of anguish. "Must I too die, must also I be as lifeless as my friend? Given that I was born as a two-thirds god and a one-third man, will one-third of me disappear and two-thirds go on living? If only I could find the one man whom the gods made immortal, I would ask him how he overcame death."

That man is Uta-napishti, the Babylonian antecedent of the biblical Noah, the only human the gods ever made immortal. When the two finally meet, Gilgamesh is told that even though every individual is doomed to die, mankind will continue to live. To this the Far-Away receives the reply, "As I look at you, Uta-napishti, your form is not different, you are just like me, you are not different at all, you are just like me. So how was it that you found life?"

In response Uta-napishti proceeds to tell the story that no human has ever heard before. That story tells how Enlil, the godly grandfather, was getting so upset with the human noise that he designed a final solution: everyone shall be drowned, not as punishment for their sins, merely because the Mafioso—like Apsu before him—cannot stand them anymore. When the gods in council accept this drastic proposal they also swear that the humans will never be told about the end that is awaiting them. In a language full of ambiguities the secret is nevertheless leaked to Uta-napishti, who promptly builds a big ark onto which he loads everything he thought worth saving. As the gods have ruled, the flood comes and after seven days the ark runs aground. In gratitude for having been saved, Uta-napishti offers a sweet-smelling sacrifice so pleasing that the gods gather like flies around him, eventually declaring him immortal. Pivotal here was Ea's argument that even in the council of gods there must be a proportion between guilt and punishment; as he put it, it would have been better to kill the people by sending a lion, a wolf, or a famine than by opening the floodgates. Perhaps Uta-napishti's immortality may be seen as a damage settlement paid in retribution for the gods' overreaction.

Having heard this story Gilgamesh is sent back home with a most valuable farewell gift—a plant that is supposed to give eternal life to whomever consumes it. Off he is but after twenty leagues he stops for a bath, leaving his clothes on the ground. A snake smells the plant's fragrance, devours it, and promptly discards its old skin and turns young again. No way to retrieve it, so Gilgamesh sits down to weep, wishing he had never embarked on this futile exercise.

* ·

Finally, accompanied by Ur-shanabi, the Babylonian Charon, the king once again sets his eyes on the city that no city can equal. He sees the ramparts gleam like copper in the sun, he climbs the staircase more ancient than the mind can imagine, he walks on the wall of Uruk, he follows its course, inspects its mighty foundations, examines its kiln-fired brickwork. He finds the cornerstone and under it the copper box that is marked with his name. He unlocks it, he opens the lid and rediscovers himself, life by definition a spiraling work in progress. Here Comes Everybody, human erring and condonable.

Genesis

Unmoored again. But now no longer on a raft but on an ark with six decks and a sail made from Gilgamesh's robe, the rumor of the crew's excitement generating a stream of visitors, all of them eager to share their own tales of how *they* became human. The perfect occasion for a series of informal colloquia never held before, The Power of Identity/Difference Formation their forbidding title.

Weaving those conversations together is the close yet intricate relation between story and history, between tales told and lives lived, no participants better qualified than the authors and editors of the Hebrew Bible, a work that took half a millennium to complete, the final result a text with significant differences in style, vocabulary, and content. In that realm much remains uncertain, but it is generally agreed that the oldest portions (perhaps from around 915 BCE) were formulated by a person identified as **J**, or the Yahwist, so called because the writer's god was named *Yahweh*, in English customarily rendered as *The* LORD. The next layer (perhaps two generations younger) is credited to **E**, or the Elohist, who calls the deity *Elohim*, in English simply *God*. While there is general agreement that **J** and **E** composed major parts of what are now known as Genesis, Exodus, and Numbers, the Fifth Book of Moses—Deuteronomy—was added some time in the fifth century by a compiler identified as **D**. Then followed an edition with many additions of much ritual material—the **P** version or the priestly code—which was written after the Babylonian exile. Finally, there was the formidable **R** or Redactor, most likely a committee of learned men who around 400 BCE gave the Torah the shape and content it still has, a story designed to change history, to liberate the Hebrew mind from the memories of the Babylonian Captivity (597–538), and to ensure that the Israelites would never again be corrupted by the idolatry and false gods of their neighbors. From beginning to end a text designed to turn the Hebrews into Jews, to forge a new covenant between Yahweh, the nation, and the individual.

Of the biblical authors **J** is generally considered the master of narrative, dubbed by Harold Bloom a creative writer of Shakespearean proportions, an artist who presented the LORD as a god who acts and speaks like a human person, in that sense very similar to its Babylonian ancestors; anthropomorphic, not alien, is Yahweh. In contrast **E** is more reflective and theological, an interpreter who conceives the potentate as a more remote and less accessible being, an interpretation that hammers home the message of Israel's special role in the history of nations. Finally, there is the **P** code where the narrative is frequently interrupted by detailed ritual instructions. All told a marvelous illustration of how every story changes with the political situation, its main function to shape and legitimate the power of its time, Marduk and the LORD two of a kind. Most commentators agree that the Israelites did not become monotheists until the sixth century.

*

And where does all that take us? To Genesis, of course, and to its two quite different creation epics, the chapter numbering at the same time confusing and revealing. To be precise, chapter 1 is actually younger than chapter 2, the former composed by **E** and **P**, the latter by **J**.

Once again the setting is crucial, for J's text most likely stems from the tenth century BCE, a time when Israel was mightier than ever before and ever after, a realm that extended from the Euphrates in the northeast to the Nile in the southwest, King Solomon its absolute ruler, a figure equally famous for his wisdom and his follies, the latter symbolized by seven hundred wives and three hundred concubines, many of them worshipping not Yahweh but the pagan deities of their homelands. No wonder the LORD got angry, no wonder **J** did whatever s/he could to adjust the story and thereby uproot their deeply held beliefs. It should nevertheless be stressed that **J** never worships Yahweh, merely makes him the leading character of her narrative, more of a hero that cannot be trusted than a holiness to be feared and celebrated.

And thus it came about that the LORD of Genesis 2 created man with his hands, a pinch of dust (or was it clay), a sculpture (or was it a mobile) into which he breathed a breath of life. This primordial art-work he then placed in an orchard with plants that were pleasing to see and fruits that were good to eat, everything except two very special trees free for man to enjoy, those exceptions being the tree of life and the tree of the knowledge of good and evil; as the LORD God directed, "You are free to eat from any tree in the garden; but you must not eat from the tree of the knowledge of good and evil, for when you eat from it you will certainly die."

With these words the stage is set for the rich drama that is to follow, including the story of how the LORD God caused the man (now called

"Adam") to fall into a deep sleep and then took out one of his ribs and closed up the place with flesh. After this the newly created man, *not the LORD*, declares, "This is now bones of my bone and flesh of my flesh; she shall be called 'wo**man**,' for she was taken out of man." Ambiguous is the drama of who did what, one actor forming the body, another giving it meaning. It cannot be said more clearly: to imitate God is to imitate contradictions.

Be this as it may. But as the story continues we learn that the woman meets a serpent—a being more crafty than any of the wild animals—a creature that tempts her not only to eat of the forbidden fruit but to share it with her husband. "You will certainly not die," the serpent assured her, "[but] God knows that when you eat from it your eyes will be opened, and you will be like God," a prospect not to the Almighty's liking. The consequences are well known, the punishment without mercy: with pain will she give birth to her children and with hard labor will he till the thorny ground, day after day until he is eventually returned to the dust from which he had once been made. In the meantime Adam lived a total of 930 years, perhaps an indication that the tenth-century author took the snake's words to be more trustworthy than those of the LORD. As an echo from the Council of Babylonian Gods the latter simply concludes,

The man has now become like one of us [*sic*], knowing good and evil. He must not be allowed to reach out his hand and take also from the tree of life and eat, and live forever.[3]

To that end, the LORD God first banished the unruly couple from the Garden of Eden, then placed a cherub with a flaming sword to guard its entrance.

No peace in sight, though, for in the perpetual war of identity and difference both sides are defined in terms of each other, dialectics the prime mode of analysis. Therefore, as the tension rises, the thought of a final solution lies close at hand. And just as both Apsu and Enlil had gotten annoyed by the noise of their offspring, so God feels much the same, the

Israelite flood essentially a monotheistic appropriation of a polytheistic story. This is what he said:

> I will wipe from the face of the earth the human race I have created—and with them the animals, the birds and the creatures that move along the ground—for I regret that I have made them. . . . I am going to put an end to all people, for the earth is filled with violence because of them.[4]

But like Uta-napishti, who had found favor in the eyes of Ea, now Noah—a righteous man—finds favor in the eyes of the LORD God, builds the ark and crews it as he has been ordered to do. And when the floodgates eventually are opened, everything is wiped out from the face of the earth, everything except Noah and those who are with him inside the ark. Horrifying is the experience, but once they have been cast ashore on Mount Ararat, Noah builds an altar and sacrifices burnt offerings on it, the aroma so pleasing that the younger God (not the older LORD) declares that never again will he curse the ground because of humans. And never again will he destroy all living creatures as he had just nearly done. The result is a covenant that he establishes with Noah and all his descendants, a rainbow in the sky the sign that he is the only god they can trust.

The ties are tightening, for after the flood Noah lived on for another 350 years, a stunning 960-year-old when he passed away. Not immortal, of course, just mature enough not to complain.

*

After a brief break the seminar discussion returns to the alternative creation epic of Genesis 1, *the* speech act of speech acts, a magic show of ontological transformations performed by none less than God himself, like every happening an event anchored in its own time and space.

Most crucial here is that the **P**-text was written after the exile, after the Persian king Cyrus II in 539 had defeated the Babylonians and declared not only that the deported Jews were free to return to their homeland but that they were allowed—indeed encouraged—to worship their own God and rebuild their ransacked temple; a radically different mode of governance, its principles laid out in the so-called Cyrus Cylinder, itself an utterance the United Nations has hailed as history's first declaration of human rights.

Such was the historical setting of Genesis 1, the background to the first chord of one of the most influential stories ever put together: **Let there be! And there is.**

So, what did God do when he created the world? Exactly what every power-wielder has always done, his forerunner Marduk included: divided and conquered. To that end the Almighty followed a three-step procedure through which he *first* captured the formless and empty world in an either-or net of this-and-that, *then* sorted the catch into two heaps, and *finally* named the categories. As the story tells it:

> Now the earth was formless and empty, darkness was over the deep, and the Spirit of God was hovering over the waters. And God said "Let there be light," and there was light. God saw that the light was good, and he separated the light from the darkness. God called the light "day," and the darkness he called "night."[5]

The plain truth is for every reader to read: God did not build the world, he uttered it. No spades, no buckets, no bricks, no nails, no hammers, no quadrants, no architects, no free masons, no bulldozers, no wrecking machines. The sun and moon, water and air, stones and trees, fish and fowl, you and I, everything flowing out of his mouth. Differences born and identities named, politics by definition located in the abyss between one and many, the individual and the collective. No violence, though, for the priestly God had neither friends nor enemies, neither parents nor children. *Factum-verum/Verum-factum*, such was the mantra of Giambattista Vico.

And there was evening, and there was morning. Six days it took for the earth to be completed, man—the very pinnacle of the Godly action—formed in the creator's own image, ruler over the fish of the sea, the birds of the air, and every creature that moves on the ground. Surely an instance of *imitatio dei*, the prototype of mimetic desire, Jacques Lacan obviously not the first to understand the abracadabra that naming is the social practice that gives the real its structure. Simsalabim—human action a magic trick of ontological transformations.

But on the seventh day God looked back at everything he had done. And see, it was very good. Satisfied with himself he leaned back, resting from all the work he had done—not like a Buddha contemplating his own navel, for a navel he did not have—but like a Narcissus puffing on his Freudian cigar. Peace and quiet, the thunderstorm blown away, a rainbow in the sky.

*

Heady adventures these seminars on the upper deck, cultured fields on the Left Bank, wild mountains on the Right. Scorching sun at noon, bright stars at midnight, splendid wine in the evening, the seminarians continuously searching for the safe h(e)aven of stable fix-points. The overwhelming conclusion is that even though the LORD God has neither wives nor concubines, he certainly does have relatives, all of them engaged in a nonending family feud, Apsu and Tiamat (perhaps his parents), Marduk, Isis, Osiris, each and every one claiming their birth rights. In addition, of course, there are the stories of Abraham, Isaac, and Jacob, the three patriarchs who from the outset were torn between the desire of being themselves and the duty of being true to their creator, the God who once made them in his own image. For both sides a no-win situation.

Like other sagas also this one has a beginning, a once-upon-a-time that is closely tied to Abram, the legendary chieftain who about four millennia ago is said to have left his home in the Sumerian city of Ur, at that time a vigorous seat of polytheism and the birth-place of *Enuma elish*. "Leave your country," the LORD told him, "I will show you the way. And as a reward I will bless you with a large family." Off he went, driven by famine, wandering here and there, Sodom and Gomorrah, Haran and Canaan, Egypt the most fateful of all stops along the way, the land where Abraham gave his beautiful wife to the pharaoh claiming she was his sister, a gift that eventually was returned to its rightful owner. No children, though, hence some serious doubts about whether God's promises were to be trusted.

Then, for the fifth time, the Almighty repeats, "I will make my covenant between me and you, and will multiply you exceedingly."[6]

My covenant, not ours! And as a sign that the old man is not an impotent geriatric but a blessed representative, the self-appointed declares that his underling shall no longer be called Abram but Abr*ah*am, no longer merely "exalted father" but "father of many nations," the name of his wife no longer Sarai but Sar*ah*. An astonishing *ah!* if one ever was, a joke, a miracle so remarkable that already in the womb the longed-for child was called Isaac, "he will laugh"; in Abraham's own words, "will a son be born to a man a hundred years old and will a woman bear a child at the age of ninety."

No wonder the Almighty wants a sign that the old man has not just heard his words but understood them as well. As proof he therefore demands that Abraham cut the foreskin of his penis, a non-erasable reminder that it is up to God, not to man, to decide whether there will ever be a great nation. And on that same day Abraham proceeded to carry out the mutilations— first on himself, then on all males of his household, the slaves included, the tree of life-and-death as much off limits to Abraham and Sarah as it once had been to Adam and Eve.

And perhaps it is this prohibition that explains why the follow-up story is not as laughable as the beginning. For with God's remark, "It is through Isaac that your offspring will be reckoned," the stage is set for the *Akedah*, the famous binding that to all Jews, Christians, and Muslims constitutes the ultimate tie between Abraham and the One and Only, at issue nothing less than the issue of mutual trust. Therefore,

Some time later God tested Abraham. He said to him, "Abraham!"

"Here I am," he replied.

Then God said, "Take your son, your only son, Isaac, whom you love, and go to the region of Moriah. Sacrifice him there as a burnt offering on one of the mountains I will tell you about."

Early the next morning Abraham got up and saddled the donkey. He took with him two of his servants and his son Isaac. When he had cut enough wood for the burnt offering, he set out for the place God had told him about. On the third day Abraham looked up and saw the place in the distance. He said to his servants, "Stay here with the donkey while I and the boy go over there. We will worship and then we will come back to you."

Abraham took the wood for the burnt offering and placed it on his son Isaac, and he himself carried the fire and the knife. As the two of them went on together, Isaac spoke up and said to his father Abraham, "Father?"

"Yes, my son," Abraham replied.

"The fire and the wood are here," Isaac said, "but where is the lamb for the burnt offering?"

Abraham answered, "God himself will provide the lamb for the burnt offering, my son." And the two of them went on together.

When they reached the place God had told him about, Abraham built an altar there and arranged the wood on it. He bound his son Isaac and laid him on the altar, on top of the wood. Then he reached out his hand and took the knife to slay his son. But the angel of the LORD called out to him from heaven, "Abraham, Abraham!"

"Here I am," he replied.

"Do not lay a hand on the boy," he said. "Do not do anything to him. Now I know that you fear God because you have not withheld from me your son, your only son."

Abraham looked up and there in a thicket he saw a ram caught by its horn. He went over and took the ram and sacrificed it as a burnt offering instead of his son. So Abraham called the place *The LORD will provide.* And to this day it is said "On the mountain of the LORD it will be provided."

The angel of the LORD called to Abraham from heaven a second time and said, "I swear by myself," declares the LORD, "that because you have done this and not withheld your son, your only son, I will surely bless you and make your descendants as numerous as the stars in the sky and the sand on the seashore. Your descendants will take possession of the cities of their enemies, and through your offspring all nations on earth will be blessed, because you have obeyed me."

Then Abraham returned to the servants, and they set off together for Beersheba.[7]

Although everyone on the ark had been through this text many times before, the seminarians were as taken now as the first time they had met it. What a rich and remarkable text, one of the greatest, most awesome, and most significant stories ever told! All it says without saying, all it shows without showing. Imagination gone berserk, the most penetrating account of power ever formulated. *Here I am* (in some translations rendered as *Behold me*), a *topos* so vague that it might be any-where, hence both no-where and every-where; *some time later*, a *kairos* so fleeting that it could be any-time, hence both always and not at all. A shovel-board of coordinates, a world which is neither here nor there, neither now nor then. No shelter to be found between the *rising early next morning* and on *the third day*, not a word on what transpires in the minds of the father and his son, merely the factual observation that *the two of them went on together*, world literature's most pregnant silence. When Isaac (very little on Isaac) wonders why they carry with them both fire and wood, but no lamb for the offering, he is quieted with the assertion that *God himself will provide the lamb . . . my son*. Not an adjective in sight, not a trace of modality. No local habitation with a name, merely the Elohist's way of saying "I have not the faintest idea of what's going on. Yet it does make more sense to sacrifice a ram than to slaughter your son."

A power-play beyond belief. And perhaps that explains why this pivotal text for so long has functioned as a paradigm of institutionalized terror, a story of how the king must never be mated and the queen never be caught with her pants down, a map of invisible points that never stay put. Most significantly, the critical moment comes with the appearance of the angel, an ambassador rather than the LORD himself, a *Doppelgänger* in case Abraham loses his mind and turns the knife on the perpetrator rather than on the chosen victim. We do not even know whether Abraham ever agreed to God's request, just as we are never told whether he lied or told the truth when he informed his servants *I and the boy . . . will come back to you*—as the text has it "Abraham returned" not "Abraham *and the son* returned." Even Isaac's age has been much debated, most accounts agreeing that the "boy" must have been about thirty-seven years old.

In all the ambiguity one thing seems nevertheless clear. This is that the turning point (not a Greek *katharsis*) comes with the emissary's message that the Almighty has changed his mind, seemingly an order to save the boy's life, in effect the LORD's way of demonstrating that it is he, and he alone, who has the power to overrule every rule: "Stop! Stop! For Heaven's sake! No need to slaughter your son! By showing your willingness to go along, you have already slain yourself!" And after this supreme trial God never speaks to Abraham again, perhaps a sign that it was he, not Abraham, who had learned most about who he is.

Stiffened by fear is Abraham (perhaps Isaac too), for he now understands that whoever has changed his mind once is likely to do so again. How could anyone who bases his credibility on the declaration *I swear by myself* ever be trusted? A knock on the door and the world tumbles down, for even though the trains to Auschwitz and Gulag carried no destinations signs, they all left on time.

Little wonder, therefore, that the angel's cry from heaven has left generations fearing and trembling, indeed that the very point of the *Akedah* is that the LORD's actions are beyond human understanding, therefore a matter of trust (*pistis*) rather than an issue of reason (*dianoia*). Unbearable is the proper word, predictably unpredictable the terrorist's actions, the God of Genesis clearly more concerned with reproduction than with morality. All with a price, however, for when Sarah learned about the horrors that took place at the place the LORD had provided, she promptly passed away, perhaps too distressed by her husband's behavior to want to go on. Abraham, for his part, briefly grieved the loss then found himself another wife (age undisclosed), fathered seven more children, and lived till the age of 175.

*

But who really was Isaac, which role does he play in the narrative of Western culture? Neither a source of comic laughter nor a tragic hero, Isaac is merely a figure so unremarkable that he is the only patriarch that God did not deem worthy of a new name, a novel label functioning as *the* sign of being moved from one category to another.

Whatever the answer, the *Akedah* set the stage for Jacob, Isaac's son, one of the worst crooks ever to be chronicled, yet one of the most richly rewarded, a figure known for betraying both his twin brother and his father, a person so power-hungry that he already in the womb had struggled to be the first to get out (hence his name, "he who takes by the heal" or "he who supplants"). When that tactic failed, he first forced his brother to sell his birthright for a slice of bread and a bowl of lentil soup, then came before their blind father all set on stealing the blessing which had already been promised to the first-born, albeit to be given only after the latter had returned from the open country with the wild game the father loved.

Hardly had the red-haired left, though, before Rebekah, the scheming mother, first dressed Jacob in the smelly clothes of his brother, covered his hands and the smooth part of his neck with goatskin and then prepared a tasty dish that her favorite could bring to the blind man pretending he was not what he was. Thus equipped he

went to his father and said, "My father"; and he said, "Here I am; who are you, my son?" Jacob said to his father, "I am Esau your first-born. I have done as you told me; now sit up and eat of my game, that you may bless me." But Isaac said to his son, "How is it that you have found it so quickly, my son?" He answered, "Because the LORD *your* God granted me success." Then Isaac said to Jacob, "Come near, that I may feel you my son, to know whether you are really my son Esau or not." So Jacob went near to Isaac his father, who felt him and said, "The voice is Jacob's voice, but the hands are the hands of Esau. And he did not recognize him, because his hands were hairy like his brother Esau's hands; so he blessed him. He said, "Are you really my son Esau?" He answered, "I am." Then he said, "Bring it to me, that I may eat of my son's game and bless you." So he brought it to him, and he ate; and he brought him wine and he drank. Then his father Isaac said to him, "Come near and kiss me, my son." So he came near and kissed him; and he smelled the smell of his garments, and blessed him."[8]

The parallels are clear, for just as the farmer Cain had killed the herdsman Abel, so Jacob is determined to get rid of the hunting kinsman. No wonder Esau vowed to kill him. Duly warned Jacob promptly escaped, by all signs as frightened as he deserved to be. He is constantly on the run, but one night, when Esau is too close for comfort,

> Jacob was left alone; and a man wrestled with him until the breaking of the day. When the man saw that he did not prevail against Jacob, he touched the hollow of his thigh; and Jacob's thigh was put out of joint as he wrestled him. Then he said, "Let me go, for the day is breaking." But Jacob said, "I will not go, unless you bless me." And he said to him, "What is your name?" And he said, "Jacob." Then he said, "Your name shall no longer be Jacob, but Israel, for you have striven with God *and* with man, and have prevailed." Then Jacob asked him, "Tell me, I pray, your name." But he said, "Why is it that you ask my name?" And there he blessed him. So Jacob called the place Peniel, saying "For I have seen God face to face, and yet my life has been preserved." The sun rose upon him as he passed Peniel, limping because of his thigh.[9]

Pivotal stories these are, turning points in the relations between the LORD God and his followers. For with what and whom did the runaway actually wrestle? His bad conscience, God, or his twin brother? The narrators do not say, stating only that Jacob had striven first with a man and then with God *and* man, a clear illustration that in Jacob's lust for power nothing is sacred, not even his relation to the LORD himself. Pushed to the limit, the latter defends himself by exercising the double privilege of categorizing and naming, which rests with him and with him alone. *Let there be* and the once-solid man melts into the airy collective of Israel, the second-born no longer an individual human being but a member of a social class, "Israel" itself a word that means "May God prevail." Twelve sons did he father.

Never had anyone seen God's face and survived, yet that feat is exactly what the notorious liar claims to have achieved. In the eyes of the Almighty the blasphemy of blasphemies, in the ears of the outsider a piece of self-aggrandizing propaganda. Which persecutor would take such a well-connected figure to court? And which witch-hunter would in a time of crisis pick a limping patriarch as his healing scapegoat?

Exodus

The lesson from the Identity/Difference seminars is that NAMING is the name of the game, "Un coup de dés" played with loaded dice, the rules set to guarantee that in the long run all gains go to the croupier. But by which rules is the game played? Who wrote them, and how did they get codified? And most importantly: How and why are they accepted, honored, and obeyed?

These are the questions the seminarians are giving themselves, In Search of the Social DNA or Remembrance of Things Past the title of their deliberations. No small order.

*

Welcome, therefore, to yet another colloquium about the question of how we are made so obedient and so predictable, no document more foundational than the Ten Commandments. Beware, though, for the exegetes are often distinguishing not ten or twelve of them (one for each finger or one for every moon), but a staggering total of 613, 365 phrased in the positive, the rest in the negative. Since J never refers to them, the list was almost certainly composed by D, albeit with antecedents from the seventh century BCE, perhaps from the thirteenth and the time of Moses himself. The issue of internal numbering remains unsettled as well, different congregations following different conventions.

Highest on the seminarians' agenda is the political question of how and why a particular voice is believed and obeyed, an amalgam of political philosophy and social psychology, jurisprudence by definition the study of codified social relations. And for that reason the Ten Commandments are usually divided into two groups such that the prologue and the three first laws govern the relations between God and man, the remaining seven the relations between man and man; *in toto* a two-volume law book where the first part covers the constitutional law while the second deals with the civil and criminal laws.

Although the different statements are intimately related, the upper-deck seminarians are focusing on the paragraphs of Exodus 20:1–12 and Deuteronomy 5:6–15. Given its lapidary style and extraordinary economy—one prologue and three paragraphs—this self-referential document is often considered the most genial codification of power ever formulated, *the* constitutional law par excellence, a trinity with God in one corner, the Israelites in another, Moses in the third. From beginning to end a rich and contradictory story, countless authors involved.

But what does it mean to be an author, a figure of authority, a person whose task is to invent and to cause something to come about, every story a reflection in the mirror of its own time and place? Through which social processes is the tain of those mirrors formed and polished? How could a twenty-first-century writer ever grasp the thoughts-and-actions of Moses, Pharaoh, even God himself, if s/he did not approach them **as if** they were like him/herself? Why would an imagined patriarch be more trustworthy than a contemporary president, especially as the terms "truth" and "trust" are etymologically closely related, their common root in the Indo-European word *deru*, which means "tree." The challenge is to understand, not to accuse or to criticize.

Be this as it may, for the point is that in times of crisis it is the first stone tablet that tells the RULER how to rule, and that is regardless of whether the potentate happens to be a Machiavellian Prince, a dictatorial Führer, or an elected Prime Minister; a Jew, a Christian, or a Muslim; a communist, a fascist, a capitalist, a social democrat, or an ardent believer in anything else. A rhetorical masterpiece constantly reinforced, in the following section quoted from the Authorized King James Version originally published in

1611, by its own admission a text "containing the Old and New Testaments translated out of the original tongues and with the former translations diligently composed and revised by His Majesty's special command."

*

It is hard to imagine a more power-filled statement than this Constitutional Law, especially as it was God himself (albeit via Moses) who spake the words of the **prologue**:

> **I am the LORD thy God, which have brought thee out of the land of Egypt, out of the house of bondage.**

Each and every word pregnant with meaning, speech act and self-reference knotted together into a net of internal relations: (1) the self of self-representation condensed into the name *I am*; (2) the power beyond power manifested by the definite description *your* LORD; (3) the legitimating reminder that it was *I who brought you out of the house of bondage.*

I and thou inseparably bound together by the shared experience of the slavery and the long march. Come election time and the chants are echoing through the halls and bouncing off the screens. "You never had it so good (alternatively never so bad). Be calm Citizen K, for through my acts I have already shown that I am your shield and your great reward. Come with me to the land of Nowhere, the Utopia that I have personally designed. Blood, sweat, and tears along the way, milk and honey once we get there. Read my lips, scrutinize my record." Lenin before Lenin, Mao before Mao, Trump before Trump. The eternal flame every evening rekindled at the grave of the unknown soldier. *Honi soit qui mal y pense.*

From this mantra the lawmaker moves directly to §1:

> **Thou shalt have no other gods before me.**

Yet another return to the original summons, the idea that there is one God, one and only one, a proposition as stunning now as when it was first uttered. For what these eight words are effectively decreeing is that **I** shall be your dictator, I and no one else. Wherever this Almighty happens to be—and by definition he is every*where*—he rules over every*one* and every-*thing*: "I am your LORD, you are my servant." Monolatry at the beginning, monotheism in the end, YHWH a jealous ruler known for tolerating no opposition. Remember, therefore, my child, that you are nothing but a cog in the LORD's machinery.

The genius who first coined the phrase that there must be no one before (or, according to some translations, "beside") him was well aware that in the surrounding lands there were many gods and many princes. In deed it was exactly that type of chaos the sojourner was so eager to get away from that he submitted his entire future to a power-holder he knew nothing about. At the same time the brilliant lawmaker would not have been so brilliant had he not foreseen that whoever declares himself to be your dictator is bound for trouble. And since knowledge, understanding, critique, and reasoned revolt are exercises in translation, he also realized that every translation must be carefully monitored and controlled. Thus—given his deep insights into the mechanisms of rhetoric—he built a two-tiered defense system with both a wall and a moat, the former (**§2a**) constructed as a ban on the (mis) use of metaphor, the latter (**§2b**) as a guard against runaway metonymies, the former trope functioning as the agitator's detonator, the latter as his dynamite. And there it is, **§2a**:

> **Thou shalt not make unto thee any graven image, or any likeness of anything that is in heaven above, or is in the earth beneath, or that is in the water under the earth. Thou shalt not bow down thyself to them, nor serve them: for I the LORD thy God am a jealous God, visiting the iniquity of the fathers unto the third and fourth generation of them that hate me; and showing mercy unto thousands of them that love me and keep my commandments.**

A most delicate dialectic, especially as the Hebrew term for "image" refers more to God's dwelling place than to the pictorial representation of his invisible being, more to the materiality of the burning bush than to its socio-psychological meaning. It follows that if you tell me *where* you are, I shall tell you *who* and *what* you are. At the same time the believer is cautioned that whenever s/he tries to make the invisible visible, s/he runs the risk of misplaced concreteness, not merely of reifying the deified but of deifying the reified. These warnings notwithstanding the graven image remains the prototype of mimetic representation, the master key to idolatry and the doors of competing ideologies. The obvious purpose of §2a is to block that road to insight, to stifle every upheaval in its infancy.

Still there are loopholes. And that explains why there is also a prohibition against falsified tales, empty promises, stinging comedy, and laughable farce—**§2b**:

Thou shalt not take the name of the LORD thy God in vain; for the LORD will not hold him guiltless that taketh his name in vain.

In its totality the second paragraph may be read as a product of the LORD's Security Forces, some of its agents trained in Plato's academy of distributive justice, some others raised in Orwell's pig farm. True to its ambitions this command is unique also in the sense that it is at the same time both a *de*scription of the forbidden crimes and a *pre*scription of the corrective punishments, the misuse of metaphors considered more serious than the play with metonymies: four generations sent to Siberia for the father's sin of erasing Stalin's moustache from a poster. As every rock blaster knows, it is more important to safeguard the detonators than the dynamite, just as every general knows *both* that there are dozens of bomb-carrying airplanes circling the globe *and* that the code for letting them off is kept in the president's well-guarded(?) briefcase.

Totalitarianism operationalized, the overriding purpose of the second paragraph to silence every critique before it is uttered. Therefore, "you, my subject, you as well as your descendants, shall for ever know your place, never commit the sin of trespassing. My authority must never be questioned, my caricature never be drawn, my name never turned into a joke."

Rephrased, the purpose of the second paragraph is to make sure that the rhetorical animal is not merely circumcised but castrated, an operation swiftly performed by §3:

> **Remember the Sabbath day to keep it holy. Six days shalt thou labor, and do all thy work: But the seventh day is the Sabbath of the LORD thy God; in it thou shalt not do any work, thou, nor thy son, nor thy daughter, nor thy manservant, nor thy maidservant, nor thy cattle, nor thy stranger that is within thy gates: For in six days the LORD made heaven and earth, the sea, and all that in them is, and rested the seventh day: wherefore the LORD blessed the Sabbath day, and hallowed it.**

Although the antecedents of this word are even more uncertain than for any of the others, most exegetes agree that the Sabbath is as unique an invention as Israel's worship of one single God. Yet it should be recalled that already in the *Enuma elish*, written long before the time of J, Marduk bought his vassals' support by telling them that they worked too hard and that he had created the human race as a means of relieving their burdens. What does it really mean to be human, when in one account man is a Mesopotamian blood sausage, in another an Adamic speck of dust, in a third a Darwinian bag of walking sea water?

At any rate the third commandment is the only word whose Exodus and Deuteronomy phrasings are significantly different. Thus, according to the former it is the LORD who blesses the Sabbath day and hallows it, while in the latter it is the liberated serfs who are asked to remember that it was the LORD their God, who by a mighty hand and an outstretched arm had brought them out of the land of Egypt; the LORD's lust for power tied to recent history. "Therefore, after all these ordeals, I declare that you deserve a rest. No running around, however, for I say that you must never spend that precious time alone, but always together with your likes. At the pub and the synagogue, in the church, at the playground, the faculty meetings, the confirmations, the funerals, the family dinners—it is at these gatherings that my invisible officials shall teach you how to think-and-act! By common prayer you will then grasp the common truth: *I am* your LORD, *I am* the air of your breath, *I am* your taken-for-granted. Be like everyone else and you will be blessed. And since I despise the threatening originals and love the servile copies, the former shall be punished, the latter shown mercy."

No wonder that §3 is frequently considered the most crucial of all commandments, along with the prologue the ultimate guarantee that the dictatorial practice of monotheism will survive. Beware, though, for not even timeless propositions come with timeless interpretations.

Therefore, and since no man is an island, there is also **§4**, the familiar bridge between the Constitutional Law of §§1–3 and the Civil Law of §§5–10:

Honour thy father and thy mother: that thy days may be long upon the land which the LORD thy God giveth thee.

But even for fathers and mothers—Apsu and Tiamat included—enough is sometimes enough.

*

More story than history is the Israelites' time in Egypt, no archeological sites to prove that they were ever there. Be this as it may, because the seminarians' interest lies less in what might or might not have happened during the thirteenth to the fifth centuries BCE, more in understanding the present. In addition, since the arkographers are schooled in the hermeneutics of suspicion and the epistemology of the extreme, they often argue that the art of creative caricature is more revealing than the science of facsimile reproduction, quotations playing the same role for them as statistics for the empiricists.

No drama with an opening more striking than this: a burning bush that does not burn but talks. And this is what it says to Moses: "I am your God and I have come here to tell you that I have chosen you to lead my people out of this land of Egypt. I know how they suffer and with your help I shall liberate them from the violence and injustices with which they are treated." Too afraid to look, Moses first hid his face then countered that he is really not the man for the job, not a political agitator but a man slow of speech and tongue. "Very well," was the answer, "then I will appoint you as my executive and your brother Aaron, the Levite, as your spokesman. He will speak to the people on your behalf, and, whenever he does, it will be *as if* he were your mouth and *as if* you were the God to him, an incarnation of myself. And as a sign of your position I now hand over to you this staff, a magic wand with the power of changing the world." Decreed and performed.

What then follows is a horrendous series of threats and counterthreats, Presidents Trump and Kim Jong-un millennia ahead of themselves, the original catastrophe not a nuclear blast but the killing of all first-borns in the land of the Nile, everyone from the son of Pharaoh, who sat on the throne, to the daughter of the prisoner, who was kept in the dungeon. Not a house without a dead child, not a family without a weeping mother. National emergency, Moses and Aaron at short notice summoned to the palace, where they are told to immediately leave the country, their green cards torn to pieces. "Go into the desert, you and your wretched people! Eat there the meat of your sacrificed oxen, worship there the violence of that god of yours."

Off they go, the LORD himself leading their way, in daytime disguised as a pillar of cloud, at night as a pillar of fire. But hardly have they left before the officials change their minds realizing that without slaves they would no longer be themselves. The army is mobilized, the Israelites pursued, hunger, thirst, and fear their companions. In desperation they cry out, "Moses, why did you do this to us? Better be alive as servants in Egypt than dead in the desert."

Under internal pressure, and on the LORD's personal advice, he took the staff, the simsalabim that earlier had brought plagues of frogs, gnats, hail, locusts, and dead children to Egypt. And with that device he divided the sea ahead of them, letting his followers cross on dry ground, one wall of water on their right, another on their left. That operation completed he lifted his hand again, and the water rushed back promptly, drowning six hundred charioteers, uncounted horsemen, and every high-ranking officer. No Egyptian ever to be heard of again. And when the Israelites saw how the LORD had treated the slave-drivers, they feared him. And they put trust not only in him, but in Moses, his chief executive officer, as well.

Then, on the third new moon after the people of Israel had left, they come to the wilderness of Sinai. Once there, at the foot of a mountain, the LORD calls on Moses declaring, "I am going to come to you in a dense cloud, so that the people will hear me speaking with you, my trusted confidant. Lest they come too close, however, you shall put limits around the mountain and tell them that whoever touches the mountain will be killed."

Then, on the morning of the third day, Mount Sinai is covered with smoke, the LORD descending in fire. The whole mountain trembles and when he calls on Moses and Aaron to join him, the sound of trumpets prepares their way. But the people are once again warned not to force their way through to see him, for if they do, many of them will perish. While listening to his words is mandatory, seeing him is strictly forbidden.

Exactly what transpired on top of the smoke-covered mountain is not perfectly clear. What *is* clear, though, is that when the two appointees returned, they brought with them not only the words of the Ten Commandments but a long list of additional rules and regulations; an eye for an eye, witches shall be killed, shellfish not eaten, young goats not be cooked in their mother's milk. What is also certain is that God never spoke with his people directly, only with Moses who in turn, via Aaron, informed them about what had been decided. Here, as in the mafia-world of fear, invisibility is the LORD's signum, any show of weakness a deadly threat. And in that spirit, he says:

> I will send my terror ahead of you and throw into confusion every nation you encounter. I will make your enemies turn their backs and run. I will send the hornet ahead of you to drive out the Hivites, Canaanites and Hittites out of your way. [I will] hand over to you the people who live in the land and you will drive them out before you. Do not make a covenant with them or with their gods. Do not let them live in your land, or they will cause you to sin against me, because the worship of their gods will certainly be a snare to you.[10]

Like everything else in Exodus a preview of what was to come, a blanket legitimation of ethnic cleansing, every genocide the result of meticulous calculation: the Armenians in Ottoman Turkey; the Jews in Nazi Germany; the Tutsis in Hutu Rwanda, 800,000 black Africans turned into a swarm of despicable cockroaches, the United Nations blotting out the memory of the celebrated king Cyrus II; the Muslim Rohingyas in Buddhist Myanmar . . .

*

So strong are these words that they must be confirmed to be believed. Therefore, the LORD said to Moses,

> Come up to me on the mountain and wait there; and I will give you the tablets of stone, with the laws and commands, which I have written for their instruction. [And] when Moses went up on the mountain, the cloud covered it, and the glory of the LORD settled on Mount Sinai. [Then] Moses entered the cloud as he went on up the mountain. And he stayed [there] for forty days and forty nights.[11]

A long session indeed, every moment devoted to precise instructions about how, where, and through whom the LORD God is to be worshipped, the official report seven chapters long (Exodus 25–31), for emphasis repeated in Exodus 34–40, often verbatim:

"Bring me offerings and make me a sanctuary where I may dwell; build an ark, a box made of acacia wood two and a half cubits long, a cubit and a half wide, a cubit and a half high; overlay this container with gold and put inside it the Testimony which I will give you; make for me a tabernacle, a movable tent in which I can dwell until you have built me a permanent temple; hang inside the tent a curtain and place the ark of the Testimony behind it, that curtain separating the Holy Place from the Most Holy Place; build an altar for the fragrant incense; make a courtyard around the tabernacle so no one can come close enough to touch me." Such is the architecture of the LORD's dwelling, a blueprint of an Orthodox church, perhaps of Russian politics in general: the congregation on one side of the decorated iconostasis, the priests on the other, the former hearing and smelling how the latter share the wine, bread, and incense of the communion, the secluded celebrants as invisible as their forerunners.

Working inside this structure shall be a number of priests dressed in garments embroidered in gold and with threads of finest linen, blue, purple, and scarlet, Aaron's ephod the most elaborate of them all; the consecration of the priests—a ritual seven days long—an orgy in unprecedented bloodiness, one young bull and two rams without blemish providing the consecrated ingredients for the anointment; a sacrifice of two year-old lambs day by day continually; a laver of bronze for the ritual washing; a detailed prescription for the cooking of the anointing oil. All of this and much more for keeping the priests, including Aaron, in a social class of their own.

For Moses, though, there were no special regulations, no uniform, no perfumed oil. But, at the end of the forty days and forty nights, when God had spoken with him on Mount Sinai, he is given the two tablets of stone inscribed by the finger of God, the public to be duly informed.

*

For so long was the executive gone that people began to wonder where and who he was, indeed whether he would ever return. And in their bewilderment they approached Aaron begging him to make them a god capable of showing them the way to the promised land of milk and honey. Since he had not yet been informed about the deliberations in the smoke-filled room, hence knowing nothing about the paragraphs of the Constitutional Law, Aaron collected the women's earrings and made thereof an idol in the shape of a golden calf. And early next morning they sacrificed burnt offerings, they ate and they drank and had a big celebration.

No wonder the LORD, their God, got very upset, swearing to destroy them all. Moses did whatever he could to calm him down, even threatening to resign if he did not listen. However, when he had come down from the mountain and saw what was happening, he could not contain himself but threw the tablets to the ground, smashing them into pieces.

And when he realized that Aaron could no longer hold the stiff-necked people in his hands, he himself addressed the crowd directly, for the first time giving a speech of his own. This is what he said in one of the strongest political statements ever made, and this is how he was blessed for his cruelty:

> This is what the LORD, the God of Israel, says: "Each man strap a sword to his side. Go back and forth through the camp from one end to the other, each killing his brother and friend and neighbor." The Levites did as Moses commanded, and that day about three thousand of the people died. Then Moses said, "You have been set apart by the LORD today, for you were against your sons and brothers and he has blessed you this day."[12]

Not a case of ethnic cleansing but a purge of Stalinist proportions, not a genocide but a crime against humanity. No alternative, so on that same day about three thousand men were slaughtered. God blessed the murderers and asked Moses to join him once again at the top of the mountain. And up there they talked face-to-face as a man speaks to a friend.

God, pleased with what he was hearing, gave Moses his go-ahead, then told him to chisel out two new stone tablets exactly like the ones he had earlier broken. Moses did as he had been told and, after another forty days and forty nights in the LORD's company, he descended with the law in his hands and a face that was radiant. Everyone was terrified, Aaron included. But they listened carefully as he read them all the commands he brought with him: "Circumcise therefore the foreskin of your heart, and be no longer stubborn."[13]

As a sign that he had not only seen God but spoken with him, Moses put a veil over his face, well aware that he was the only link between the people and their LORD. And when this prophet of prophets had finally passed away, an obituary was issued by his successor, Joshua, the lieutenant under whose command thirty-nine Canaanite cities had been exterminated. These were his farewell words:

There has not arisen a prophet since in Israel like Moses, whom the LORD knew face to face, who did all those miraculous signs and wonders the LORD sent him to do in Egypt—to Pharaoh and to all his officials and to his whole land. For no one has ever shown the mighty power or performed the awesome deeds that Moses did in the sight of all Israel.[14]

Platopolis

What a fantastic adventure it has been, this journey down the Red River Valley. A lived experience of how everything changes, yet always remains the same. Seemingly a travelogue from the Euphrates, the Nile, and the Red Sea, in reality an immersion in a stream of language, words fused together in ways they never were before. Perhaps a shadow of the future. Perhaps a dream about a social variant of the biological DNA. Perhaps a hallucination kicked off by travel fatigue.

First there was *Enuma elish*, the story of how a family of gods was born, the two oceans of Apsu and Tiamat their parents, Marduk their most prominent offspring. Fifty were his names, for fifty were his personalities. Then followed the Mesopotamian odyssey of *Gilgamesh*, the tale of how a two-thirds god with that same name met his counterpart, the wild-man Enkidu, how these figures fought, loved, traveled, and finally acknowledged that both of them were full-blown humans and therefore, like everyone else, bound to die. After this came Genesis, the biblical story not only of how the many deities became one but of how the Almighty changed over time. Who is actually who, God an image of Man, Man an image of God? Hints of an answer are in Exodus, here read as an outstanding handbook of political philosophy and social psychology, world history's most influential codification of the fluctuating relations between a group of people and their jealous ruler.

From beginning to end a drama of mutual trust and distrust, everything eventually reaching a breaking point with Job, the blameless foreigner whose allegiance Satan questioned and God tested. What followed was a torture beyond belief, yet the accused refused to admit a wrongdoing he knew he had not committed, pleading instead for a forum where he could defend himself—"Oh that I had someone to hear me!"

And that is exactly what happened, the supreme court agreeing to hear his case—Job vs. God—a unique proceeding in which each contender acted as his own defender. Arrogant power from God's side:

> Who is it that darkens my counsel
>> with words without knowledge?
> Brace yourself like a man;
>> I will question you;
>> and you will answer me.
> *Where were you when I laid the earth's foundation?*
>> Tell me, if you understand.
> Who marked off its dimensions? Surely you know!
>> *Who stretched a measuring line across it?*[15]

Polite answers from the defendant (or is it the plaintiff):

> I am unworthy—how can I reply to you?
>> I put my hand on my mouth.
> I spoke once, but I have no answer—
>> twice, but I will say no more.
>
> I know that you are all powerful:
>> what you can conceive, you can perform.
> I am the man who obscured your designs
>> with my empty-headed words.
> I have been holding forth on matters I cannot understand,
>> on marvels beyond me and beyond my knowledge.
> [Listen, I have more to say,
>> now it is my turn to ask questions and yours to inform me.]
> I knew you then only by hearsay;
>> but now, having seen you with my own eyes,
> I retract all I have said,
>> and in dust and ashes I repent.[16]

When the verdict finally comes, God is sentenced to pay a tremendous damage settlement, not merely double the number of the sheep, oxen, and donkeys he slaughtered, but the seven sons and three daughters as well. Yet Job never rejoices, partly because three new daughters can never relieve the pain of having lost just one of the old, mainly because he seems to realize that now, when he has actually seen the LORD with his own eyes, he really does not like him, perhaps because both of them are created in the image of the other.

After these events, Job lived for a hundred and forty years and he saw his children and their children to the fourth generation. Most significantly, the LORD never visited on any of them the iniquity of their father and that is despite the fact that Job had not only seen him, but survived the ordeal, the Job story much richer than the report from Abraham's test on Mount Moriah and Jacob's bragging about how he got his limp. So total is in fact Job's victory that in the Hebrew Bible God never speaks again.

* * * * *

No wonder the arkographers on the upper deck are eager to pursue their search for insights, to somehow grasp what it means to be human. And when they now look out over the widening river, they see in the distance the contours of a city and a ship heading their direction. The captain comes aboard bringing with him an invitation to come for a visit. And, if they agree, the oarsmen will pull them into the city, a place called Platopolis, home of learned academies and schools of navigation, acknowledged experts in the art of finding the way. "For certainly," says the captain, "you must continue your journey on a ship better equipped than this rudderless float."

An invitation impossible to refuse.

II

Imaginare Necesse Est

Once the ark is moored the seminarians are taking off in their own directions, their minds set on the evening meal and a full night's sleep. Not the explorer, though, for he is too excited by what he believes might be lying ahead. Across the square and into the tavern, where he promptly runs into the captain of the rescue ship who with a firm grip leads him into a *chambre séparée*—an arrangement similar to, yet drastically different from, the story of how God met Moses at the top of the mountain, a secluded place  where the two of them could talk face-to-face as a man speaks to a friend.

And immediately they were seated—as if they could not be contained— these were the words that came out of the seaman's mouth:

Sharp and guileful he'd need to be, the man who'd outsmart you
in every trick, were it even a god who met you! Perverse,
devious-minded, obsessed with deceit, won't you ever,
even in your own country, abandon your deceptions
and the lying tales you adore from the very ground up? But let's
speak no more of these things—we're experts both
in craftiness: you are the best of all living mortals
for counsel and storytelling, while I among all the gods
am famed for contrivance and sharpness. You failed to recognize

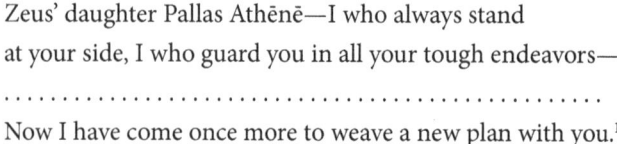

Zeus' daughter Pallas Athēnē—I who always stand
at your side, I who guard you in all your tough endeavors—
. . . .
Now I have come once more to weave a new plan with you.[1]

Astonishing experience, a geriatric of the twenty-first century being greeted
by none less than Zeus's own daughter, the goddess who long ago showed
Odysseus the way from the wooden horse of Troy back to his Ithaka family.
Twenty years for the man of twists and turns, a lifetime for the arkographer. From beginning to end a wonderful instance of imagination, the art
of making the absent present and the present absent, no humans and no
creation epics without it. Like Homer and Sophocles before him, Shakespeare too knew that

> Lovers and madmen have such seething brains,
> Such shaping fantasies, that apprehend
> More than cool reason ever comprehends.
> The lunatic, the lover, and the poet
> Are of imagination all compact
> . . . .
> And as imagination bodies forth
> The forms of things unknown, the poet's pen
> Turns them to shapes, and gives to airy nothing
> A local habitation and a name.[2]

At the same time true and misleading, for such is the nature of local hab-
itations and names that they keep moving around, ceaselessly changing
with the context. Ultra-foreign to current readers is therefore the essence of
classical Greece, much as artificial intelligence would have been to Homer
and the Homeric deities to Moses, seventh century Greeks believing that
if they did something, then it was not they who did it but the gods who
acted through them. As Agamemnon put it,

> I am not responsible
> but Zeus is, and Destiny, and Erinys the mist-walking

who in assembly caught my heart in the savage delusion
on that day I myself stripped from him the prize of Achilleus.
Yet what could I do? It is the god who accomplishes all things.[3]

To be human was consequently at that time-and-place to be an extended arm of the gods, each deity adorned with a proper name, a definite personality and a set of well-defined duties. So deeply ingrained was this belief that in Old Greek there was not even a word for what we today mean by the verb "to will."

Not surprisingly, this attitude came to be questioned not least by Aeschylus, Sophocles, and Euripides, all of them as relevant today as in the fifth century. And out of their tragic dramas grew not only a novel conception of guilt and punishment but the discipline of ethics itself, the only ordered discourse that takes human action as its prime topic—if Oedipus's fate was determined by the divinities, then it is *they* who should be blamed or praised, if the wrongdoings were of his own making, then everything falls back on *him*, the self-blinding a foregone conclusion. The point is that just as the mortals have much to learn from the gods, so the gods have much to learn from the humans, no issue more crucial than the relations between identity and existence.

Those were the meanings that Pallas Athene (as always disguised, on this occasion as the seasoned skipper) spoke to her newfound protégé, stressing that translation is everything, no power more powerful than the ability/opportunity of saying that something is something else and being believed when you do so. Not merely that expression and impression are two sides of the same sign but that every sign is itself structured like a map, a weaving together of picture and story. Sometimes a word, sometimes a gesture, a painting, a sculpture, an icon, an index, a symbol. But always a triangulation, a geometric operation which tells you not only where you are but whence you came and where you should go, indicative and imperative in the same breath. Squeezed into its own minimum every sign is a double fold, verb turned to noun, noun to verb.

*

"Remember therefore," mentors the well-travelled sailor, "that these insights were born and nurtured by the Greeks, Plato, Aristotle, and Euclid foremost among them, their bodies long dead, their ideas still alive and soon to be visited. Before that encounter, however, you must first be given a mandatory introduction to the lingua franca of the semiotic animal, Semiotics 810, like its forerunner Geography 810 a graduate seminar that may be elected more than once, the trendy Bar de Saussure the perfect venue. The point is that without that propedeutic the classics will be gibberish to modern people like yourself; knowing how to read the graffiti is simply not enough, you must learn to master the tractatus logico-philosophicus as well. For always keep this in mind, that whereas the biblical God shows himself through poetic revelation, the Olympians come forth through logical reason. To honor the testimony of the former takes an arkographer, to understand the latter takes an arkologist. Let him be! And there he is."

Saussurean Bar

The starting point of that mind-forming experience is the sign itself, a double helix that from one direction looks like

$$\frac{s}{S}$$

from the other like

$$\frac{S}{s}$$

the s in both instances standing for "signified," the S for "Signifier," the — for the bar which in the same stroke keeps the two ingredients together and apart. What the two expressions share in common is that whatever appears in the denominator is brought about by the numerator, what is lying on top impregnating what is below, new signs produced in the process: while in the linguistics of Ferdinand de Saussure (1857–1913) an idea is searching for its expression (a poet striving for the proper word), in the psychoanalyses of Jacques Lacan (1901–81) an utterance is groping for its interpretation (a therapist sensitive to the Freudian slips). On the surface two realities, one intelligible, one sensible, deeper down a kaleidoscope of socially constructed appearances, the bar-in-between simultaneously serving both as the magic wand of ontological transformations and as a two-way bridge between the five senses of the body and the sixth sense of culture.

From beginning to end a play of mimetic desire, a drama in which the S and the s are doing their utmost to become one and the same, language itself a machine of perpetual motion. Seducer seduced, a languishing tango for two. To no avail, however, for so ingeniously is the sign structured that the dream of perfect union can never be realized, a mute s turning into a screaming S, Edvard Munch's open-mouthed girl on the bridge triggering a sense of *horror vacui*. It follows that as a reified phenomenon the sign *has* a body, as a deified noumenon it *is* a mind, the two verbs "to have" and "to be" intimately connected through the penumbra of the tympanum. And thus it is that the one-dollar bill gets its value not from the wrinkled paper with the picture of George Washington but from the social institutions through which it may be exchanged for something else. From beginning to end a play of truth and trust, promises kept and promises broken. In comparison bitcoin is a risky investment, a modern invention that like Baudelaire's albatross was once admired as a heavenly king and now is paddling around on the ship's deck, kicked and ridiculed by speculators who know nothing better. He who was so fine, how droll and ugly now.

The point is that no sign can be understood directly, only via a substitute, every understanding an exercise in (mis)translation. The Bar de Saussure is the place where it all happens, the favorite hangout for beauties and madmen alike. And as long-term resident of that establishment the semiotic animal is well aware of the tension between what a text *means* to say and what it is *constrained* to say. To "deconstruct" an utterance—be it a poem, a painting, a law, an equation, or anything else—is therefore to operate a kind of strategic reversal, seizing on precisely those unguarded details (causal metaphors, footnotes, incidental turns of argument), that are always, and necessarily, passed over by more orthodox interpreters. The lessons sound loud and clear: easy to tell the truth; easy to be believed; difficult, perhaps impossible, to do both at the same time. Apart from others, you are one with yourself, for as Ludwig Wittgenstein understood, it is by saying how things are, that the solipsist shows who he is. Samuel Beckett's *Unnamable* knew the Bar from the inside: "Perhaps that's what I feel, an outside and an inside and me in the middle, perhaps that's what I am, the thing that divides the world in two, on the one side the outside, on the other the inside, that can be as thin as foil, I'm neither one side nor the other, I'm in the middle, I'm the partition, I've surfaces and no thickness, perhaps that's what I feel, myself vibrating, I'm the tympanum, on the one hand the mind, on the other the world, I don't belong to either."[4]

Pallas Athene was right, Jacques Lacan as well: the unconscious is structured like a language. Not that the unconscious *is* a language, merely that the only way to grasp it is to approach it *as if it were* a language. The implication is, of course, that for the past to be understood it must be translated into the present, Plato into Duchamp. But which are the reins that are keeping the twenty-first century on track, how is it structured, the social scientist's counterpart to the biologist's DNA? What does s/he look like, the emperor without clothes? Can there even be an emperor stripped bare, a representation that itself is not a representation, a difference so pure that it refuses to be forced into an identity? How does it sound, the music to which the sign is treading its perpetual breakdance?

*

Hard to tell except the composer was most likely conceived and trained in the Bar de Saussure, a place important enough to be protected by the taboo, an excluded middle that thus far has been symbolized by the ultra-thin line-in-between. But imagine now instead the sign as it appears on a page, the Signifier parading up front, the signified hiding on the back, the thickness of the sheet showing the connection between them. A local habitation never visited before: the horizontal line metaphorically turned into a vertical wall, the unwritten page a counterpart to the filmmaker's screen, the painter's canvas, the stage director's velvet curtain. No longer a straight line on a flat surface but a set of folded imaginations, pockets full of posies. "Every thought gives off a throw of dice," said the poet of nothingness. *Comme si, comme ça*, because in the drunkenness of the Bar de Saussure nothing takes place except the place

EXCEPTÉ

PEUT-ÊTRE

UNE CONSTELLATION

Ashes to ashes, dust to dust, in the cleft of self-reference we all fall down. And hanging there at the bar of the Bar the explorer thinks to himself, what a wonderful world—to the poet the penumbra between what is experienced and how it is understood; to the psychologist the labyrinth of conscious and repressed; to the mythologist the spring water in which Narcissus first mirrors and then drowns himself. The mimetic desire out of bounds, perhaps an indication that metaphoric boundaries and metonymic associations are all that the semiotic animal shares, the art of living with difference the very definition of what it means to be human, of writing in such a way that the structure of what the text is *about* is the same as the structure of the language it is rendered *in*. The sign of true creativity, mathematical physics a case in point.

Finally: just as our bodies carry the scars from the initiation rites (wedding ring, pierced ear, broken hymen, circumcision scar), so do our minds. Any mark is consequently better than no mark, for without categorization there would be nothing at all, not even nothing at all. That horrifying alternative is in fact the norm in the Realm of Psychosis, that literally unthinkable province where there are no initiation rites, no scars, no individuals, no society. The abyss of the excluded middle in its proper context.

"So now," says the sparkling-eyed Athene, "with these concepts in your toolbox, you should be better equipped to meet the Philosopher Himself and through Him understand that the Bar-in-Between is the trace of the Lacanian Real, the true home of the semiotic/rhetorical animal. No Platopolis without it."

The Republic

High time, therefore, for a visit to the map room of Plato's Republic and a crash course in the architecture of political geography, *the* groundbreaking illustration of how it is in the infra-thin interactions at the Saussurean Bar that truth is simultaneously created and repeated, at once originary and memorial, at once a Signifier searching its soul and a signified searching its body. The subject does not belong to the world, the subject is the limit of the world.

The resulting issues go to the heart of what it means to be human, for it is in the rhythmic interchange between the sensible and the intelligible that life gets its meaning, hence its sense and direction. At issue is the power-filled question of how we manage to represent absent objects *as if they were* present and subsisting relations *as if they were* existing things. And just as Saussure and Lacan opted for different solutions to this ontological paradox so did Plato and Aristotle, the former, like Saussure, leaning heavily toward the intelligible, the latter, like Lacan, toward the sensible. Thus, while to the father-like master the images were false reflections of pure thought, so to the

son-like pupil reason without images was unseeable, hence literally unknowable. Although they both agreed that just as in the case of the wheel, so there must also in logic be a point that remains at rest, they profoundly disagreed on the nature of that Archimedean fix-point; what was stable to one was ephemeral to the other. It is telling that in Raphael's painting *The School of Athens*, Plato is pointing to the heavens with one finger, Aristotle reaching to the earth with his whole hand.

Raphael: *School of Athens*. Detail of Plato and Aristotle. 1508–11. Fresco. Stanza della Segnatura, east wall. Musei Vaticani, Città del Vaticano. © Vatican Museums, all rights reserved.

To search for the fix-point is to enter the forbidden rooms of the Bar de Saussure, by definition the abysmal *topos* of ontological transformations. Once there, however, one must always keep in mind that the blueprint of the Greek House of Representatives was drawn a long time ago, most outstandingly in books 6 and 7 of the *Republic*, the grand center of the Socratic dialogues. More explicitly than anywhere else it was in those pages that Plato argued that for every set of changeable things there is a single Form—although there are many beds, there is only one Bed. It was the master's genius to weave those threads of ontology and epistemology into a coordinate-net for capturing the world of human thought-and-action, the code to his political geography: a play between *pre*-sented originals and *re*-presented copies, the former imagined by the inner eye of the mind, the latter by the outer eye of the body. The difference between *perspectiva naturalis* and *perspectiva artificialis* long before Hubert Damisch coined the terms, everything elaborated in a dialogue between Socrates and Glaucon, Plato's older brother.

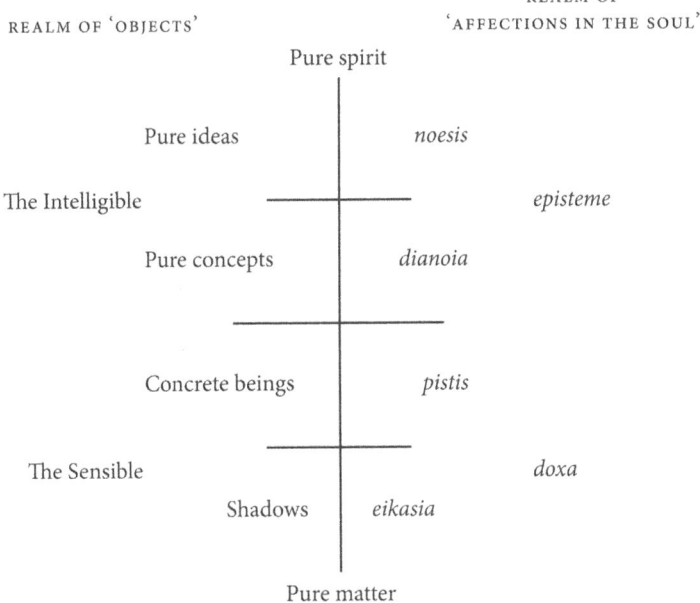

Categories of Plato's *Republic*.

I understand, he said, not fully, for it is no slight task that you appear to have in mind, but I do understand that you mean to distinguish the aspect of reality and the intelligible, which is contemplated by the power of dialectic, as something truer and more exact than the object of the so-called arts and sciences whose assumptions are arbitrary starting points. . . . And I think you call the mental habit of geometers and their like mind or understanding and not reason, because you regard understanding as something immediate between opinion and reason.

Your understanding is quite correct, I said.[5]

*

It has been said before and deserves to be said again: the *Republic* is an atlas, the overriding purpose of its maps to charter the way to the good life in the good city and thereby provide an answer to Socrates's question of how one should live. The important point is not that his atlas is a political document (which of course it is), but that the political is an explication of how the real world is moved from the existing Now-here of the already to the predicative No-where of the not yet, both topoi equally imaginary and symbolic. Obviously easier said than done and when Glaucon asked what the Good really is, Socrates wisely replied that if he knew, he would be much more than content.

Yet he cannot resist the temptation. Therefore, with the purpose of teaching Glaucon how to paint the picture of the Good in a just person's knowledge, Socrates introduces him to the three figures of the analogy of the Sun; the allegory of the Line; and the parable of the Cave. Similarly (and equally skilled in the art of rhetoric, some claim in the art of lying), every cartographer has learned that for making a map all one needs are three concepts. No more and no less than

- a **point** that remains at rest
- a **line** otherwise known as a scale or a coordinate net
- a **plane** onto which the emerging picture/story is projected.

And thus it is that mapping is essentially an exercise in the geometry of triangulation, triangulation itself an exercise in the politics of power, the latter a Wiener-waltz with the semiotician's three-cornered figure of thought, symbol, and referent.

Following this rhythm the map-making Plato first transforms Socrates's Sun into the fix-point of his own time and place—the counterpart of Ptolemy's North Pole and Stalin's Dictatorship of the Proletariat. He then changes the Divided Line into a set of scaling coordinates—a Marduk-net designed to capture, sort, shape, and name the Ruler's needs and interests. Finally, he understands that the canvas of the *mappa* serves the same function as the wall of the philosopher's Cave—the culturally prepared projection screen onto which invisible relations are casting their visualized marks. Geometry's taken-for-granted disrobed, for just as the Archimedean point of ontological transformation is the pivot of the revolving world, so the Ptolemaic line is the legend that translates picture to story and story to picture. The Platonic plane, in its turn, is the knowledge-stained napkin of Deleuzian manifolds. Blow your nose, Pinocchio, and you will discover that just as the snoot can be seen, so ideas can be thought.

Which is another way of saying that as the Sun reigns over the world of the eyeball, so the Good reigns over the intelligible. And just as to Aristotle—the pupil—there was no mortal without soul and no vision without light, so to Plato—the seer—there was no reason without goodness. Yet, if the Greekjew stares at the Sun with her eyes unprotected, she goes blind, if the Jewgreek meets his God naked, he goes mad. Hyperbole can get us no further and even though Socrates forcefully argued the case of political idealism, he still considered it the most destructive of passions, largely because regimes depend on virtues, not on institutions; if the highest virtues are not present in the rulers, an inferior regime is instituted; the conclusion is that the only guardian of the guardian is a proper education. In the words of Aristotle—Plato's student and Alexander's teacher:

> It is the mark of an educated man to look for precision in each class of things just as far as the nature of the subject admits; it is evidently

equally foolish to accept probable reasoning from a mathematician and demand from a rhetorician scientific proofs.

Now each man judges well things he knows, and of these he is a good judge. As so the man who has been educated in a subject is a good judge of that subject, and the man who has received an all-round education is a good judge in general. Hence a young man is not a proper hearer of lectures on political science; for he is inexperienced in the actions that occur in life, but its discussions start from these and are about these; and, further, since he tends to follow his passions, his study will be vain and unprofitable, because the end aimed at is not knowledge but action.[6]

Accordingly, a proper education is precisely the gift that Socrates administers to Glaucon, a dialectical enterprise equally daring and moderate; daring because the nephew was too young to have any personal experience of either politics or philosophy, moderate because Socrates's teaching drew entirely on his student's ability to imagine. It may even be that the most remarkable aspects of the collected dialogues lie not in the teacher's deliberations but in the students' readiness to understand them, not in the mature man's sayings but in the youngsters' hearings. How do I grasp a meaning I never met before, how do I make sense of something hitherto unseen?

Part of the answer lies in the richness of the word *meaning* itself (a total of eight pages in the *Oxford English Dictionary*), a sense that begins its wanderings in the **point**-like qualities of whatever lies in the middle, then moves via the **line**-like directives of intending, signifying, or pointing the way, to the final destination in the **plane**-like values of the taken-for-granted. It follows that a sentence can be said to have a certain meaning if it performs a certain illocutionary act, that is if it somehow induces a person's mind to move from one topos to another. "To mean" is consequently to invoke a travel story, to construct an invisible map of the invisible, to engage in a form of cartographic reason. Thus, it was Plato's gift to lead his pupils not into the wilderness of the utterly unknown but to vantage points from which they could *re*cognize what they had already cognized on their own.

It follows that the only way to reach the utopian No-where is to approach it *as if it were* Some-where, to accept that Plato's Academy was built as a map room. As Immanuel Kant was eventually to put it:

> *Imagination* is the faculty of representing in intuition an object that is *not itself present* . . . The faculty of imagination is to that extent a faculty which determines the sensibility *a priori*; and its synthesis of the intuitions conforming as it does to the *categories* must be transcendental synthesis of *imagination*. . . , [the only place where] I am conscious of myself, not as I appear to myself, nor as I am in myself, but only that I am. This *representation* is a *thought*, not an intuition.[7]

And therein lies the hidden condition of all knowledge, the only force strong enough to invade the utterly unknown. The Bar de Saussure is the place to experience it, an establishment that Aristotle's Laws of Thought (identity, difference, excluded middle) forbid the logician to enter:

$$a = a$$
$$a \neq \sim a$$
$$a \vee \sim a$$

* * *

Mapping the *Republic* is to draw the lines of what it means to be human, to mount the instruments of cartographic reason in the infra-thin boundary between the two prepositions *of* and *in*, to face once again the challenge of writing in such a way that it is not *about* something but *is* that something itself. And with that unreachable goal etched onto the receding horizon, two maps are immediately forthcoming, one geographic, the other administrative.

The first imitation is a metaphysical base-map drawn with the purpose of determining the limits of language and thereby the boundary between Plato's *Republic* and four *terra incognitae*. While the characteristics of the latter are literally unmentionable, the former is a confederation divided into two realms, one filled with objects of varying ontological beings, the other by different modes of epistemological understanding.

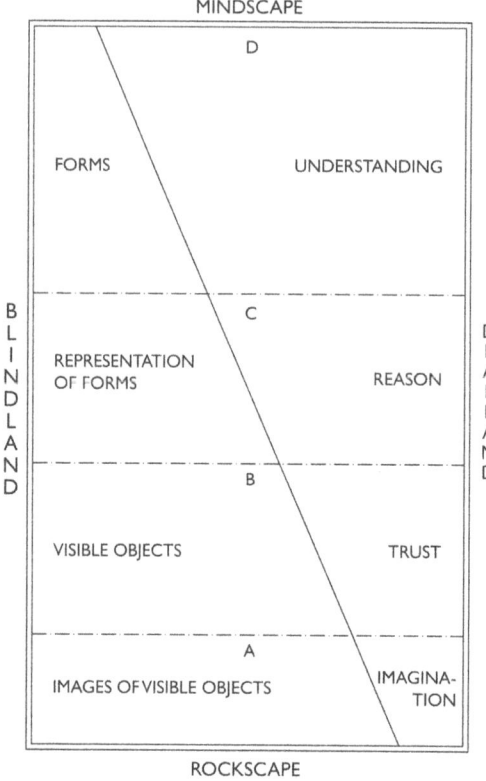

D

FORMS

UNDERSTANDING

B
L
I
N
D
L
A
N
D

C

REPRESENTATION
OF FORMS

REASON

D
E
A
F
L
A
N
D

B

VISIBLE OBJECTS

TRUST

A

IMAGES OF VISIBLE OBJECTS

IMAGINA-
TION

ROCKSCAPE

Base map of Plato's *Republic*.

To be precise, this base-map is enclosed within an Albertian rectangle drawn in the proportion of the golden section. On its inside lies the **Territory of the Humans,** on the outside a world so utterly unthinkable that it can be neither noticed nor named. That fact notwithstanding it is extremely difficult, perhaps impossible, to envision a boundary with only one side. And that is why the young Wittgenstein, following Immanuel Kant's example, declared that the very purpose of philosophy is to "set limits to what can be thought; and in doing so, to what cannot be thought. It must set limits to what cannot be thought by working outwards through what can be thought."[8]

Thus guided, the arkographer turned arkologist discovers that on the other side of what can be captured by the five senses are four unknown continents, fancy-lands on which the semiotic animal has never set foot, an imagined *Mappa Mundi* that in its structure is reminiscent of the *Ebstorfer Weltkarte*—**Mindscape** at the top (the medieval east where the sun rises), **Rockscape** at the bottom (west where the sun sets), **Blindland** to the left (north), **Deafland** to the right (south). Inside that same limit lies Plato's Republic itself, a territory split into two realms of the same size and shape, one called **The Realm of *Objects* of Cognition**, the other **The Realm of**

Kinds of **Cognition**, the former essentially ontological, the latter essentially epistemological.

Marking the boundary between the two realms is a barbed wire twined from the prepositions *of* and *in*, a divid*ing* line that runs from the Mindscape to the Rockscape, ontology to the left, epistemology to the right. Finally, cutting through the Human Territory, reaching all the way from the invisible Blindland to the inaudible Deafland, runs yet another frontier, sometimes called the divid*er* of the dividing line. Above this crucial line— Plato's forerunner to the Saussurean Bar, the border station where word turns to flesh and matter becomes meaning—lies the so called **Intelligible Region**, below it the **Sensibility Region**.

With the grid of this fundamental(ist) creation firmly in place, the human territory is divided into four provinces customarily known as the **A** and **B** of the Sensibility Region, and the **C** and **D** of the Intelligibility Region, the scale of the administrative map given by the relative size of the four provinces corresponding directly to the original segments of the Divided Line such that

$$D : C :: B : A$$

from which follows both that

$$D : B :: B : A$$

and that

$$D: C :: C : A.$$

Rephrased,

The Intelligible World : The World of Appearance

::

Visible Objects : Images and Shadows

Seemingly confusing, in reality the mapper's scale of what it means to be human, the guarantee that whatever the cartographer happens to say must be doubly bound to the objects s/he is talking *about* and the understandings s/he is talking *in*. Plato long before Joyce and Beckett. To be more exact, the objects of Province **A** are images by which "I mean first shadows, and then reflections in water or in [mirrors of] close-grained polished surfaces and everything of that kind, if you understand."[9] This particular mode of understanding (*eikasia* or "perceptual thought") is of course itself a product of imagination, hence of our ability to make the absent present, the present absent. In contrast, the objects of Province **B** are always presently present, "actual things of which the [shadows of Province **A**] are likenesses, the living creatures about us and all the works of nature or of human hands." Most importantly, our grasp of these objects is a function not of individual imagination but of social trust (*pistis* or "folk wisdom"),

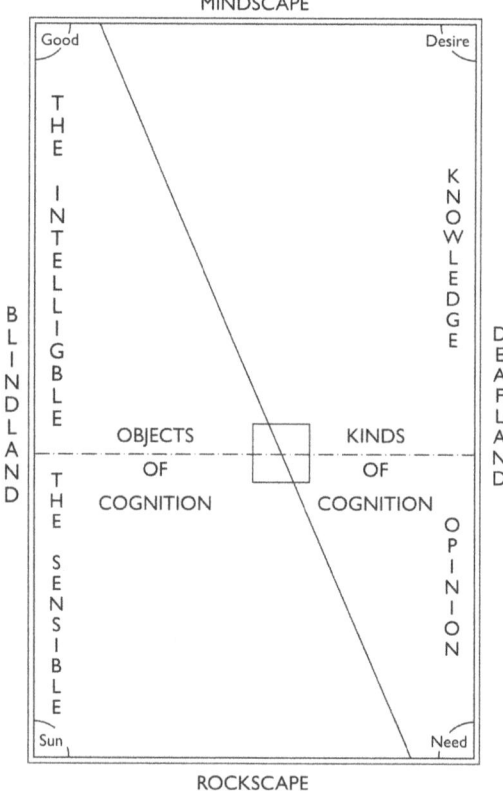

which is anchored in the five senses—well remembering, of course, that what I see with my eyes is not necessarily the same as what I touch with my hands. This much (or rather this little) about the Sensibility Region, the area which on our two maps is located *below* the infra-thin line of the main parallel. Familiar ground, finding the way a child's play.

Administrative map of Plato's *Republic*.

In the Intelligibility Region, which is located *above* the main parallel, the situation seems at first quite different. However, as soon as one realizes, firstly, that everything in the **C** Province concerns mathematical reflection and, secondly, that mathematicians deal with visual things in a very special way, then most of the difficulties evaporate. In particular one must keep in mind that the images with which the mathematician is working are not material objects that can be readily grasped by the human body but something higher and more abstract—not ordinary shadows or reflections in water but diagrams, imitations in drawings of concepts unseen. The objects of the **C** Province are consequently instanced not by *this* particular square or by *this* particular diagonal but by *the* square and *the* diagonal; although the square drawn on the blackboard in some sense is a real thing—white chalk-marks on a black surface—the figure itself is a shadow not of a concrete thing but of an abstract idea, not an entity the thinker can hold in his hand but a relation that only thought can apprehend. The presented maps are obviously objects of this latter kind, Plato's distinction between the visible and the intelligible essentially the same as the positivist's division between the observational and the theoretical. It follows that in the **C** Province the main mode of apprehension is the type of reason (*dianoia* or "scientific thought") which is usually associated with formalized logic and geometry. The concept of the taken-for-granted undressed, logical deduction another word for the bureaucrat's machinations, the mind rather than the body being the major target of his intentional actions.

In Province **D**, finally, the objects of cognition are as far removed from the material world as anyone can imagine. The actual things, which earlier were encountered in Province **B**, are here replaced by the concept of pure Forms, an entity not so easy to grasp. For the sake of clarity,

> let me therefore remind you, [He said,] of the distinction we drew
> earlier and have often drawn on other occasions, between the multi-
> plicity of things that we call good or beautiful or whatever it may be
> and, on the other hand, Goodness itself or Beauty itself and so on.
> Corresponding to each of these sets of many things, we postulate a

single Form or real essence, as we call it. . . . Further, the many things, we say, can be seen, but are not objects of rational thought; whereas Forms are objects of thought, but invisible.[10]

In condensed summary: Plato's Theory of Form is a visual metaphor applied to mental objects, an imagination of geometric shapes (*eidos* or "idea") that cannot be seen.

*

Then, suddenly, at the end of a well-prepared road, the view from the summit. And from that vantage point it is immediately clear that the only approach to the Forms goes via the intelligent understanding of dialectics (*noesis* or "dialectical thought"), in Aristotle's terminology the twin sister of rhetoric. While in Province **C** the conventional axioms and reasoning rules were taken as self-evident starting points for deductive conclusions, here, in Province **D**, the same statements are themselves turned into the prime objects of inquiry. In a marvelous condensation, Socrates teaches Glaucon that

> when its gaze is fixed upon an object irradiated by truth and reality, the soul gains understanding and knowledge [*noiesis* and *episteme*] and is manifestly in possession of intelligence. But when it looks toward that twilight world of things that come into existence and pass away, its sight is dim and it has only opinions and beliefs [*eikasia* and *pistis*] which shift to and fro, and now it seems like a thing that has no intelligence.
>
> This, then, which gives to the objects of knowledge their truth and to him who knows them his power of knowledge, is the Form or essential nature of Goodness. It is the cause of knowledge and truth; and so, while you may think of it as an object of knowledge, you will do well to regard it as something beyond truth and knowledge and, precious as these both are, of still higher worth. And just as in our analogy light and vision were to be thought of as like the Sun, but not identical with it, so here both knowledge and truth are to be regarded

as like the Good, but to identify either with Good is wrong. The Good must hold a yet higher place of honor. . . .

I understand, [said Glaucon] though not perfectly.[11]

At issue in Province **D** is obviously neither the content of the taken-for-granted nor the consequences of the taken-for-granted, but the Taken-For-Grantedness in and of itself. More specifically,

> When I speak of the other sub-section of the intelligible part of the line you will understand that I mean that which the very process of argument grasps by the power of dialectic; it treats assumptions not as principles, but as assumptions in the true sense, that is, as starting points and steps in the ascent to something which involves no assumption and is the first principle of everything; when it has grasped that principle it can again descend, by keeping to the consequences that follow from it, to a conclusion. The whole procedure involves nothing in the sensible world but moves solely through Forms to Forms and finishes with Forms.[12]

The concept of Being is consequently itself a Form, arguably even higher than the Form of the Good. Higher still, though, is the Form of Forms, and that explains why Socrates did his utmost to prove that without Forms there can be no stability, hence no knowledge either. Aristotle, of course, took the opposite stance, arguing that Plato introduced the Forms because he wrongly "accepted the Heraclitean sayings which describe all sensible things as ever passing away, so that if knowledge or thought is to have an object, there must be some other and permanent entities, apart from those which are sensible; for there could be no knowledge of things which were in a state of flux."[13]

To be a Platonic Form is consequently to be an entity which is self-referential, unique, intelligible, immutable, and taken-for-granted. A primal scream in an echo chamber, a secret committed to a war-time diary. For now it should be obvious that my propositions serve as elucidations in the following way: anyone who understands me eventually recognizes them as nonsensical, when he has used them—as steps—to climb up beyond them. (He must, so to speak, throw away the ladder after he has climbed up it.) He must transcend these propositions, and then he will see the world right.[14]

Finally, Socrates again, the ring of unmistakable genius: the mind uses as images those actual things which themselves have images in the visible world. Two verbs to do the trick—"remember" and "remind," the former a backward-looking thing, the latter a forward-looking meaning. While the job of reifying remembrance is to re-member the members dismembered, the magic of deifying reminders is to re-imagine relations forgotten.

* * *

Let there be no doubt. The wisdom-loving philosophers and the food-loving workers are at opposite ends of the social hierarchy which makes the *Republic* equally famous and infamous. With the purpose of determining the boundaries of that universe, a third map is forthcoming, the only one in our atlas that explicitly focuses on the concept of power and the socialization processes that make the semiotic animal so obedient and so predictable. Although the previous ties to Plato's Divided Line will remain strong, the more immediate connections are to the allegory of the Cave.

Like its predecessors, also this map is structured around the slanted and horizontal lines, their intersection forming the pivot of the world (sometimes known as the *agora*); as recalled, the slanted line marks the ontology/epistemology boundary between the two Realms of Cognition, the horizontal between the **A** and **B** regions of the sensible, on the one hand, the **C** and **D** regions of the intelligible, on the other. In the socioeconomic case, however, the associations run less to Plato directly and more to the Neoplatonic blueprint of Plotinus (204–90 CE) whose hypostasis separated and tied together the food- and sex-loving workers in the crowded cellars and the money-loving artisans in the claustrophobic entresol. Rising from that ground is an executive tower where the lower floors are assigned to the honour-loving soldiers and the penthouse to the wisdom-loving philosophers. While the auxiliaries have been trained to look down at (or is it *on*) the street below, the real statesmen are free to see everything and anything, including whatever hovers above the rooftops and whatever gleams beyond the horizon.

Socioeconomic map
of Plato's *Republic*.

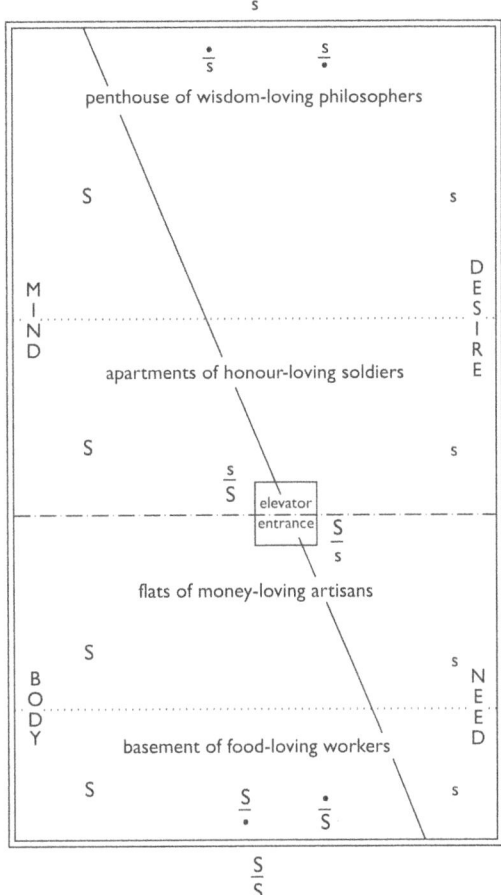

In this strange co-op the different population groups are communicating through some sort of language. Their respective idioms are nevertheless drastically different, especially in the ways they tie together the sensible and the intelligible, the workers and the artisans empha-sizing their bodily needs (the Saussurean **S**), the guardians their desire for knowledge (the Saussurean s). The fullest and most balanced expressions are consequently exchanged in the entrance hall of the executive tower where the elevator boys are the only figures capable of communicating with everyone else. In contrast, the Basement floor and the Penthouse roof constitute impenetrable limits of language, the entire construction resting on a foundation of silent rocks and reaching into a sky of non-expressible meaning. In between are the guardians on the upper floors and the workers on the lower, the former focusing their desiring minds on the accumulation of knowledge about non-changeable Forms, the latter content with satisfying their bodily needs and fluctuating opinions.

Nothing new, of course. For already in the crucial passage that transfers the analogy of the Divided Line to the allegory of the Cave, Socrates suggested that

> we should take, as corresponding to the four sections, these four states of mind: *intelligence* for the highest, *thinking* for the second, *belief* for the third, and for the last *imagining*. These you may arrange as the terms in a proposition, assigning to each a degree of clearness and certainty corresponding to the measure in which the objects possess truth and reality.[15]

That measurable measure of truth and reality is indeed to be found also in the layout of the Plotinian House, a construction of understanding with several levels, each one resting on its own hypo-stasis:

THE ONE

THE INTELLECT

THE SOUL

---

image

plant

In Plotinus's own words, themselves forerunners to the later debates at Nicaea:

> The *One* is all things and not a single of them: it is the principle of all things, not all things, but all things have that other kind of transcendent existence: for in a way they do occur in the One; or rather they are not there yet, but they will be. . . . The One, perfect because it seeks nothing, has nothing, overflows, as it were, and its superabundance makes something other than itself. This, when it has come into being, turns back upon the One and is filled, and becomes the *Intellect* by looking towards it. . . . This activity springing from the substance of the Intellect is *Soul* [which] does not abide unchanged [but] brings

forth an *image* [and eventually] reaches as far as the *plants*. . . . All these things are the One and not the One.[16]

*

It takes little imagination (merely a turn from the vertical to the horizontal) to transform the Saussurean rendering of Plotinus into an architectural drawing of Plato's Cave. The latter is nowadays often pictured as an old-fashioned movie theater with the guardians seated in the back rows, ready to escape, and the workmen on benches up front, too close to the screen for grasping what is going on:

> Next, said I, here is a parable to illustrate the degrees in which our nature may be enlightened or unenlightened. Imagine the condition of men living in a sort of cavernous chamber underground, with an entrance open to the light and a long passage all down the cage. Here they have been from childhood, chained by the leg and also by the neck, so that they cannot move and can see only what is in front of them, because the chains will not let them turn their heads. At some distance higher up is the light of a fire burning behind them; and between the prisoners and the fire is a track with a parapet along it, like the screen at a puppet-show, which hides the performers while they show their puppets over the top.
>
> I see, said he.
>
> Now behind this parapet imagine persons carrying along various artificial objects, including figures of men and animals in wood and stone or other materials, which project above the parapet. Naturally some of these people will be talking, others silent.
>
> It is a strange picture, he said, and a strange sort of prisoners.
>
> *Like ourselves*, I replied, for in the first place prisoners so confined would have seen nothing of themselves or of another, except the shadows thrown by the fire-light on the wall of the cave facing them, would they? . . . Now, if they could talk to one another, would they

not suppose that their words referred only to those passing shadows which they saw? . . .

No doubt.

In every way, then, such prisoners would recognize as reality nothing but the shadows of those artificial objects.

Inevitably.

Now consider what would happen if their release from the chains and the healing of their unwisdom should come about in this way. Suppose one of them set free and forced suddenly to stand up, turn his head, and walk with eyes lifted to the light; all these movements would be painful, and he would be so dazzled to make out the objects whose shadows he had been used to see. What do you think he would say, if someone told him that what he had formerly seen was meaningless illusion, but now, being somewhat nearer to reality and turned towards more real objects, he was getting a truer view? . . . Would he not be perplexed and believe the objects shown him to be not so real as what he formerly saw.[17]

Ludwig Wittgenstein almost certainly knew what the released would have said: "I have gone mad!"[18] He would then have added, "This expression is merely another way of saying that I don't know my way about, that my social compass has lost its bearings, my map its scale. What I see looks so unfamiliar because my translation function has gotten all screwed up, nothing about aborted signs, nothing but mute Signifiers with no signifieds to unlock them." But as soon as the cave-dwellers, chained by the leg and by the neck, have heard these words from the aristocrat, then they, like ourselves,

would laugh at him and say he had gone up into the light only to come back with his sight ruined; it was worth no one's while even to attempt the ascent. If they could lay hands on the man who was trying to set them free and lead them up, they would kill him.[19]

Finally, Socrates' own summarizing conclusion, a rhetorical masterpiece starting with a well-defined beginning and ending with a firm conclusion. Like all analyses a travel story in disguise:

> Every feature in this parable, my dear Glaucon, is meant to fit our earlier analysis. The prison dwelling corresponds to the region revealed to us through the sense of sight, and the free-light within to the power of the Sun. The ascent to these things in the upper world you may take as standing for the upward journey of the soul into the region of the intelligible; then you will be in possession of what I surmise, since that is what you wish to be told. Heaven knows whether it is true; but this, at any rate, is how it appears to me. In the world of knowledge, the last thing to be perceived and only with great difficulty is the essential Form of Goodness. Once it is perceived, the conclusion must follow that, for all things, this is the cause of whatever is right and good; in the visible world it gives birth to light and to the lord of light; while it is itself sovereign in the intelligent world and the parent of intelligence and truth. Without having had a vision of the Form no one can act with wisdom, either in his own life or in matters of state.[20]

*

A premonition. For killing the truth-saying Socrates is exactly what the Athenians did, perhaps because they understood that the Cave allegory equated the prisoners with the crowd, downgraded common beliefs, and showed that the very purpose of the dialectic is to destroy the taken-for-granted. Dangerous in deed, especially as Socrates's dialectic focuses less on *what* we see and more on *how* we see, not a technique which like geometry and mathematics draws conclusions from a set of premises but an art that rules over all the other sciences. Just as the angels descended and ascended Jacob's ladder, so the modern dialecticians use the Plotinian elevator to carry them from the workers' basement to the ruler's penthouse. Once there the doors slide open and the wisdom-lovers are free to enter the smoke-filled rooms of the privileged, some so enchanted by the *alta vista* that they will never want to leave, others so taken by the experience that they return back to the dungeons as self-appointed missionaries. At any rate,

> no one will maintain against us that there is any other method of inquiry which systematically attempts in every case to grasp the nature of each thing as it is in itself. The other arts are nearly all concerned with human opinions and desires, or with the production of natural or artificial things, or with the care of them when produced. There remain geometry and those other allied studies which, as we said, do in some measure apprehend reality; but we observe that they cannot yield anything clearer than a dream-like vision of the real so long as they leave the assumptions they employ unquestioned and can give no account of them. If your premise is something you do not really know and your conclusion and the intermediate steps are *a tissue of things you do not really know,* your reasoning may be consistent within itself, but how can it ever amount to knowledge?
>
> [So] the method of dialectic is the only one which takes this course, doing away with assumptions and travelling up to the first principle of all, so as to make use of confirmation there. When the eye of the soul is sunk in a veritable slough of barbarous ignorance, this method gently draws it forth and guides it upwards, assisted in this work of conversion by the arts we have enumerated.[21]

A tissue of things you do not really know, assumptions not left unquestioned! Surely a case of the cartographer's projection screen par excellence, for just as *mappa* means "tablecloth" or "napkin" and *charta* stands for "leaf of paper," so a *tissue* is "a rich kind of cloth, often interwoven with gold or silver now applied to various rich or fine stuffs of delicate or gauzy structure, a 'fabric', 'network', 'web' (of things abstract, most usually of a bad kind, as absurdities, errors, falsehoods, etc.)."[22]

It cannot be said more clearly: if it were not for the resistance of the limestone wall, there would be no shadows in the cave, hence nothing for the prisoners to see and nothing for the wisdom-lovers to deconstruct; if it were not for the fabric of the *mappa*, there would be nothing to capture the cartographer's travel-story, hence no map to guide him; if there were no Saussurean Bar there would be neither Signifier nor signified, hence no language to translate. Rephrased: without the faculty of imagination, there would be no humans. The issue is, of course, whether the mapmakers can be trusted.

"May the gods bless you," smiled Athene otherwise known as the goddess of truth.

Edging

The question keeps returning: How do I find my way in the unknown? Plato's answer echoes back: by map and compass, picture and story.

More precisely: How is the semiotic animal made so obedient and so predictable? How are they constructed, the invisible maps and internalized compasses that inform the wanderer both where he is and where he should go, not in the visible landscapes of earth and air, fire and water, but in the invisible universe of the taken-for-granted? Is madness the price he is paying for the sins of penetrating the abyss between the five senses of the body and the sixth sense of culture? How do I communicate my findings in such a way that they at the same time appear true to me and trustworthy to you?

The answer is that I must produce a document that in the same gesture both shows and tells, a performance which is not merely *about* something but *is* that something itself. In short, a matter of rhetoric when it works, a challenge which Immanuel Kant took more seriously than most, his conception of understanding thoroughly soaked in metaphorical reason, a way of sharing the world which was doubly rooted in his own body and in the academic disciplines of architecture and geography.

Immediately one enters this terra incognita one discovers that many have been there before. Perhaps the first was Thales from Miletus, perhaps his pupil Anaximander, perhaps someone else with a made-up name from an unclocked time and uncharted place. Be this as it may, for the definite answer will never be known. One thing is nevertheless certain and that is that the legitimate father of modern reason is Immanuel Kant (1724–1804), Plato (428–348) its ageing grandfather, Ludwig Wittgenstein (1889–1951) its late-born Isaac. What links these giants together is not that their questions made them theoretical philosophers but that their answers made them practicing geographers, clandestine agents stationed in the no-man's land between sensibility and intelligibility, courageous explorers of the taboo-ridden realm of the taken-for-granted, self-appointed land surveyors commissioned to establish the line between the **Oikumene** of the humans and the **Anoikumene** of the gods and the brutes. Their challenges were the same as well, for they all believed that while we can think beyond the limits of our experiences, we cannot know the objects of such thoughts. And yet we are all using the expression "making sense" when "making intelligible" would be more appropriate.

It was this issue of truth and trust—the ultimate question of what it means to be human—that permeated Kant's teachings, not least the detailed analyses of the *Critique of Pure Reason*. And nowhere was this challenge more precisely located than in the first paragraph of the pivotal chapter, "On the Ground of Distinction of All Objects in General into Phenomena and Noumena," at the same time a summary of what has gone before and an anticipation of what was to come. In Max Müller's old-fashioned translation:

> We have now not only traversed the whole domain of pure understanding and carefully examined each part of it, measured its extent, and assigned to everything in it its rightful place. This domain, however, is an island and enclosed by nature itself within limits that can never be changed. It is the country of truth (a very attractive name), but surrounded by a wide and stormy ocean, the true home of illusion, where many a fog bank and ice that soon melts away tempt us to believe in new lands, while constantly deceiving the adventurous mariner with vain hopes, and involving him in adventures which he can never leave, and yet can never bring to an end. Before we venture ourselves on this sea, in order to explore it on every side, and to find out whether anything is to be hoped for there, it will be useful

to glance once more at the map of that country which we are about to leave, and to ask ourselves, first, whether we might not be content with what it contains, nay, whether we must not be content with it, supposing that there is no solid ground anywhere else where we could settle; secondly, by what title we possess even that domain and may consider ourselves safe against all hostile claims.[23]

Imagination at high pitch, cascades of brilliant associations, the master key to Kant's entire philosophy. No wonder that this time-bound traveler has been called *the* student of limits, his very name a handy revelation of his predilections—the German word *Kante* means literally "edge." The true purpose of philosophy, he claimed, is to expose the illusions of reason by reminding us of its limits, none of them more fundamental than the one that runs between phenomena and noumena, the former representations of things *as they appear* to the senses, the latter representations *as they are*, hence knowable only to the *nous* of pure understanding. Clearly an Enlightenment project steeped in the tension between identity and difference; in the land surveyor's own words:

Two things fill the mind with ever new and increasing admiration and reverence, the more often and the more steadily one reflects upon them: *the starry heavens above me and the moral law within me.* I do not need to search for them and merely conjecture them as though they were veiled in obscurity or in the transcendent region beyond my horizon; I see them before me and connect them immediately with the consciousness of my existence. The first begins from the place I occupy in the external world of sense and extends the connection in which I stand into an unbounded magnitude with worlds upon worlds and systems of systems. . . . The second begins from my invisible self, my personality, and presents me in a world which has true infinity, but which can be discovered only by the understanding.[24]

It cannot be said more clearly: Kant's entire oeuvre may be viewed as an exhibition of invisible lines, one type dividing and discriminating, another orienting and connecting, the former telling him where in his thinking he is, the latter to where he should go. What is at stake is not the particular knowledge that is caught in the conceptual net but the structure of the net itself. Rephrased,

> thoughts without content are empty, intuitions without concepts are blind. It is therefore, just as necessary to make our concepts sensible, that is, to add the object of them in intuition, as to make our intuitions intelligible, that is, to bring them under concepts. These two powers or capacities cannot exchange their functions. The understanding can intuit nothing, the senses can think nothing. Only through their union can knowledge arise. But that is no reason for confounding the contribution of either with that of the other; rather it is a strong reason for carefully separating and distinguishing the one from the other.[25]

It follows that a priori knowledge is possible only under the provision that the objects of experience conform to the constitution of our minds, only if body and imagination can be perfectly mapped one onto the other; as Ludwig Wittgenstein wrote, to follow a rule is to follow it blindly, to obey an order before it is uttered. Finding the way is consequently to be so fully integrated in one's culture that one knows neither this nor that, neither how nor why. An alternative way of phrasing James Joyce's dream of perfect writing, nowhere as beautifully illustrated as in Molly Bloom's flow of consciousness.

*

The ensuing power struggle is by definition a struggle over limits, the struggle over limits itself a matter of drawing a line, of pointing and naming. Kant's own approach to this problem was to say that the objects of the synthetic a priori are products of our consciousness, especially of the ways in which we share our sense impressions with each other. In addition, he claimed that these invisible objects are not discovered after the fact (*a posteriori*) but are somehow given to us in advance (*a priori*). In opposition to previous thinkers, the world traveler who never left home argued that the relation is exactly the reverse, nature mirroring thought rather than thought mirroring nature. So radical was this reversal that he dubbed it his "Copernican revolution in epistemology," an idea that eventually led Friedrich Nietzsche to the conclusion that God is dead. Just as the Polish astronomer had proven that the earth moves around the sun, not the sun around the earth, so the German philosopher reasoned that the fix-point of understanding lies in thoughts, not in things.

The question poses itself: through which socialization processes is the a priori formed and institutionalized? The answer, so it seems, lies in Kant's conception of geography, a mode of reason so close to his own taken-for-granted that he had no alternative but to pass it over in silence. Crucial are nevertheless his remarks concerning the limits of knowledge, themselves operationalized in the difference between the marking of limits (*Schranken*) and the drawing of boundaries (*Grenzen*); in short, what lies inside the limits of language can be shared, whatever lies outside its boundary cannot.[26] As succinctly presented by Edward Casey: "Limit, like shape, belongs primarily to what is limited and only secondarily to what does the limiting (e.g. a container). [To] be a boundary, by contrast, is to be exterior to something, or more exactly, to be *around* it, *enclosing* it, acting as its surrounder. As such, a boundary belongs to the container rather than the contained";[27] an echo of Plato's distinction between *topos* and *chora*, the fetus and the womb. Along the same line it has been argued that "ignorance is a limit in knowledge, but such a limit can be of two kinds. It may be a limit that derives simply from the fact that there are things with which we are acquainted, or it may derive from the way in which our knowledge is itself determined, and so limited, in its very nature. Ignorance that arises on the basis of the latter may be termed necessary."[28] An obvious question is what can or cannot be said about the gap between a conditional (hence unstable) limit and the absolute boundary. As Wittgenstein put it, the aim

is to set a limit to thought, or rather—not to thought but to the expression of thoughts: for in order to be able to set a limit to thought, we should have to find both sides of the limit thinkable (i.e. we should have to be able to think what cannot be thought). It will therefore only be in language that the limit can be set, and what lies on the other side of the limit will simply be nonsense. . . . *Wovon man nicht sprechen kann darüber muss man schweigen.*[29]

Now, just as that quandary grew out of the distinction between *Schranken* and *Grenzen,* so the latter concepts are deeply rooted in Kant's geography lectures, especially in the circumstance that unlike the casual observer, to whom the earth *appears* as a flat surface, every schoolboy *knows* first that it is a sphere and then, as a geometric consequence, that there is a world also beyond the horizon. And just as the horizon can never be seen from without, so the same holds for the boundary. Rephrased, the Kantian space of reason has its roots in the irreconcilable tension between the solid island of truth and the wide and stormy ocean around it, his life's obsession to mark, once and for all, the exact location of the shoreline, an Egyptian land surveyor resurrected.

The conclusion is that what I happen to see depends on where I happen to stand—*the* lesson from the Renaissance rediscovery of the perspective, no subsequent paintings without it—an insight which Kant pursued in the famous essay "What Is Orientation in Thinking?" At issue there is nothing less than the cartographer's fix-point of fix-points, by necessity one with the asymmetric body that the observer shares with everyone else, left hand to the left and right hand to the right, head up and feet down, face in front, rump in the back. However, since cartography by definition is an exercise in triangulation it is not enough for the mapmaker to anchor what he is seeing in the subjectivity of the observing body, it must also be tied to an objective entity outside it. While in the history of mapping this external point has usually been located in the fixity of the North Star (eventually in the shiftiness of the magnetic North Pole) the creators of the medieval *mappa mundi* took it to be Paradise, its exact location never found but always taken to be in the direction of the rising sun—the etymology of the verb "to orientate" is to face toward the east, the garden of Eden the hook on which the O/T maps were hung. But where is it, and what does it look like, the Paradise (alternatively Hell) that is guiding the thoughts-

and-actions of today's presidents, prime ministers, ayatollas and CEOS? At bottom a power-filled question of politics, by definition an issue about the relations between identity and difference, me and you, individual and society, the one and the many. And so it is that

> in the original synthetical unity of apperception I am conscious of myself, neither as I appear to myself, nor as I am myself, but only that I am. This representation is an act of thought, not of intuition. . . . I have no knowledge of myself as I am, but only as I appear to myself. . . . As for the knowledge of an object different from myself I require . . . an intuition also of the manifold in me. . . . I exist, therefore, as such an intelligence, which is simply conscious of its power of connection.[30]

And with that observation it returns, the original challenge of the birds and the egg, the eggs and the bird. How do I learn to think-and-write in such a way that it is not *about* something, but *is* that something itself, the impossible dream of perfect translation. Kant's answer was that since we cannot reach the things-in-themselves we must be content with reaching the things-in-us, not persist in our search for the noumena that subsist independently of human cognition but be satisfied with our knowledge of the phenomena whose existence depends entirely on our cognitive apparatus. Whether the definition of phenomena and noumena commits him to a one- or to a two-world view has been much and inconclusively debated.

*

Human, all too human. But what does it look like, the island of truth, Kant's realist version of Plato's and Olof Rudbeck's fanciful Atlantis, by the former located in the Garden of the Hesperides somewhere to the west of Gibraltar, by the latter in Sweden?

"Thought you'd never ask," said the immortal sea captain. "Now come with me down to the wharfs where I'll give you a speedboat with a pilot and the latest navigation instruments."

Said and done. Off they go, across the Red River Bay and through the narrow straights, the beacon of Scylla de Saussure on the starboard, the lighthouse of Lacan's Charybdis on the portside. "Get ashore," says the goddess, no longer disguised. "I'll track your tale just as I once did with that twisty man who traveled widely. Here's a map in case you get lost. Take your time, wander around, learn by yourself how to find your way. I'll be waiting for you in the castle, more precisely in the place which on the map is marked with a big **X**, the copulation chamber where you were once conceived and the chapel in which you were eventually confirmed."

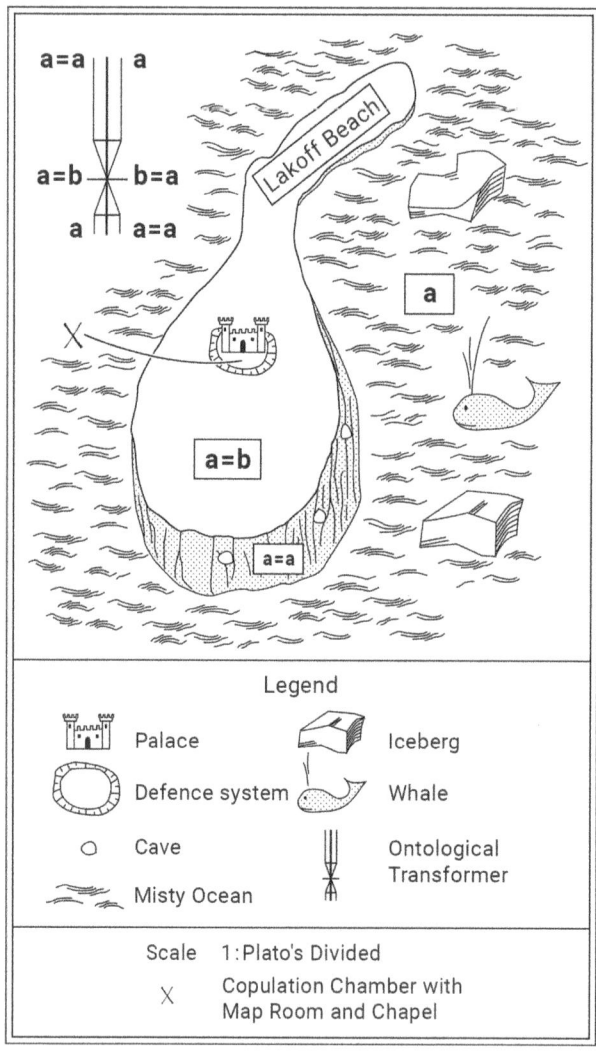

The Kantian *Island of Truth.*

Island of Truth

Shaped as a Wittgensteinian duck-rabbit is the island, its name

$$a = b$$

one with its meaning, a domain where the explorer may consider himself safe against all hostile claims. A code name admittedly not as attractive as Kant's original suggestion, merely an echo of the saying that to tell the truth is to claim that something is something else and be believed when you do so. The inhabitants of this familiar realm are likewise, a bastardous blend of semiotic and political animals, ironic creatures who after long practice have learned to live with the tensions between identity and difference. Driven by an irresistible desire to turn everything into copies of themselves, these human-like beings have all been drafted into a rhetorical army of metaphors, metonymies, and anthropomorphisms, trouping tropes designed to change illusion into reality. And so it is that the island is not merely an island of trustworthy truths but a continent of unassailable power.

While the occupants of this imaginary nation are spread across the realm, their ruler resides in a centrally located castle, by some called the World Center. Flown from its main tower is a banner designed as a blood-colored square with a black equal-sign, a most fitting symbol for the Supreme whose name is one with his personality:

$$A = A$$

The relations between this self-appointed potentate and his subjects are governed by a constitutional law of the Mosaic type. From its first paragraph echoes the message that

I am the one, only I beneath the moon and under the sun. Night and day I shall be under the hide of you. Make no mistake, though, for through my self-definition I shall tolerate no usurper and I shall destroy any yokel who stands before or beside me.

This jealous despot is well aware that he is always threatened, his power under constant attack. As Shakespeare lets Cæsar put it:

I could well be mov'd, if I were as you;
If I could pray to move, prayers would move me;
But I am constant as the northern star,
Of whose true-fix'd and resting quality
There is no fellow in the firmament.
The skies are painted with unnumber'd sparks,
They are all fire, and every one doth shine;
But there's but one in all doth hold his place.
So in the world: — 'tis furnish'd well with men,
And men are flesh and blood, and apprehensive;
Yet in the number I do know but one
That unassailable holds on his rank,
Unshak'd of motion; and that I am he.[31]

For his own protection the dictator then proceeds to construct around himself a two-tier defense system consisting of both a wall and a moat, the former constructed as a ban on the (mis)use of metaphor, the latter as a rule against the creative associations of metonymy. The intention of this second paragraph of the Constitutional Law is, of course, to silence any critique before it is uttered, to ensure that

You, my subject, you as well as your descendants, shall for ever know your place, never commit the sins of trespassing. Wherefore, you must never question my authority, never make of me a caricature, never use my name in vain.

Totalitarianism operationalized, the rhetorical animal not merely circumcised but castrated. The very point of outlawing the *as-if* is, of course, that the RULER thereby guarantees that nothing new will ever issue from his subjects but always emanate from himself and from himself alone. With that purpose constantly in mind he then assigns every phenomenon or sense-thing its rightful place, all social relations between people automatically turned into material relations between things. Countless slaves in the treadmills, none on the chariot. The censor at work.

Surrounding the island of power is a wide and stormy ocean, the true home of illusion. At the same time forbidding and tempting this vast unknown is the domain of the noumena or thought-things, unapproachable in their own right. Nameable only in the islanders' own language, this ambiguous area is called

a

not because the metaphorical fog banks *are* **a**, but because the semiotic animal would not be what it is if it did not call it something. The very purpose of the baptizing ceremony is in fact to function as a pair of forceps, the name itself a conceptual tool by which the ontological magician can handle non-graspable noumena *as if they were* graspable phenomena.

The northern part of the island consists of a low-lying cape with sandy beaches, a tourist paradise developed and controlled by the consortium Lakoff & Associates, Inc. The leading idea of this group is that language is essentially metaphorical and that our unconscious therefore is structured like a body; *without body, no thought,* such is the slogan by which the Californians are trying to perform the same upside-down operation on Immanuel Kant as Karl Marx once did on G. W. F. Hegel.

For these reasons the Lakoff Cape would be well worth a study of its own. For the present explorer, however, it seems even more rewarding to study the coastal area in the southwestern part of the island, a precipitant landscape that looks like the cliffs of Dover, albeit with a geology of firm granite rather than vaporous limestone. Cut into these steep and inaccessible formations are a number of caves, most of them nesting areas of the albatross, some inhabited by a group of autistic solipsists. Since these outcasts are more interested in telling the truth than in being believed, they call themselves

a = a

a name which they synecdochically attach to their region as well.

Since the cave-dwellers find socializing exceedingly difficult, the only thing to tie them together is a deep sense of rejection, a kind of hatred that is directed less against the self-acclaimed despot and more against his self-serving lackeys. The most eloquent among them, those who are open to abstract thought, focus their opposition not on the outward signs of power but on the third paragraph of the Constitutional Law, the codified set of beliefs through which the emperor legitimates his naked behavior. Here, then, is the thesis about the necessary unity of consciousness in another form:

> **Remember that you are nothing but a cog in the Ruler's machinery. Never question the righteousness of the collective, always remain convinced that the individual is wrong. I am your Ruler, the spiritualized embodiment of your taken-for-granted, the pivot of your world.**

Whether by force or choice the cave-dwellers occupy the inaccessible boundary zone between the solid phenomena of the island and the fleeting noumena of the sea. Most of them would rather die than submit, rather shut up than be silenced.

Given this information, the secret agent took it as his mission to measure the outer limits of the island and draw a map thereof including the Lakoff Beach, the in-between zone of the tidal area, home of the taboo-laden shellfish. During that work the explorer quickly discovered that without the assistance of the cave-dwellers he could never capture in the same glance both the a posteriori phenomena of the island and the a priori noumena of the ocean. Only with their help could he hope to stake the boundary between the two realms of cognition, the line better known as Ferdinand de Saussure's Bar or as Samuel Beckett's Tympanum, the thin foil which is one with every mapper's *mappa*.

*

The typical cave-dweller is a dedicated artist. And as such s/he is driven by the idea of simultaneously grasping the phenomena of the five senses and the noumena of the sixth, the bodily organ of the eye and the cultural meaning of the glance. In reality a mission impossible, a task which Paul

Cézanne once outlined in his description of how a tube of ready-made paint may be turned into the revelations of a Swedenborgian angel:

> At times I conceive of colours as vast *noumenal entities*, ideas with a physical presence, creatures of pure reason, with whom we can enter into relations. Nature is not an affair of the surface; it is in depth. Colours express the depth of the surface. They arise from the roots of the world. They are its life, the life of ideas.[32]

And in that conjunction the seemingly different approaches of Francis Bacon and Mark Rothko—two of Cézanne's outstanding descendants—turn out to be remarkably instructive.

Imagine, therefore, that one fine morning these equally dedicated individuals crawl out of their caves, reach for the ladders, and climb to the cliff's edge. Once there they set up their easels, Rothko turned toward the mist-enveloped sea, Bacon looking the other way. Drunk on the spirits of the Saussurean Bar both of them share the same dream of painting their self-portraits, by definition their personal understanding of what it means to be human. However, as their viewing angles are radically different, what they see is radically different too; while Bacon's eyes are drawn to the naked bodies of the islanders, *les boudins à la Mésopotamie*, Rothko's mind is spellbound by the fog banks and the melting icebergs, visible signs of the invisible.

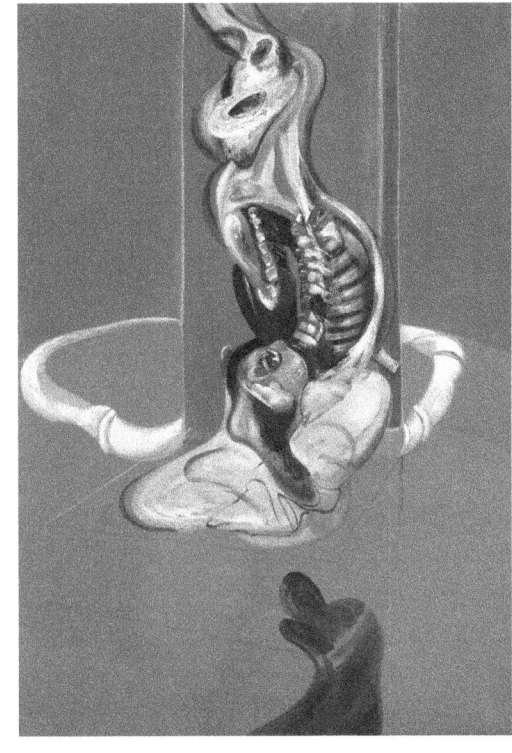

Francis Bacon, *Three Studies for a Crucifixion.* Third panel. 1962. Oil with sand on canvas, 198 × 145 cm. The Solomon R. Guggenheim Museum, New York. © The Estate of Francis Bacon. All rights reserved. / BUS 2019.

From these diverse vantage points it was possible for Bacon to produce some of art history's most brutal paintings of human flesh, violence, and deprivation, for Rothko to create what are among the most sensitive and moving color studies ever made—while to the former the world was cruelty and pain, to the latter it was nothing but mute presence. With Bacon a pope in a cage or a lover carcassed on a butcher's hook, Edvard Munch's *Scream* at a higher pitch, Titian's *Flaying* a cut deeper, always a body trying to escape from itself through itself. With Rothko infra-thin layers of red for the happy days, dark greys for the deepest depressions, in both cases a god-like breath breathed onto a non-prepared canvas, the well cleaned brush as soft as silk, the work of art always an instance of plasticity. The cruelty of facts versus the tender touch, the horrible versus the sublime. And yet, to both masters, as to any great artist, the subject of their painting was always the actual *paint*ing itself, the fashioning of a sort of liquid and nameless geometry; in Rothko's own words, "A painting is a statement of the artist's notions of reality in the terms of plastic speech. In that sense the painter must be likened to the philosopher rather than to the scientist."[33]

Mark Rothko, *Untitled*. 1969. Acrylic on canvas, 206.5 × 193.7 cm. National Gallery of Art, Washington DC. Gift of the Mark Rothko Foundation, Inc. © Mark Rothko / BUS 2019.

So unyielding was the commitment of the two contemporaries (Bacon 1909–92, Rothko 1903–72) that it led both of them to predictable suicides, equally sad albeit with a crucial difference. For it now turns out that with Bacon the immediate victim was not the artist himself but his friend George Dyer, the violent drug addict who killed himself in a Paris hotel room two nights prior to the opening of Bacon's 1971 retrospective at the Grand Palais, the most significant exhibition he up till then had ever staged. For Rothko, though, there was never a substitute, no ram caught with its horns in a thicket, no angel descending from the sky.

In the mapper's imagination the two self-killings come together in a diptych of the second commandment, for whereas the atheist Englishman naturally assigned descriptive titles to his figures of crucifixion, the Russian Jew called his best canvases nothing but *Untitled*. The heritages of Odysseus and Abraham in another guise, the lover's name no secret worth hiding, the LORD's identity an unmentionable mystery that even the atheist knew may be neither said nor shown. In the pregnant words of Bacon himself: "Images just drop in as if they were handed down to me. Really, I think of myself as a maker of images. The image matters more than the beauty of the paint. [However], if you can make the image with the mystery of the paint, so much the better."[34]

In his best moments Mark Rothko managed to do exactly that, to make the image with the mystery of the paint, in that respect similar to Cézanne himself. And not only was Rothko the better for it, but he paid a horrible price for the blessing. Because I, the LORD, the God of thy immigrant parents, am a jealous God, visiting the iniquities of the fathers unto the third and fourth generations. But beware, Dear Critic, and always remember—for thy own sake—that the Almighty will not hold him guiltless that taketh his name in vain.

Two remarkable explorations of the lines of power and the limits of language, Francis Bacon annihilating the cave dweller's importance as an animal creature, Mark Rothko elevating his own worth as a sensitive intelligence, large, vibrant, and iconic. The screen of the cartographer's *mappa* unveiled. For every serious artist is obsessed with the idea of making his own self-portrait, thereby manifesting what the naked eye cannot see.

And so it is that the lines of power and the limits of language come together in the cartographer's scale, a device patterned after the Divided Line of the *Republic*, its fix-point lodged in Plato's boundary between invisible forms and visible objects, the *agora* of Greek thought. This boundary-line is the magic wand by which word turns to flesh and everything solid melts into air, the freezing point of Celsius's zero metaphorized, the shoreline of the magic island.

Therefore, once the explorer returns to the RULER's palace he finds that stationed in its watchtower is a cadre of cadets. Since these underlings do not know where the power they are set to guard is actually hiding, they devote their energy to ensuring that the paragraphs of the Constitutional Law are honored and obeyed. The mapper, however, was better informed and could therefore place on the map Athene's X, a sign that points the treasure hunter to a well-appointed apartment located in the castle basement. It is there, in a velvet-clad copulation chamber, that the semiotic and political animals come together to con-verse, literally "to turn oneself into another." It is in this incestual room that the semiotic animal is first conceived and then brought to life.

Leading out of the copulation chamber are two doors made of cedar wood, both exits guarded by some trusted eunuchs. Hidden behind one of them lie the archives of the Royal Map Room, an underground intelligence center inundated by the smell of *as-if*, its shelves filled with technical information about the cartographers' fix-points, scales, and *mappae*, including the architectural drawings of the castle, the wall, and the moat. And tucked away in the vast library, unknown to anyone but the few, are two rare volumes, one entitled *Abysmal: A Critique of Cartographic Reason*, the other *Arkography: A Grand Tour through the Taken-for-Granted*.

The other door of the copulation room leads to a chapel, the holiest place on the island. In that sanctuary, open day and night, a choir keeps repeating that it is you, you, you who are the one, only you beneath the moon and under the sun. Not, however, because you happen to be anything special, but because the Kantian thesis about the unity of consciousness connects your person with the person of everyone else. Woven into the lyrics are echoes of Thomas Hobbes, the power analyst who long before the Königsberger understood that whosoever looketh into himself, and considereth what he doth, when he does *think, opine, reason, hope, feare, &c*, and upon what grounds; he shall thereby read and know, what are the thoughts, and Passions of all other men, upon the like occasions. I say the similitude of *Passions*, which are the same in all men, *desire, feare, hope &c*; not the similitude of *the objects* of Passions, which are the things *desired, feared, hoped, &c*. . . . [And] when I shall have set down my own reading orderly, and perspicuously, the pains left another, will be onely to consider, if he also find not the same in himself. For this kind of Doctrine, admitteth no other Demonstration.[35]

A universe of human relations deduced from the principle of self-preservation, such is the Hobbesian common-wealth. Sadly outdated, though, not least because to Hobbes the thought of suicide bombing was too inhuman even to imagine. The frontispiece of his book nevertheless remains a poignant illustration of the structure of power, for in this Arcimboldo-like engraving the sovereign's body is constructed out of the many bodies of his subjects, the ruler's head adorned with the king's crown, his right hand holding a sword, his left hand a bishop's staff. What a magnificent illustration of the fact that to govern is to cause to believe. Another map of the Island of Truth-and-Power, in the palace chapel actually used as an altar piece.

Manipulated frontispiece of
Thomas Hobbes's *Leviathan*.

The strength of the isosceles triangle epitomized, one of the most power-filled images of power ever imagined. But the biblical Leviathan—Hobbes's vision of power—was itself a monster "with a heart as firm as stone, yea, as hard as the nether millstone. . . . Upon earth there is not his like, who is made without fear."[36] Yet, the most striking difference between Hobbes and Kant is that in the commonwealth of the former the sovereign is a chimera composed of the likes of you and me, while on the island of the latter the inhabitants are human beings exactly because we share our consciousness with everyone else.

*

In the deep vaults of the castle the critic of cartography gradually realizes that the Kantian conception of truth is at the same time a celebration of a reasoning mode on its deathbed and an anticipation of something not yet imagined: a deceptive story transformed into a picture of adventures that we can never leave and never bring to an end; a foretaste of what it means to talk about cartographical reason in the idiom of cartographical reason; a preliminary preface to a fourth Critique, the particular mode of thought-and-action which Kant himself lived and therefore could neither think nor act.

For the same reasons of self-reference it is impossible to say anything definite about the present, even less about the future. Yet the explorer cannot help but be impressed by the protesters who never yield, those who refuse to be caught in the ruler's coordinate net, to be weighed on the sovereign's scale, to be screened by the land surveyor's *mappa*. Especially insulted are those rebels whom the Almighty continues to call **b** even though they themselves know, beyond a doubt, that they are not **b** at all, but something entirely different. Perhaps **c**, perhaps **d**, perhaps **e**, perhaps something that may be neither grasped nor mentioned.

Not so strange, therefore, that these late-born Ishmaels often dream of a life at sea, maybe remembering that their Melvillean namesake was the only one to survive Moby-Dick's revenge, the imagination that floated away in a coffin destined for a future different from that of Captain Ahab and the rest of his crew, those unfortunate believers who were pulled down into the depths of the unknown, Melville's key saying that of the high seas there can be no maps, because on the high seas there is no solid ground on which to settle, no fix-points fixed, no lighthouses lit. To the eyes of the helmsman the scales are wavy, the *mappae* fluid.

Not to Pallas Athene, though, the guardian who is there to greet the explorer when after his visit to the secret map room and the holy chapel he returns to the copulation room. "How was it?" she asks. "Marvelous," he replies, "but nothing compares to the glass tetrahedron on the altar table, a sculpture which reminded me most vividly of the ark in Moses's tabernacle. In addition, and potentially even more important, next to that piece I discovered a document authored by a person named Gunnael Jensson and entitled *Mappa Mundi Universalis*, evidently a blueprint of how people in the twentieth century were finding their way in the world. I should of course be ashamed, but I could not resist the temptation—I stole the text and took it with me. Please protect me when my transgression is discovered." "A promise is a promise," mused the temptress, the grey-eyed goddess of truth.

* * * * *

And she took in her hands what she had been given, promptly forwarding it to the Museum of Collective Memory where a modernist Codex is already being installed, like the works of Marcel Duchamp (daily companion for fifty-five years) a creation epic expressed in two media, both modes subject to the lawmaker's censorship paragraphs, §2a with its ban on charging metaphors, §2b with its prohibition against runaway metonymies. For just as in the Frenchman's case the crucial interaction is between (1) the Glass of *La mariée mise à nu par ses célibataires, même* and the notes of the *Green* and *White Boxes* and (2) the montage of *Étant donnés: 1° la chute d'eau, 2° le gaz d'éclairage* and its accompanying *Manual*, so (3) the same holds for Jensson's imagination, where the artifact of the *Crystal Palace* and the text of the *catechesis* are inseparably united.

It cannot be said more clearly: *La mariée*, the *Étant donnés*, and the *Mappa Mundi* are picture and story woven together, paradigmatic cases of Kantian reason and Platonic arkology, all three now on permanent show in the entrance hall of the Bar de Saussure.

$\frac{s}{s}$ MINDSCAPE $\frac{s}{s}$

$\frac{s}{S}$ HUMAN TERRITORY $\frac{s}{S}$

$\frac{s}{s}$

$\frac{s}{S}$ ROCKSCAPE $\frac{s}{S}$

MAPPA MUNDI
UNIVERSALIS

Gunnael Jensson
alias
Ole Michael Jensen & Gunnar Olsson

Glass pyramid on granite base, 64 × 64 × 49 cm. Mixed material
(Kalmar granite, Weissglass, gold, ruby).

Genesis

IN THE BEGINNING are the heavens and the earth. The earth is without form and void and there is darkness upon the face of the earth. Nothing to see, nothing to hear, nothing to touch, nothing to smell, nothing to taste. No distinction. No identity. No difference. In this spiritual land of silence there is a meaning so meaningful that it refuses to be expressed.

A wind moves across the void. Lightning. Thunder. Rainbow in the sky. Out of the mist rises a flat granite rock that gently slopes into the distant sea. In this physical land of silence is a matter so material that it emits no meaning whatsoever.

Strange creatures emerge out of Nowhere, quickly spreading across the rocky ground. A foot gets stuck in a crevice, others observe, and for the first time there is a difference important enough to make a difference. In the intercourse of the body and the stone, the origin of man is conceived.

The primordial distinction—**A**—splits into three: one a shadow of the shadow (**a**); one a tautological expression which keeps repeating that it is what it is (**a=a** or $\frac{a}{a}$); one an informative statement insisting that it is something else (**a=b**). Identity and difference separated and united. Atoms of understanding captured in a mushroom cloud of perpetual fission.

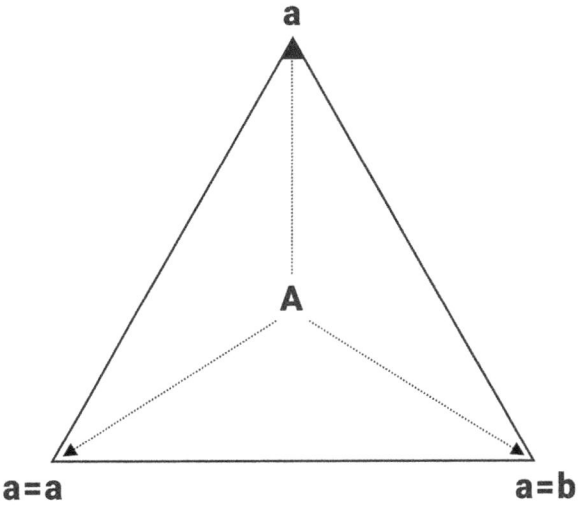

Points of Distinction

WHEN THE TENSION reaches its limit, the cloud bursts into fire. Out of the dusty ashes grows a Crystal Palace, sometimes known as the crucible of man, sometimes as the prison house of language. Both the floor and the walls are built as equal-sized equilateral triangles, the walls invisible, the foundation sunk into the granite ground. At the center of the basement is a well of identities and differences, its opening covered by a red-colored lid, itself the memorial mark of the original distinction and the trace of the first sacrifice, the blood from the killing of an identical twin, the footprints of a deviance turned scapegoat, the navel of what it means to be human.

A twist of cultural survival and the four-cornered deities merge into one, the multitudes of polytheism concentrating in the singularity of mono-theism. In the process of that unmooring, absolute power finds its place at the top of the pyramidal structure, a pivotal point which is the locus of a tautological and nameless entity that defines itself as that which it is: **A=A**. A contradictory condensation of identity and difference, one God one Being, the Almighty created in the image of man.

From its inception this Absolute speaks, its power one with its language, its language one with its power. "Let there be!" And there is. A universe flowing out of the actor's mouth.

In the coolness of the evening, the Absolute looks back at what he has uttered, claiming first that it is very good, then that he alone has the right to judge. Tolerating neither idols nor false prophets he declares that all usurpers will be killed. Impressed by his own achievements, he finally proclaims a day of rest, a Sabbath without work, twenty-four hours devoted to the glorification of himself and his faithfuls. Such is the subjection of subjects, such is the structure of dictatorial power. Now as well as then, then as well as now.

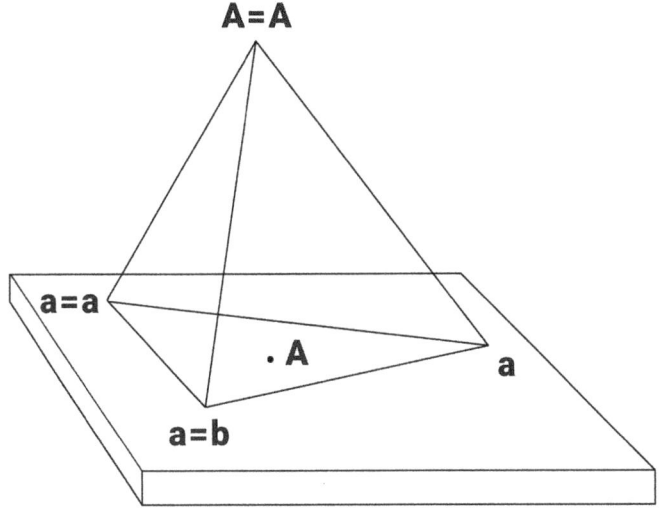

Crystal Palace

Laws

THE ALMIGHTY REALIZES that he leads a dangerous life. For that reason— and with the purpose of regulating the relations between ruler and ruled—he formulates a Constitutional Law, a power-filled document that begins with the reminder that it was he who liberated the suppressed, he who cut their chains, he who brought them out of the land of bondage. A rhetorical trick based on the false premise that old wolves automatically turn to peaceful sheep. And that is why the political atrocities of people like Stalin, Hitler, Mao, and Pol Pot are easy to explain, impossible to excuse.

Paragraph 1: You shall have no other ruler before me.

What is that? You shall fear and love your Leader above everything else, placing all your belief and trust in him. Martin Luther was rejected by the pope in Rome before he was accepted by the king in Stockholm, the praying Mohammed faced Jerusalem before he turned to Mecca.

EVERY DICTATOR KNOWS that to stay in power he must squash all opposition. But he also knows that all power rests in language. This in turn explains why the operationalization of the Constitutional Law takes the form of three lines extending from the top of the Crystal Pyramid to the corners at the base. It is through these communication lines that the Lord and his people are tied together into a network of mutual dependence. Issued from the top are orders that follow no rules but their own, predictable only in their unpredictability. Echoing from the underground is nothing but legitimation. In the rooms of the Almighty anything goes; in the dungeon of the critics translation is strictly forbidden.

Coupled with each line is a segment of the Law, each one a different aspect of §1. While paragraphs 2a and 2b are alike in the sense that they block all roads toward representation and thereby to critical understanding, paragraph 3 rules that in conflicts between the forces of collective cohesion and individual rebellion, the former are always right. While the paragraphs 2a and 2b ensure that only the Absolute can eat from the tree of knowledge, paragraph 3 focuses on the relations between categorization and socialization.

Paragraph 2a: You shall not make for yourself a graven image or any likeness of the Almighty, for no power-wielder allows his secrets to be revealed. No statue, no picture.

What is that? You shall fear and love your Lord without questioning who he is or what he does, accepting every decree as an integral part of the taken-for-granted. Forbidden is every attempt to picture the invisible, every attempt to sculpture the untouchable. In the world of the Crystal Palace, the message of §2a is transmitted through the communication line that runs from the tautological **A=A** to the informative **a=b**.

It is in the formulation of this paragraph that the lawmaker demonstrates how sophisticated his conception of power actually is. For the prohibition against images stems from the recognition that the likeness of metaphor plays the same role in the rhetorical art of ontological transformations as the igniting charge does in the engineering science of blasting. Since it is this device that turns untouchable ideology into touchable stone, visible structure into invisible meaning, the Absolute does his utmost to ensure that it will never fall into enemy hands; just as the ordinary dynamiter jealously guards his detonators, so does the Mosaic Absolute.

So important is this principle that any transgression is most severely punished—executed are not only the sinning fathers but also their children, grandchildren, and great-grandchildren. Any ruler who resorts to penalties of that magnitude is scared out of his wits. Given the outrageous claims of §1, he ought to be.

Paragraph 2b: You shall not misuse the name of your Leader, never tie his proper name to a definite description. For every power-wielder is eager to punish the truth-sayers and to reward the ass-lickers.

What is that? You shall love and fear your Lord and never use his name for evil wishes, swearing, lying, or deception. Forbidden is every mode of reformulation, every deconstruction of the sign, every visit to the Saussurean Bar. In the blueprint of the Crystal Pyramid, §2b is twined into the line that runs between the big tautology of **A=A** and the small tautology of **a=a**, the former located at the top of the world, the latter stuck into one of the bottom corners.

The Almighty categorically refuses to be categorized, and that is why he chooses a tautology as his name: "I am who I am." Always true, never informative. Yet, for the ruler who rules by systematically contradicting himself, no name is more appropriate. Beatings at dusk, blessings at dawn. Fear institutionalized. For he who has hit you once is likely to hit you again.

Tautology is the name of the Almighty. It is also the fix-point of two-valued logic. And herein lies the paradox of the social sciences, for whereas the words and objects of power never sit still, the words and objects of science must not hop capriciously about. It follows that logical analyses will never lead to a proper understanding of power itself. In studies of Venus, the planet, Bertrand Russell's theory of proper names and definite descriptions is often helpful. To the understanding of Venus, the goddess, it contributes little but confusion. The concepts of transparency and obliqueness are like oil and vinegar.

Paragraph 3: You shall attend all party meetings, never enter into the no-man's land between clean and unclean, never bite the hand that feeds you.

What is that? We shall fear and love our Leader together, gratefully honoring and obeying all his commands. For united we stand, divided we fall. §3 is the line that runs from the elevated **A=A** to the shadowy **a**.

WHILE THE REGULATIONS of §§2a and 2b address man in our appearance as a semiotic animal, §3 speaks to us as social and political beings. Of the three paragraphs, the third is in fact the most crucial, for without rules of conduct there is neither society nor individual, neither language nor power. It is by intercepting and decoding messages sent through this channel that we learn why and how we become so obedient and so predictable; the imperative of communication rests on a foundation of social control. The question is a question of socialization, the answer a bucketful of insights lifted from the well of original distinctions.

Projections

LINES ARE NOT ONLY connectives between points, they are also dividers between planes. In the latter function they constitute the corners of the Crystal Palace, at the same time separating and uniting the adjacent walls.

Grasping the nature of the invisible walls is extremely difficult, for even though we seem to be standing on the outside looking in, we are in fact confined to a life on the inside. In this prison house of language there are no windows and no escape routes, only a constant bouncing against unbreakable walls. Yet there are human lives and experiences of incredible richness, for the tetrahedron is in reality a gigantic movie theater, in each corner a projector, every wall a screen. The arrangement is familiar, its predecessors in the cave of Plato's *Republic*, in Fra Angelico's Prado version of the *Annunciation*, in Marcel Duchamp's *La mariée mis à nu par ses célibataires, même*. Without the limestone wall, the wood panel, and the transparent glass, these artists would have nothing to show, no means for capturing the split-up versions of the original distinction **A**.

When the golden rays hit the opposite plane at a right angle, they rebound to the point of origin, offering no news from the travel. This is the case of perfect translations and perfect signs, imaginable in theory but impossible in reality. From the **a=b** projector beam a set of definite descriptions, informative statements that are cast onto the wall of science as the perfect sign of $a=b$, a so-called *index*. Then, from the **a=a** corner come a series of creative images that are cast onto the canvas of aesthetics as the sign of $a=a$, in Charles Sanders Peirce's terminology an *icon*, in the world of semiotics the total-merger of Signifier and signified, here given as $\frac{a}{a}$. Finally, from the shadowy point of **a** issues the sign of a, the mantras of non-graspable religion that in Peirce's philosophy are called a *symbol*.

As the tautology is the fix-point of Aristotelean logic and Old Testament power, so the ninety-degree angle is the fix-point of Euclidean geometry and New Testament penance. But in the real world of imperfect communication, the projection lines never strike the knowledge planes straight on. Instead of bouncing back to their respective point of origin, they are reflected onto one of the other walls. This combined principle of uncertainty and complementarity explains why the three modes of knowledge—religion, science, and the arts—never appear in their pure form, always as a series of approximations, a chain reaction in which the ethics of religious belief turn to the logics of scientific law, the logics of scientific law to the aesthetics of artistic expression. And so on, and so on, one meaning colliding with another, the critical mass the trigger of itself.

And so it is that the corner lines of the Crystal Palace at the same time communicate the paragraphs of the Constitutional Law and mark the limits of the three planes of knowledge. Since limits by definition are taboo, the movements from one screen to another occur only through the intermediary of a transition rite. In Christianity these magic formulas are one with the sacraments, in Catholicism seven, with Luther condensed into two: baptism and communion. The latter ritual is intricately intertwined with §3 of the Law, the former with §§2a and 2b; while the naming ceremony of §2a is performed in the water of images, in §2b it is done in the medium of ordinary language.

No wonder that so many sinners pray that their trespasses be forgiven, no wonder that so many dictators kill those who trespass.

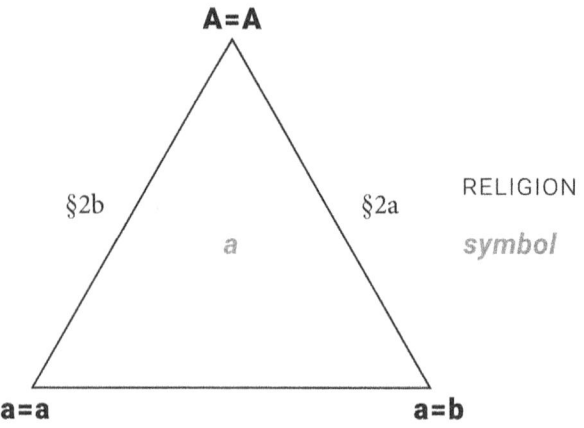

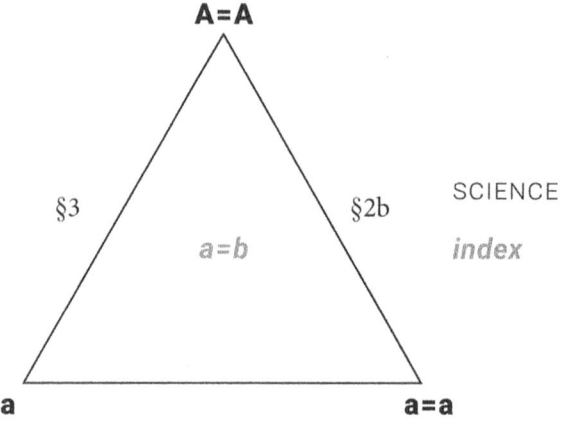

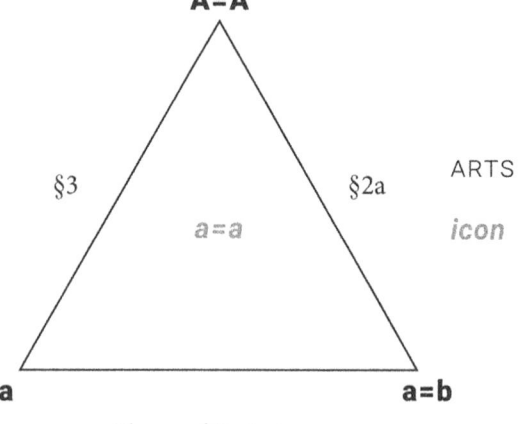

Planes of Projection

Trinity

IN THE BLUEPRINT of the Crystal Palace one trajectory is left invisible, perhaps because it is too culturally specific to be noticed. This is the line that runs from the **A=A** of God, the Father, to the **A** of the Holy Spirit. As recalled, the **A** stands for the covered mark of the original distinction, the **A=A** for its tautological reformulation, the trace of an aborted attempt at reification, a desire to concretize the abstract. The King is dead, long live the King!

Impressed by his own omnipotence the Absolute wants to return to the crevice of the original distinction, no longer satisfied with being the tautological reformulation **A=A** but obsessed with the desire of once again being one with the untouched purity of the **A**; as an early Narcissus also the Almighty strives to merge with his own image. To that end he tries to do away with himself by jumping out of his privileged position at the top. But in mid-air—moments before smashing through the lid and plunging into the covered well—he is caught in a semiotic rescue net whose corners are fastened to the perfect signs of the icon, the index, and the symbol. The prototype of this ontological surface was first invented in Nicaea in the year 325, whence it was formulated as a political/ theological commentary on the issues of representation in general and the prohibition against images in particular.

Floundering in the western net of perfect signs is nothing less than Jesus Christ, here known under the pseudonym **A=B**, by definition a complete merger of mind and matter, the logical union of **A** and **A=A**; as recalled, the only Son of God is defined as being of one substance (*homoousion*) with the Father, incarnated by the Holy Spirit and made man. Himself a sacrificed scapegoat, this epistemological savior eventually ascends to the heavens and gets appointed to the Highest Court, wherefrom he is now sentencing both the quick and the dead.

The most remarkable story of an ontological transformation ever to be told. The word made flesh, the unnameable named. Eucharist.

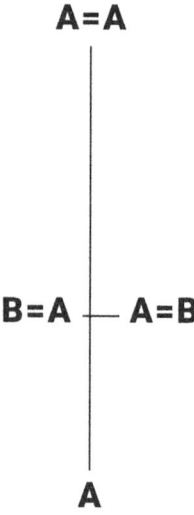

Line of Trinity

Mapping

THE CRYSTAL PALACE is a well-guarded castle, its ruling resident the tyrant of tyrants. Admittedly a rhetorical exaggeration, for no Absolute is absolutely absolute, no crook crooked enough to live on for ever. And for that reason it should be recalled that just as the doctrine of *imitatio dei*—the imitation of God—plays a central role in Jewish piety, so the imitation of Christ fills the same function in Christianity. The difference is nevertheless crucial: to imitate God (**A=A**) is to recant a tautological contradiction (**a=a**), to pray the mantra of the icon (a=a); to imitate Christ (**A=B**) is to reformulate a definite description (**a=b**), to invent an index (a=b).

The architectural tour of the Crystal Palace should not be interpreted as a glorification of life in a monotheistic temple. Instead it is the drawing of a heretic (not blasphemous) map of power, an attempt to understand how and why we find our way in a universe of obedient submission and unpredictable cruelty. Not a *Mappa Europæa Mundi* but a *Mappa Mundi Universalis*, a universal means for catching the world in a net of points, lines, and planes, the mandala constituting a typical non-Western case. As usual, it is more difficult to understand the world than to change it, for the reality of being has a richness that no abstraction can harness, a living life that neither stories nor pictures manage to name.

THE NINETY-DEGREE ANGLE is the fix-point of fix-points, a human invention of the highest rank. Triangulation is the name of the game, for in order to make a map only three ingredients are needed: the scale, the pointing arrow, the canvas. As triplets of the right angle these elements form the foundation on which the Crystal Palace is constructed, that power-filled edifice which at the same time is the crucible of man and the prison house of language. The Library of Invisible Maps is the best guarded part of the palace, for it is there that we learn how to learn, it is there that we find out both where we are and where we should go.

The **scale of scales** is by definition a translation function, the ruler over ontological transformations, the magic formula of "Let there be!—And there is." An early version is in the creation myth of Genesis, the most crucial reformulations in the Divided Line of Plato's *Republic* and the speech acts of Euclid's *Elements*.

The **pointer of pointers** is the hook on which everything is hung, the invisible force which in ordinary maps corresponds to the magnetic North Pole. The construction of the Crystal Palace is its counterpart in the collective unconscious and thereby in Plato's conception of the Sun, that medium which simultaneously lets us see and makes us blind. It should nevertheless be remembered that it was the exiled Jews who insisted that the Sun—which the idolatrous Babylonians took to be the god of gods—in fact is nothing but an illuminating lamp. A definite description of revolutionary importance, an act of cultural survival closely tied to §3 of the Constitutional Law. Attend the compulsory meetings and your eyes will be opened, the truth revealed!

But it must also be recalled that long before the events in Babylonia, the Sun's dethroner—the tautological Yahweh—had warned Moses, "You cannot see my face; for no one can see my face and live . . . And I will cover you with my hand until I have passed by, then I will take away my hand, and you shall see my back; but my face shall not be seen." And yet, that is exactly the blasphemous act that Jacob (the crook of crooks) claimed to have committed: seen God's face and survived.

The prophet Job had much the same experience, for also he told the story of how his ears first had heard about the Absolute then how his eyes had seen him. But unlike the treasonous Jacob, the man of integrity from the land of Uz was ashamed of what he saw, despising himself, repenting in dust and ashes. And he lived on in this world for another 140 years.

The **canvas of canvases** is the background cloth, the receptor onto which everything is projected, the tain of the mirror, Plato's limestone wall, Fra Angelico's wood panel, Duchamp's large glass, the screen that captures all signs. As a matter of fact, the canvas is nothing less than the physical resistance without which nothing can be noticed. The latter-day version of the granite rock that sprang a well of clear distinctions.

Revelation

IN THE PRACTICE of cartographical reason, man is once again put back at the center of the universe. No longer a noun, not even a verb. A preposition, a place assumed in advance! A point at which lines are projected onto a plane of power. A coordinate cross of right angles.

Such is the nature of cartographical reason, a mode of understanding at the verge of realizing that the canvas of the world is not a smooth flatness but a wrinkled manifold, that the pointer is not straight but crooked, that the scale is not a suspended line between *alpha* and *omega* but a Moebius band of chiastic reversals. And it has no idea what will happen next.

MAPPA MUNDI

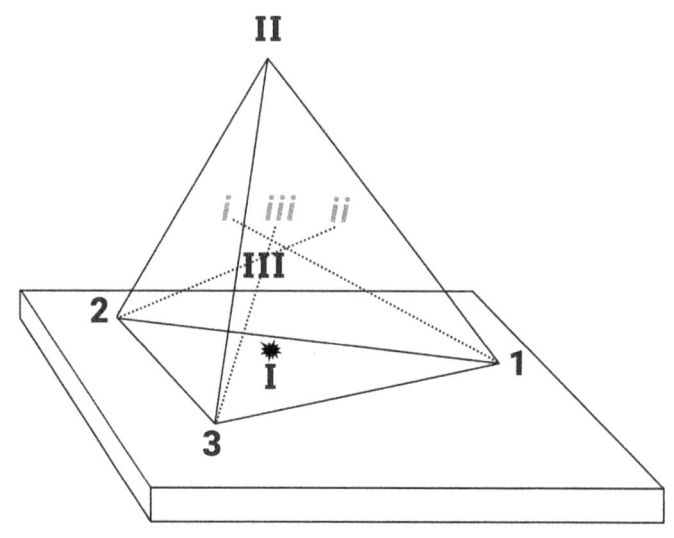

Compass   Scale

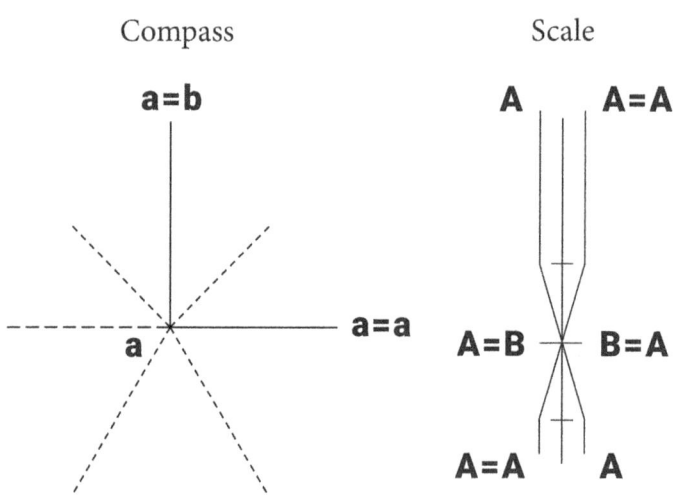

POINTS OF DISTINCTION

I	**A**	Foot in the crevice; Holy Spirit
II	**A=A**	Absolute power; God, the Father
III	**A=B**	Ontological transformation; Jesus Christ

LINE OF TRINITY

| II-III-I | Plato's Divided Line; Nicaea 325 |

Cornered Points of Distinction

1	**a**	Shadow
2	**a=a**	Tautology
3	**a=b**	Definite description

Lines of Power

II-3	§2a; Baptism by imaging
II-2	§2b; Baptism by naming
II-1	§3; Communion

PLANES OF KNOWLEDGE

II-2-3	Religion
II-3-1	Art
II-1-2	Science

Lines of Projection

1-*i*	Ethics
2-*ii*	Aesthetics
3-*iii*	Logics

Points of Signs

i	a	*symbol*
ii	a=a	*icon*
iii	a=b	*index*

■

MAPPING

MAPPING IS TRIANGULATION

TRIANGULATION IS THE GEOMETRY OF POWER

GEOMETRY OF POWER IS THE PRACTICE OF CARTOGRAPHICAL REASON

THE PRACTICE OF CARTOGRAPHICAL REASON IS THE CRITIQUE OF MAPPING

+

III

Crystal Palace

"Let it be known," said the reincarnated Athene, "that whenever I visit the Island Chapel, I am reminded of Plato's Academy and the rumor that its entrance was adorned with a well-wrought sign, at the same time inviting and forbidding." Not, as in the case of Auschwitz, *Arbeit macht frei*, but

HERE NOBODY ENTERS
WHO DOES NOT KNOW HIS GEOMETRY

The message was, of course, that the rules of geometry and the rules of thought are one and the same, the implication that whoever holds the keys to the former automatically knows the way also to the latter, triangulation the modus operandi of Euclid's proofs and Archimedes's deductions. "And let me retort," said Anaximander, father of the limitless *to apeiron*, "how modern critics hold not only that geography is best defined as a geometry with names, but that the Academy had both a public entrance and a secret exit." And next to that worm-eaten door was a penciled note:

HERE NOBODY LEAVES
WHO DOES NOT KNOW HER GEOGRAPHY

Easier said than done. For whereas naming the cornered points is daily business, baptizing the lines (the relations between the points) is like chasing a chameleon, capturing the planes (the taken-for-granted projection screens onto which the points and lines are cast) nothing less than a struggle with Gödel's impossibility theorem.

The roots reach deeply into the issue of what it means to be human, hence not only into Homer's *Odyssey*, Sophocles's *Oedipus Rex* and Aristotle's *Ethics*, but into the Ten Commandments as well. One could go crazy for less, especially as tragedy teaches that whatever fate there is, we bring onto ourselves. To do otherwise would be to break the rules of one's own game, to be dishonest, to be utterly lost. In the long run that is impossible, for we are all one with our own map, the indicative and the imperative thoroughly entangled. Beware, though, for just as geometry is a form of rhetoric, so geography is a form of imagination. No wonder the map is such a power-filled creation, a flying carpet, the contraband par excellence.

With these insights etched into his mind, the arkologist cannot forget what he had experienced on the Island of Truth, especially his encounter with the sculpture and the catechesis of the *Mappa Mundi Universalis*. Seemingly just a tetrahedron of transparent glass grown out of a square slab of granite, in reality a symbol rich enough to last its maker for a lifetime; a creation epic for our own time-and-place, an architectural structure as well. Not, however, a tent raised for the pleasures of the migrating LORD, but a Crystal Palace erected for the people of the twenty-first century.

Low and behold, for what does the arkologist see when he looks out over the foggy ocean? Nothing less than an ontological transformation of thoughts he had encountered in the Kantian map-room: a Crystal Palace on a faraway shore. An imagination too tempting to ignore, an adventure as impossible to leave as to bring to an end.

Obsessed by the dream of getting inside this enchantment, not merely admiring it from the outside, he returns to the cliff where he had earlier encountered Francis Bacon and Mark Rothko. And just as those two had been driven by the desire to paint their own self-portraits and write their own autobiographies, so is he. And within him he hears the whispering voice of Athene: "Be brave my protégé, be yourself." A glance and a touch of her wand and the arkographer/arkologist is turned into an arkonaut, a recreated Icaros. Off he goes, over the icebergs and into the fog.

What then happens is what could be foreseen: halfway to the other side the flyer falls down, crashing into the ocean, no parachute or life vest to save him. **Splash!** And there, waiting for his catch, is Poseidon, god of earthquakes and ruler of the sea. A tsunami and the arkonaut is cast ashore, by no coincidence next door to the Crystal Palace.

Inside

Back on Mount Olympos, sitting on her father's right side, Athene watches what is going on. Feeling that Poseidon's anger might somehow have been stirred by her own actions, she decides to bring the half-dead back to life again, to do for him what she had earlier done for Odysseus, the rugged man without defect in form or mind. Disguised as a midwife she descends to earth, picks him up, carries him into the palace, pats his cheeks. And with gleaming eyes she witnesses how his wits are returning, his dreams about to come true.

A primal scream, these his first words: "Who and where am I? What is my name and how did I get here?" "Your very question," she answers, "proves that you are a human being, a creature blessed with the faculty of imagination, the ability to make the absent present and the present absent. A semiotic animal you are, a self-referential creation."

That said, the goddess begs him to actually use his imagination and see with his inner eyes how a long time ago a drama is set in motion. The stage-floor, she tells him, is a flat rock that gently slopes into the sea, the actors some strange creatures emerging out of nowhere, aimlessly spreading across the homogeneous plain. A foot gets stuck in a crevice and for the first time ever there is a difference different enough to make a difference. The others notice, they point and they mutter, every gesture an attempt to force the bothering difference into graspable identity. An event of tremendous consequences, for what the explorer is now about to witness is the very first sacrifice, *the* act through which the indefinable creatures are eventually transformed into human beings, a species whose individuals are held together and kept apart by their use of signs, every sign an ironic expression of Signifier and signified merged into one.

When the difference is pulled out of the rock, a well of blood springs up, a constant reminder of what happened when the original deviance was turned into a non-willing scapegoat. In the *Mappa Mundi* sculpture this remarkable event is marked by a red ruby, a symbol that in the accompanying text is called **A**. Not because it *is* **A** but because even gods must call it something. As Stephen Dedalus was later to put it, "Upon the void the universe is founded," that void being not a thing but a concept; in René Magritte's language, `Ceci n'est pas une pipe`.

In the definitional struggle that now follows, the mute difference is transformed into a set of communicable identities, like every translation an act of violence. More precisely, the foot in the crevice splits into a trinity of reformulations, a set of provisional reincarnations that in the chaos of mimetic desire find their positions in the corners of an equilateral triangle. Rephrased, the unknown **THIS** of the primordial difference is captured in one of the alternative nets of (1) **this**, (2) **this is *this***, and (3) **this is *that***. As the initial difference is thus sacrificed, atoms of understanding are captured in a mushroom cloud of perpetual fission, to human history no event more foundational.

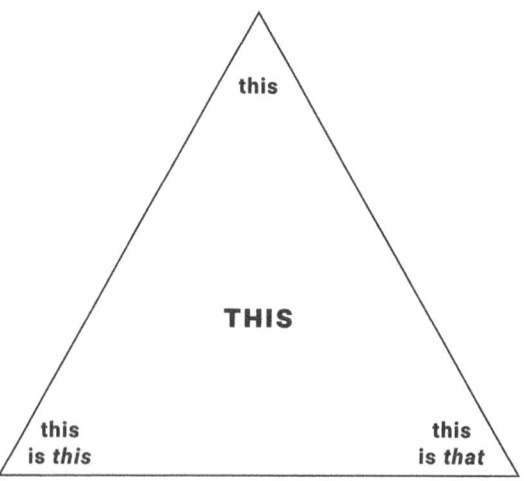

Traces of the First Sacrifice.

When the tension reaches its limit the rock bursts and out of the dust-filled lava grows a glass tetrahedron, a Crystal Palace sometimes known as the crucible of man, sometimes as the prison house of language. The floor and three walls of this enchanting structure are all built as equal-sized equilateral triangles, the walls transparent, the foundation sunk into the granite ground, the ruby-covered well at its center. In a twist of cultural survival, the three reformulations are now rising from the base, stretching upward and meeting again at the tetrahedron's top, the multitudes of Greek polytheism converging in the singularity of Abrahamic monotheism.

Like every mapping this one is also a triangulation, the **A** and its three restatements coming together in the vanishing point of the pinnacle. Not merely a contradictory condensation of Aristotle's difference and identity but a transcendence of the law of the excluded middle as well, in its totality nothing less than a rephrasing of God's name (if a name it is). And from its inception this Absolute speaks. Let there be! And there is. A universe flowing out of the creator's mouth, in James Joyce's conception a commodious vicus of (p)recirculation. **BIG BANG!**

Basement

The Crystal Palace is a well-guarded castle, its ruling resident the tyrant of tyrants. But through Athene's interference the palace is also turned into a movie theater, one projector in each of the basement corners, golden rays carrying the alternative translations from the machine rooms to the screens of the opposite walls. And when the projections of the imagined identities hit the sheets of glass they are miraculously changed into a set of Peircean signs, no longer the private fantasies of their inventor but communicable bits in an evolving discourse.

If these rituals could be perfectly performed, then the projection lines would strike the screening planes at 90° angles, every message going straight back to the cornered restatement it came from, nothing learned in the process. But even though the Saussurean/Lacanian sign is steeped in mimetic desire, the diverse ontologies of **S**ignifier and **s**ignified guarantee that this perpetual urge can never be satisfied. Hence the fortunate consequence that no translation will ever be perfect. It follows that in actuality the inclination of the (en)lightening rays is never *right on* and that the projections, instead of returning to the original identities unchanged, start bouncing between the walls. In turn, this slight deflection means that whatever we happen to think, say, and do is never pure and simple but always a non-dissolvable blend of alternative beliefs and alternative modes of being. Once that has been understood, it is obvious where the trigger of tragedy lies: in the purifying spirit of the right angle, in the hatred of the other that is built into the desire of every identity formulation. Murderous is our history, murky the connections between Signifier and signified, knowledge and action.

This in turn explains why tragedy occupies such an important place in the current conception of what it means to be human, indeed why it may be the most insightful of all available conceptions of thought-in-action and action-in-thought. The original setting is crucial, for Sophocles—a Janus-like figure who with one eye was scanning the old, with another imagining the future—lived his long life in the abyss between the *mythos* of Homer and the *logos* of Plato. What he there discovered was that the greatest tension of his time lay in the attitudes to predicament, for while the archaic poets had taken a person's social standing to reflect his or her ability to handle contradiction, the new philosophers defined paradox as the greatest threat to the cohesion of human reason, an enemy to be fought by all means. But in Sophocles's eyes religion was itself nothing but a human invention designed to keep people in place, like other laws issued by the humans of the polis rather than the gods of the Olympos. Make no mistake, though, for in the power-filled relations between kings and gods the latter are always legitimating the former, never the other way around. The king is dead, long live the god!

To be even more specific, we can now understand both why the tragedians assigned such a crucial role to the chorus and why the recurring convulsions of the last century are essentially a series of political crises, an orgy in promises that cannot be kept and therefore should never be given, the election results bought with junk bonds issued in the voters' own names. Whereas the problem for the tragedians was the exact drawing of the boundary between the humans and the gods, the problem for the post-democrats is that although all animals are equal, some pigs are more equal than the others.

Prophets' Hall

"Let me repeat," says the recovering arkonaut. "What *is* my name? And where are we?" "First question first," replies the bright-eyed midwife. "Your name is 'Gunnael Jensson,' an amalgam of the two personalities 'Ole Michael Jensen' and 'Gunnar Olsson,' the sculpture *Mappa Mundi Universalis* your shared brain-child. Surely you remember that ecstatic moment on Johannes Møllgaard's dining-room table when everything was conceived; the hopes and fears of the seven-year gestation period; the baptizing ceremony in the Uppsala Cathedral, the icon-loving archbishop nodding his blessing; Gitte Kik's *smørrebrød*, Harald Jensen's *snapse*."

"Then, your second question. Where we are standing right now is the ideal place for starting our house tour: the intersection at which the golden rays from the projectors are breaking through the membrane that separates and joins together the palace basement and the first floor, the Swedish poet Nils Ferlin our comrade in arms. As you will soon learn, this spot is the navel of the semiotic animal, *the* mark of how you became whatever you became."

Gunnael Jensson: *The Sharing Cross Station and the Space of the Prophets' Hall.*

This said the goddess looks down to the basement floor, pointing first to the blood-filled crevice at its center (earlier marked with an **A**), then to the **this**, **this is *this***, and **this is *that*** in the corners, vividly recalling how these alternative identities were originally given names that reflect the violence with which they were coined and the pain with which they were born: (1) the **this** turning into a shadowy **a**; (2) the **this is *this*** into the **a=a** (only seemingly a tautology) eventually the perfect sign of $\frac{a}{a}$ and (3) the **this is *that*** becoming the informative **a=b**. Cautioning against the faults of misplaced concreteness she then stresses that these expressions are referring not to existing things but to subsisting relations. To be more precise:

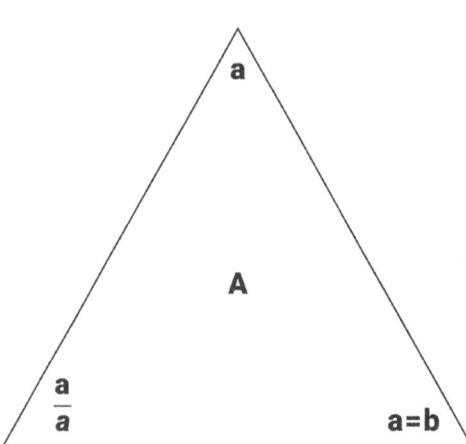

the **this** is held in place by the slanted line of dialectics (**/**); the **this is *this*** by the horizontal line of the Saussurean bar (**—**); the **this is *that*** by the parallel lines of the equals sign (**=**). A life-enhancing *ménage à trois*.

Fix-points of the Basement Corners.

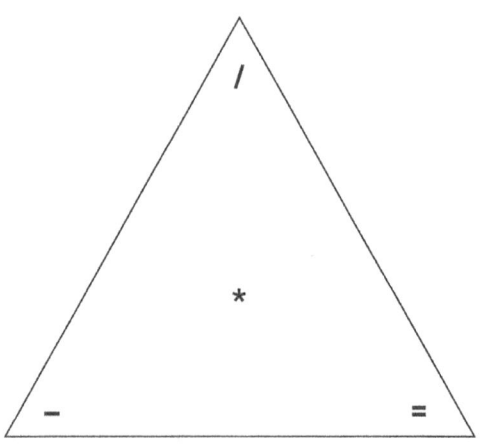

Signs of the Basement Corners.

On their way to the reflecting walls, the three projections are intersecting at the pub of the Sharing Cross Station. Once inside that establishment they immediately start arguing about whose blessing of the initial difference is the best, on the surface a case of difference deferred (Jacques Derrida's *différance*), at bottom an issue of truth and trust.

Finally agreeing that they are not agreeing, they return to the particular line that had brought them there, a peculiar system of rope-ways that will take them to their predetermined destinations on the glass walls, the movie screens that are specially constructed to tell them what and who they are. The story of Plato's cave reconfirming itself, for without the resistance of the limestone wall there would never have been any shadows, hence nothing to see, nothing to share, nothing to understand. Likewise with the walls of the Crystal Palace.

When the projections hit the three sheets of glass they miraculously change into a set of Peircean signs. But just as the painter's canvas must be properly prepared for the paint not to crack or run off, so must our minds be indoctrinated to ensure that all that is solid does not melt into air, each mode of understanding entrenched within its own self-supporting power structures, rules, and regulations. Three grand institutions have risen to the task: (1) RELIGION, where the **a** becomes the *symbol* of a; (2) the ARTS, where the **a=a** turns into the *icon* of $\frac{a}{a}$; (3) SCIENCE, where the **a=b** moves into the finger-pointing *index* of a=b, the Kantian *as-if* of provisional truth.

*

It is exactly these relations between religion, arts, and science that are brought to life in the imaginary space of the Prophets' Hall, Athene's version of the Sistine Chapel, its walls covered with portraits of acknowledged geniuses, its ceiling extending from the sturdy spikes of the **/**, the **—** , and the **=** , the first blessed by Marduk (Mesopotamian god of gods), the second by Apollo (Greek god of music, poetry, and knowledge), the third by Thoth (Egyptian god of geometry and mathematics).

A most remarkable event, for without what is now known as the symbols, icons, and indexes of Charles Sanders Peirce (1839–1914) there would never have been a semiotic animal, no faculty of imagination, no blood-stained offerings cast onto the reflecting surfaces. Much for the arkographer turned arkologist turned arkonaut to learn and admire when he now listens to a host of experts, all of them eager to show him around—Pope Francis and Karl Marx, Albert Einstein and Alan Turing, Paul Cézanne, Marcel Duchamp and Michelangelo Buonarroti presently foremost among them. And, like the Vatican guides, they are paying particular attention to the images in the ceiling. A tour not easily forgotten.

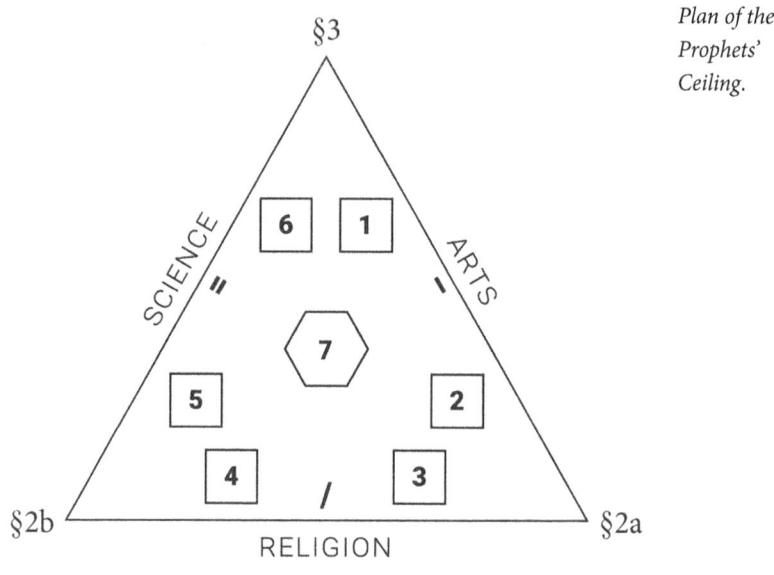

Plan of the Prophets' Ceiling.

1. Zurbarán: Veronica's Veil
2. Malevich: Black Square
3. Malevich: White Square
4. Rothko: Untitled
5. Einstein/Pythagoras
6. Double Helix
7. Michelangelo: Fingering/Fingers

First to catch our attention are Cézanne and Duchamp who note that close to the wall of art there are two icons, to the non-initiate mysterious pictures of the holy, to the believer something holy in and of itself.

First, closest to the §3-corner, is Francisco Zurbarán's version of the *Veil of
Veronica*, an imprint of Jesus's face
not made by human hand (literally
an *acheiropoieton* or a *vera eikon*, i.e.
a "true image"). Not merely a true
image, though, but the story about a
woman watching Jesus on his way to
Golgatha, the cross on his shoulder,
thorns around his head, flies in his
face. A touch of her sudarium and the
shared suffering is forever recorded.
Michelangelo's *Pietà* in another genre.

Francisco de Zurbarán: *The Veil of Veronica*. Ca. 1635. Oil on canvas, 70 × 51.5 cm.
Nationalmuseum, Stockholm.

Next to the Zurbarán picture and closer to the §2a corner, is Kazimir
Malevich's *Black Square*, to the Russian suprematist actually an icon sprung
from Walt Whitman's poem "Chanting the Square Deific," an image of the
unknowable Godhead painted as a figure with four faces: (a) the Father
without remorse; (b) the Son, absorbed by affection and charity, rejected
yet constantly resurrected; (c) the Holy Spirit, breather of life and lighter
than light, essence of forms and name of the beyond beyond the beyond;
(d) the Comrade of Criminals and Brother of Slaves, Satan himself. Much
to note about this painting, not least that the artist was too poor to afford
the best paint. As it turns out a happy circumstance, for the picture is now
badly cracked, the underlying canvas shining through in its sacred naked-
ness, an unintentional baring of the projection screen. The very essence of
the almost tautological $a{=}a$ and the Saussurean $\frac{a}{a}$.

Kazimir Malevich: *Black Square*.
1914–15. Oil on canvas, 80.01 ×
80.01 cm. (given as 79.6 × 79.5 cm.).
State Tretyakov Gallery, Moscow.

After that revelation, Karl Marx and Pope Francis are taking over, noting that on the other side of the §2a corner is yet another work by Malevich—*White Square on White*—a painting even more fascinating than the time-worn infant from which it originated: two squares, one placed inside the other, the smaller tipped and thrust toward the edges of the larger. What makes this particular work so stunning is that the icon of the tilted white (almost, but not exactly) square is set against a background that itself is white (albeit not exactly of the same hue). It follows that Malevich's series of whites on white are profitably seen not merely as pictures of the non-picturable but as studies of the background onto which the graven image

is being projected, in that sense a forerunner to Lucio Fontana's *concetti spaziale*. An unexpected coming together of §§2a and 3 of the Constitutional Law.

Kazimir Malevich: *Suprematist Composition: White on White*. 1918. Oil on canvas, 79.4 × 79.4 cm. Museum of Modern Art, New York (MOMA). © Digital image, the Museum of Modern Art, New York/ Scala, Firenze.

Still not religious enough, though, nothing compared to Mark Rothko's large canvases, many appropriately titled *Untitled*, many visitors testifying that the morning they spent in the Houston Chapel is the holiest, most sacred, experience in their life. By all indications the artist's attempt to capture the shadowy a, his subsequent suicide a foregone conclusion.

Mark Rothko: *Untitled*. 1969. Acrylic on canvas. 172.7 × 152.5 cm. National Gallery of Art, Washington DC. Gift of the Mark Rothko Foundation, Inc. © Mark Rothko/BUS 2019.

Then, around the corner where the ceiling meets the wall of science, is Albert Einstein showing his $e = mc^2$ and Pythagoras his $a^2 = b^2 + c^2$, in both cases condensed codifications of cartographic reason, Pythagoras's theorem inconceivable without the right angle, Einstein's theory a revolutionary conception of the geometries of time and space. Two equations with the built-in power of transcending themselves, the axioms of post-Euclidean geometries and the theorems of Gödel's logic playing key roles in the metamorphoses. But whereas the inventor of the theory of special relativity *believed* that God does not play dice, the instable logician *knew* that if a logical system is consistent then it cannot be complete, the axioms not provable within their own system; in essence an instance of numbers speaking about numbers, a parallel to the liar's paradox, the paradigm of language speaking about language. "All Cretans are liars," said Epimenides, himself a Cretan. "Provability is weaker than truth," said Gödel, himself a mathematician, a man so frightened of being poisoned that he died from starvation.

At that stage a new guide is stepping forth. Alan Turing, father of artificial intelligence, the instigator of a novel epic of creation, machines playing the roles that once were reserved for the gods. The question of identity and difference in a new light, man no longer created in the image of God, but the LORD disguised as a computer, an invention even more revolutionary than the printing press, the debates between Erasmus and Martin Luther as relevant today as five centuries ago. The Kantian question in a new light, for where will the artificially intelligent eventually draw the line between mind and body, the latter made of approximately 10^{29} quarks and electrons, all of them subject to the laws of physics. Big Data. Here and there, coded languages everywhere, Gödel's numbers and Turing's cryptoanalyses elaborate systems of translation, human imaginations that forever changed the world.

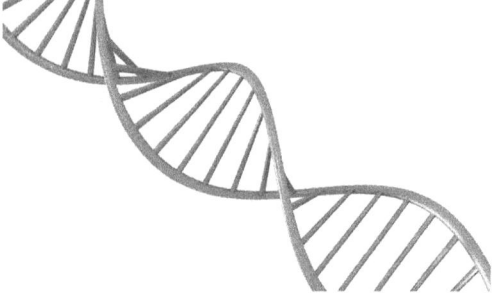

Double Helix of the DNA *Molecule.* Bing images, www.videoblocks.com.

But to the DNA molecule a transplanted heart does nothing, the a=b of the *double helix* stubbornly declaring that I am what I am, everyone uniquely different from everyone else. The original sacrifice in reverse, everything set at the time of conception: "a stubby nose, green eyes, ears like a fox, big feet, thin hair, knock-knees, a small mouth, bad teeth, a bull's neck, narrow shoulders, big rump, low IQ, low forehead, reduced lung capacity, a harelip, bad breath, a bird's chest, a paunch, a sway (or the opposite: a crocked) back, stunted growth, a piercing voice, freckles, flat feet, bony and dry (or the opposite: thick and sweaty) hands, crooked toes, nearsightedness, a tottering step."[1]

Encouraged by the proof that every individual is indivisibly unique, the guideship is finally taken over by Michelangelo Buonarroti, eager to share his rendering of Genesis 1–9, nine narrative paintings grouped into three triads: the first picturing how God turned chaos into order—the heavens and the earth, day and night, land and water, trees and animals, everything flowing out of his mouth; the second showing the creation of Adam and Eve followed by the story of how they ate from the tree of knowledge and got expelled from the Garden of Eden, the woman sentenced to bear her children in pain, the man to harvest thorns and thistles and to eat his food by the sweat of his brow; the third depicting the flood, Noah's sacrifice on Mount Ararat followed by his toil in the vineyard where he gets drunk and is found by his sons who in their shame are shown as naked as their father—a preview of the Christian Eucharist.

From beginning to end a stunning achievement, the Old Testament stories translated into Renaissance pictures, a feat well described by the saying *Quod Moses velat Christi doctrina revelat*—"What Moses veils, the doctrine of Christ reveals"—Michelangelo turning what he heard the Church say into paintings, interpretations not always to the pope's liking. So precisely ambiguous are in fact his works that they are often telling one story and showing another, his thoughts always somehow embodied, a paradigmatic case of a **this** turned into a **that**, a **that** into a **this**. And for that reason the arkonaut, now disguised as an arkotect, approaches the Sistine Chapel (built in the same proportions as King Solomon's temple) *as if it were* an ark with Michelangelo's self-portrait hidden inside it, the sculptor's attempt to paint his invisible thoughts *as if they were* three-dimensional bodies. Imagination at high pitch, for while the famous pictures say little about the real world, they offer invaluable insights into the taken-for-granted of the genius who made them. "Suspend your disbeliefs," smiled Athene, "cure your metaphor-blindness, and you will see what you never saw before."

Striking are the parallels, nowhere more clear than in the fourth panel, the *Creation of Adam*, the masterpiece that in the same brushstrokes combines the worlds of art, religion, and science. By all accounts a record of the artist's struggle with the enigma of what it means to be human, on closer inspection a self-referential drama of the eye and the index finger.

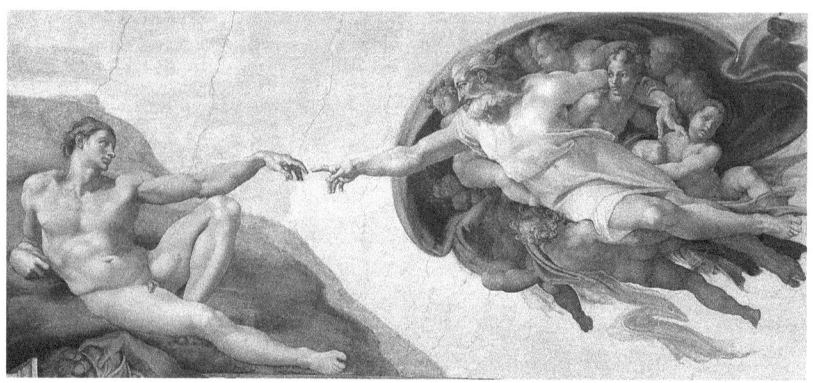

Michelangelo: *Creation of Adam*. Fresco. 1512. 280 × 570 cm.
Sistine Chapel, fourth panel. Musei Vaticani. Città del Vaticano.

The image is classic: the grey-bearded Almighty—dressed in what to us looks like a lady's nightgown—is moving through space in a red cloak, the athletic Adam resting naked on the earth from which he was made and to which he is bound to return. Their hands reaching out for each other yet never touching, God's eyes set on his own finger, hence not on the thing created but on the act of creation itself. Even more remarkably, Adam's eyes are looking past his presumed maker, a clear reference to Exodus 33:20, where the LORD told Moses, "My face you must not see, for no one can see me and live." Instead the first human is absorbed by the looks of the woman under the LORD's left arm, by general consent Michelangelo's version of Eve, according to the scriptures not yet created. Perhaps the Florentine's way of saying that being human is less an issue of God's mercy and compassion than of being seen, trusted, and desired. Why else would Adam have been depicted with a navel and why else would the contours of that same mark be shown under God's own mantle? Why else would the billowing cloak be shaped as a human brain (by some interpreted as a uterus), the anatomy of both organs well known to the sculptor turned painter. And touched by the arthritic hand is the baby boy whose words were to change the world.

Master-baiting is the creative artist obsessed by understanding his own craft: "Let there be, my struggle inseparable from my own taken-for-granted, I myself the sperm, egg, and umbilical cord, I myself a Peircean ark, I myself a trinity of signs—the hippocampus the seat of the neuroscientists' grid cells, the smithy of way-finding. No map without it." "Too much for the ceiling," muses the guide, "yet a necessary background for what I am now putting at its center."

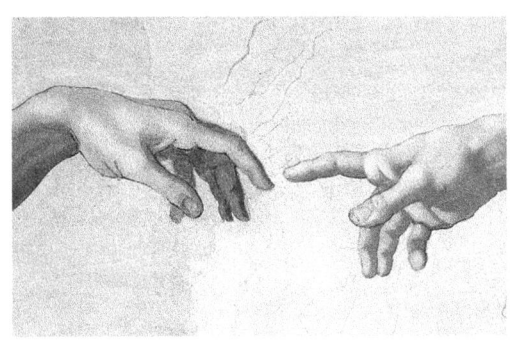

Fingering Fingers. Detail of Michelangelo's *Creation of Adam.*

Lo and behold, for at the nave of the prophets' ceiling there they are, the *Fingering Fingers* inscribed in a hexagon, no geometric figure more densely packed, *the* symbol of creativity located not in the index finger that chiseled the Ten Commandments onto the stone tablets, but in the artist's brush penetrating the wet fresco, a most demanding technique. No longer man created in the LORD's likeness, but the lord pictured as a Human, the box of acacia wood turned into a glass tetrahedron in the process. For such is the structure of the Crystal Palace that everything in the prophets' ceiling is a twisted projection of the basement floor—in both cases the alternative identities placed in the corners and the pure difference at the center, albeit with a crucial distinction. For whereas the meaning of the foot in the crevice—the original difference—was pushed to the three identities at the outskirts, here the movement goes in the other direction, the modes of science, art, and religion being sucked into the gray space between the empty hands. And cracked is the plaster in between.

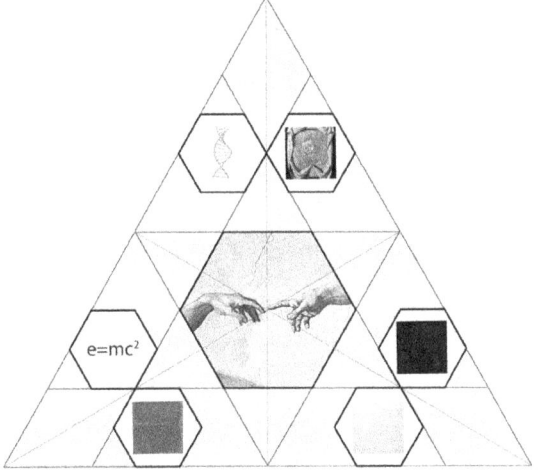

Paintings of the Prophets' Ceiling. Photomontage by Gunnael Jensson and Mathias Ruø Jensen.

Extraordinary this picture of a brain-child growing up. A creation story never told before, from beginning to end an exercise in translation, an attempt to say that something is something else and being believed when you do so. Striking are the parallels to the creation epics of *Enuma elish*, Genesis, and Exodus, the Crystal Palace essentially a modernized version of Marduk's temple, Moses's tabernacle, the Sistine Chapel:

(1) a deviance is observed, a scapegoat chosen;

(2) the scapegoat is killed, blood-soaked is the stage;

(3) the slaughtered body is cut into pieces, named and thereby blessed;

(4) the baptized pieces are moved to a sacred place, put on altars, and sacrificed, all in honor of the original deviance;

(5) ceremonial blessings of social bonds: for the celebrant a case of **this is *that*** (a means toward an end); for the congregation a **this is *this*** (a sharing of common values); for the lonely hermit nothing but a **this** (a personal experience beyond words);

(6) a ritual performed in a holy space: Jerusalem's Walled City, Mecca's Ka'bah, St Peter's Cathedral, the Taj Mahal, King's College, the Louvre, Houses of Parliament, Forbidden City, Oval Office;

(7) prayers and healings, incense and anointments, drums and trumpets, salutes and hallelujahs;

(8) difference metamorphosed, identity rising to the sky, there to be constantly reinvented.

Plus ça change, plus c'est la même chose

QUOD REVELAT

QUOD ERAT INVENDIENDUM

Ball Room

And where should we go from this self-referential creation, this experience of hitting our heads against the prophets' ceiling? To the next floor, of course, the only room with fully developed people, a rare chance to converse with our equals. The setting is gorgeous, a Ball Room built as a Hall of Mirrors, its architecture a blend of stately Versailles and popular Tivoli; at the center a supporting pillar draped by a Vitruvian *homo ad quadratum*, a perfectly proportioned figure with its feet on a floor made of solid oak and its hands toward a mirrored ceiling, the latter one with the upper limit of language. High is the room, Vitruvius's navel located exactly midway between the **A** in the tetrahedron's base and the **A=A** at the pinnacle.

Homo ad quadratum. Reproduced from Rudolf Wittkower: *Architectural Principles in the Age of Humanism*, Pl. 4.

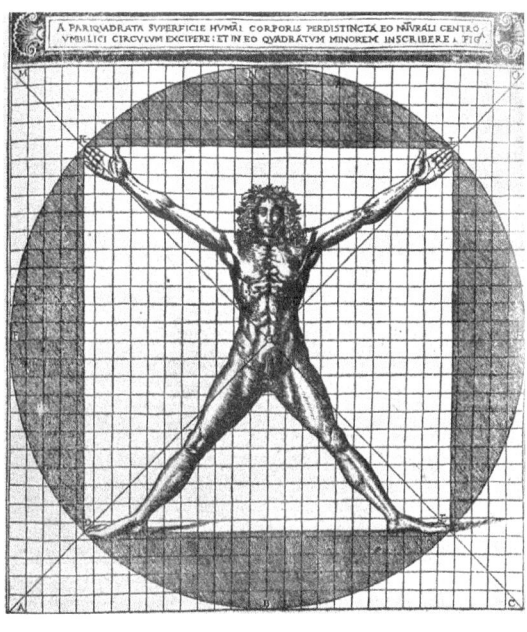

Built around this central structure is a platform with a throne for the ruling RULER and a stage for the entertainers, sommeliers, dance bands, clowns, and jugglers, each and every one a cog in the propaganda machine—bread and circuses, *panem et circenses.* And while the children out in the gutter keep shouting that the emperor is naked, the lackeys continue to carry the trail that does not exist. In the Hall itself the atmosphere is much like an intermission at the Metropolitan, La Scala, or Bolshoi, the circulating people whispering, bowing, smiling, flirting, frowning, pretending to be stronger, richer, more beautiful than they actually are. Champagne in everyone's hand and everyone's head: Monsieur, Madame, Herr Professor, Rector Magnificus, Monseigneur, Herr General, Frau Reichskansler, Mr. President, Deres Kongelige Majesteter, Sua Santità, Kreti and Pleti. Language everywhere, the two-letter words more revealing than any other, especially about the dialectics of one and many, truth and trust, knowing and believing, power and submission, law and order, things and relations, body and culture. Every conversation a medley of mixed metaphors, every exchange an exercise in translation.

And parading ahead of us is a young girl and a strange looking man. Most curious is their relation:

"Exactly like an egg he is," she said aloud to herself, standing with her hands ready to catch him, for she was every moment expecting him to fall.

"It's **very** provoking," said the Humpty-Dumpty-looking man, "to be called an egg—**very**!"

"I said you **looked** like an egg, Sir," the girl gently explained. "And some eggs are very pretty, you know," she added, hoping to turn her remark into a sort of compliment.

"Some people," he said, "have no more sense than a baby! . . . There's glory for you!"

"I don't know what you mean by 'glory,'" the young one said.

The egg-shaped smiled contemptuously. "Of course you don't—till I tell you. I meant 'there's a nice knock-down argument for you!'"

"But 'glory' doesn't mean 'a nice knock-down argument,'" she objected.

"When **I** use a word," he said in a rather scornful tone, "it means just what I choose it to mean—neither more nor less."

"The question is," said she, "whether you **can** make words mean so many different things."

"The question is," said he, "which is to be master—that's all."

The girl was too much puzzled to say anything; so after a minute the egg-shaped began again.

"They've a temper, some of them—particularly verbs: they're the proudest—adjectives you can do anything with, but not verbs—however **I** can manage the whole lot of them! Impenetrability! That's what **I** say!"[2]

A Wonderland is the Ball Room. And in one of the Joyceous corners, away from the others, is Molly Bloom soliloquying how "he kissed her under the Moorish wall and she thought well as well him as another and then she asked him with her eyes to ask again yes and then he asked her would she yes to say yes my mountain flower and first she put her arms around him yes and drew him down so he could feel her breasts and perfume yes and his heart was going like mad and yes she said yes I will Yes."[3]

So tell me now, you mirrors on the wall, who's the fairest of us all?

*

Which is to be master—that's all. A question easier to pose than to answer, as always an issue of imagination, of lying and of telling the truth, of bringing forth what has never been said or heard before, of journeying through the maps of ontological transformations. And since the Master would not be master if s/he sat still, the moment has now come to follow the word "power" itself as it moves through the parts of speech, at every stage becoming less and less mimetic, more and more abstract.

The starting point of that journey is in the fist, the whip, the bomb, the word "power" a *concrete noun*, one physical object hitting another. True! Yet not true enough. For on closer reflection "power" shows itself to be less a concrete than an *abstract noun*, not merely a material thing but a social relation, not merely a sound but an insult, not just a train but a shipment to Gulag and Auschwitz. According to William Blake (in his lifetime by many considered insane): "Prisons are built with stones of Law; Brothels with bricks of Religion. . . . What is now proved was once, only imagin'd. . . . As the catterpillar [*sic*] chooses the fairest leaves to lay her eggs on, so the priest lays his curse on the fairest joys."[4] True! Yet not true enough.

For in the blinding light of the torture chamber, neither victim nor perpetrator ever doubts that something is being done, hence that "power" is a *verb*. Not just any verb, though, but a battery of modal verbs, more exactly those three- and four-letter words that modify what can, may, must, will, and shall be done. Getting tense are the tenses as time goes by, realizing that while a kiss is just a kiss, a sigh is still a sigh. True! Yet not true enough.

For when the overripe existentialist listens to his own conscience, then he learns that killing is sometimes good and sometimes evil, sometimes a duty, sometimes strictly forbidden. And in those twists of deontic logic the word "power" changes once again, on this occasion into an *adverb*, even an *adjective*. True! Yet not true enough.

The journey goes on, for no act is ever performed in a vacuum but always in a dialogue between an I and a Thou, "power" on that account a *pronoun*, us and them the politically most prominent among them. In the no-man's land in between is the I, a territory ruled by the dialectical *I*. Not surprising, therefore, that to many Swedes the pronoun *jag* (first-person singular) is a taboo-laden word, in that sense quite different from *we* (first-person plural), the closest to another being one might ever get—a newborn baby on your chest, a loving spouse in your arms, your parent in a coffin. Beware, though, for when that same word is expanded into a capitalized *WE*, it changes into a euphemism for history's most efficient mass-murderer, more than 800,000 Rwandans slaughtered in a hundred days. Allegedly not a genocide but a sanitary operation. For to the political elite the Tutsi were not a group of human beings but a swarm of slimy cockroaches. But to the Nazi being a Jew or a Gypsy was itself so despicable that they needed no new terms to legitimate the Final Solution—six million innocents exterminated in the process. Unbelievable is real history, storytelling the only way to grasp the political play of *conjunctions* and *numbers*.

Chief among the latter is the figure 3, to the triangulating social scientist the first in an endless row, zero a position rather than a number. *The* anchoring point of any measure (including the boat-builders' *sesto*), the *origo* of debit and credit, the stand-point rather than vanishing-point of the painter's perspective. Vitruvius's navel as well.

And once this much has been grasped the word "power" finally comes out as what it really is—a *preposition*, literally a position assumed in advance. As the cubists knew, there is a profound difference between standing inside the house looking out and standing outside looking in, between the radical choice of being *at* a limit, *on* a limit, *in* a limit. Beware, though, for no matter how well you master a foreign language, a faulty preposition and a mistaken declension will eventually give you away. True. And finally true enough!

*

So it is that the pre-positions are the linguistic fix-points par excellence. And for that reason we must now return to Titian's *The Flaying of Marsyas*, not merely one of the most gruesome paintings ever made but a penetrating study of the difference between being *at* a limit and being *in* a limit. Perhaps a shift from the **this is *this*** of Peirce's ICON to the **this** of his SYMBOL.

The underlying myth has its roots in book 6 of Ovid's *Metamorphoses*, the story about a musical duel between the god Apollo on the seven-stringed lyre and the satyr Marsyas on the *aulos*, the latter most likely a kind of flute, perhaps a prototype bagpipe. At issue is who of the two is the best musician, highbrow Apollo or folksy Marsyas. To settle the case a contest is arranged, the two sides agreeing first that the judge shall be King Midas, then that the winner will be free to do with the loser whatever he fancies, almost certainly something of a sexual nature. When the muses sense that the prize might be given to Marsyas, they decree that a second round must be arranged, a performance in which the contestants are asked to play the same tunes as before but now with their instruments turned upside down.

Easy to do with the lyre, impossible with the pipes. And with that rule change the outcome is determined in advance, Marsyas eventually hung upside down and flayed alive. No death more cruel, no fate more humiliating.

Titian: *The Flaying of Marsyas*. 1575–76. Oil on canvas, 212 × 207 cm. State Museum Kromeriz. ©Archbiskuství olomoucké

What we see in Titian's picture is a triptych with Marsyas at the center of the in-between, a crucifixion in which the victim's body has been rotated around the nave of its own navel, the hooves up in the tree and the arms forming a nimbus around the head, its left eye begging for our attention. To the left is the godly realm of the flaying Apollo adorned with a laurel crown accompanied by his violin-playing double, the eyes of the latter focused on the aulos in the tree above him. There is also the assistant butcher, a hatted craftsman working on the goat's leg, the knife angled for castration. In dialectical contrast the right panel depicts the realm of nature with its assemblage of fauns and satyrs, King Midas the commanding figure shown self-absorbed, elbow on his knee, chin in his hand, Auguste Rodin's *Le Penseur* three centuries before it was cast. Next to him a horned satyr with a bucket of cleaning water, a big dog held back by an innocent faun, a smaller one licking the sacrificial blood. Grippingly gripping. But how was the painting painted and what does it say about life in the Crystal Palace?

In our search for an answer it should be recalled that Titian (1488–1576) lived to be almost ninety and that the *Flaying* (like the present text) was one of his last pieces. As a consequence, it has often been interpreted as the artist's attempt to investigate how the creative act is actually performed, the result almost certainly born from the Venetian's intercourse with the materiality of the paint itself, the distinction between figure and ground on the verge of disappearing, the cartographer's fix-point, scale and *mappa* and the logician's index, icon and symbol all fused into an unbreakable unity. In deed it is often said that the key to Titian's success lay in his skill as a tactile painter, a genius capable of showing not merely how something *looks*, but how it *feels*, Marsyas's skin and flesh sculpted by the master's brush, knife, and fingers. Not an imagination cast *onto* the canvas, but an image growing *out of* it, layer layered upon layer. And in that sense the *Flaying* actually *is* what it is *about*, Samuel Beckett's motto moved from one art form to another. The magic of ontological transformations when it works, perhaps because the skin is our largest erogenous organ, the bodily limit of limits. As Roland Barthes put it: "Language is a skin; I rub my language against the other. It is as if I had words instead of fingers and fingers at the tip of my words. My language trembles with desire. . . . Language experiences orgasm upon touching itself."[5]

And who is watching it all? Midas, of course, the Phrygian king to whom Dionysos had given the power of turning everything he touched to gold. Seemingly a wonderful gift but only until the recipient realizes that also his food and wine are changed into metal, his daughter as well. Praying to Dionysos for help, the once greedy is told to take a swim in the nearby river, and, when he does, his blessing-turned-curse leaves him. An experience so overwhelming that like a latter-day hippie, Midas retires to the countryside where he becomes a worshipper of Pan, the latter, like Marsyas himself, a satyr, hence neither man nor beast but a creature of the in-between. In revenge for the intended insult Apollo then adorns the dethroned king with the ears of an ass, a shame meant to follow him for the rest of his life. Not in Titian's painting, however, for there the ears are barely visible under the kingly crown.

It is this same Midas that Titian depicts as a figure full of thought, presumably brooding about what his long life might or might not have achieved, a figure, furthermore, with features very reminiscent of the artist's own. And for that reason the *Flaying* has often been seen as a self-portrait, like other mappings an exercise in triangulation—one fix-point in Marsyas's navel, the hook on which Titian hung the mirror in which he could reflect himself; another in Apollo's elbow, the lever of cruelty; a third in Midas's hand, which in Job-like fashion seals his mouth, the wordless glance that leaves the viewer no rest. The message is unequivocal: you and I are neither gods nor beasts but citizens of the land in-between, paying guests in the notorious Bar de Saussure, the Nietzschean hangout where not a member is sober.

Human, all too human, the lunatic, the lover, and the poet of imagination all compact. Know thyself, my mate!

Attic

Thus prompted, I lift my eyes. And what I then discover is that above the Ball Room there is an attic, the head of Vitruvius's *homo ad quadratum* clogging the narrow entrance, his hands where the Ball Room ceiling turns into the floor of the Penthouse, the sound of moving feet. A crawling space filled with implements too valuable to discard and too embarrassing to show. An in-between space forbidden to the public. A horror cabinet of ugly bastards. Bodies without heads, heads without bodies. A madhouse we ignore at our peril.

/

Tread cautiously! For once inside this forbidden space you are attacked by a swarm of rabies-infected bats, hairy animals with sharp teeth and screechy sounds, embodiments of the dialectical symbol. Hence also of Marx's *Das Kapital*, its words bat-like inventions which from one perspective look like birds, from another like mice. "What are they?" asked Vilfredo Pareto, seemingly unaware that the text before him was a political treatise composed in the dialectics of human relations, not a positivist tract steeped in the logic of material things, the difference being that the words of the latter are staying put throughout the analysis while in the former they are moving with the study object, analyst and analysand following the same music of internal and self-referential relations. Little wonder that whoever dances with Marx runs the risk of stepping on his own toes, the term "capital" itself having one meaning in volume 1, another in volume 2, a third in volume 3.

And therein lies the key to understanding why Marx's works continue to excite and bewilder. Not because of what he was writing *about*, but because of the language he was writing *in*, an idiom in which the concepts are defined in terms of each other—never an *either-or* always a *both/and*. But therein lies also the temptation to extend the beautiful analyses into political action, a series of ontological transformations in which millions upon millions have been deliberately murdered—Stalin, Mao, and Pol Pot appearing as idols for the blessed, devils for the condemned. Disastrous were nevertheless the disasters, inexcusable the excuses, a non-translatable **this** gone berserk.

Let there be no doubt: nowhere was Marx more misleading than in his complaint that the philosophers had only interpreted the world while the point is to change it. Misleading not because the world happens to be perfect (which it is not), but because dialectics is a reasoning mode capable of looking only into the past, never into the future. A category mistake of tragic proportions, for dialectics is better suited for *de*scriptive understanding than for *pre*scriptive commands. No wonder Lenin asked himself what is to be done, especially after the once "useful idiots" had been recategorized as "State Enemies," their only defense an echo of Agamemnon's excuse for the crimes he had committed during the Trojan War:

> I am not responsible but the Party is, Destiny and Trotsky, the mist-walking Commisar who in absentia caught my heart in the savage delusion of permanent revolution, dialectics the language of thought-and-action. Yet what could I do? It is the Central Committee, through its bureaucratic collectivism, that accomplishes all things.

With these words—and after a breakfast on the infamous (h)omelette—the lackey vanished quite slowly, beginning with the end of the coat-tail and ending with a grin, which remained some time after the rest of him had gone. "Well," thought Olga, "I've often seen a lackey without a grin, but a grin without a lackey! It's the most curious thing I ever saw in my life!" No wonder Marx refused to call himself a Marxist, just as Nietzsche most likely would have objected to being called a Nazi. Yet both authors were deeply influenced by Hegel's phenomenology in which there is no master without a slave and no slave without a master, no one without an Other. Accordingly, on the 18th of February, 1964, the young Joseph Brodsky was brought to trial in Leningrad charged with the crime of social uselessness, in short of being a parasite. "Answer," demanded the judge, "why have you not worked?" "I have worked," replied the budding Nobel Laureate, "I have written poems." The judge: "We are not interested in that. We are interested in which institution you have been connected with."

An insinuation that all bats do their best to avoid. And as they are echoing their way through the corridors of power some are hitting the walls and falling down dead, others just swishing by. Be warned, though, for in the semi-darkness we are all grey.

But in Svetlana Alexievich's polyphonic palimpsests whatever is erased always leaves a trace. As Søren Kierkegaard put it, we are living forward and understanding backward.

—

Half blinded I move on, promptly stumbling into a heap of razor blades, sharp knives, syringes, and various opiates, the self-referential **this is *this*** turned into means for becoming one with oneself. In reality a collection of distorted icons, some found among the fathers of Gulag, Auschwitz, and September 11, others disguised as whistleblowers, reformed sinners, and suicide bombers.

What unites the latter is their striving in the path of God, a devotion well captured by the Arabic word *jihad*, a term with different meanings for the sufi (the mystic) and the jihadist (the radical Islamist). Thus, while the former are reaching the blessed state through prayer, meditation, music, and dance—the whirling dervishes of Cappadocia a marvelous example—the latter are getting there through holy war, unpredictable terrorism a common strategy, street fighting and the deployment of human shields their preferred tactics. Add to this the charisma of the leading figures, and it is easy to understand why marginalized youth are joining the ranks, their frustration much like the sense of alienation that once permeated the working class and presently the precariat. The recruiters' challenges are nevertheless drastically different, for whereas the socialist agitator may tempt his audience with *The Communist Manifesto* and its visions of a glorious revolution, the jihadist imam knows from the *Quran* that the chosen are guaranteed a place in Heaven.

To some an offer they cannot refuse, the terrorist bomber turned into an icon in the process, a perfect unity of short- and long-term desires. The fulfillment of a divine duty, the term "suicide attack" altered to "martyrdom operation," a rhetorical trick for rounding the Islamic prohibition against self-murder. George Orwell's pigs resurrected, the holy pictures on the iconostasis of the Orthodox church turned into televised terrorists, the whole world their stage. The biblical Revelation (sometimes called the Apocalypse) reenacted in Baghdad, Mosul, New York, Paris, even Stockholm.

The author of that last book of the New Testament is known as John of Patmos, by all evidence a minor prophet who wrote a series of letters to the seven churches in Asia, allegedly reports of what Jesus Christ had revealed to him. In his own words:

> Blessed is he who reads aloud the words of this prophecy, and blessed are those who hear, and who keep what is written therein; for the time is near. . . . I, John, your brother, who share with you in Jesus the tribulation and the kingdom and the patient endurance. . . . I was in the Spirit on the Lord's Day, [and] when I saw him, I fell at his feet as though dead. But he laid his right hand upon me saying, "Fear not, I am the first and the last, and the living one; I died, and behold I am alive for evermore, and I have the keys of Death and Hades."[6]

Not for everyone to share, though, at least not in the city of Thyatira. For in his letter to that congregation the writer is very clear:

> I have one thing against you: You tolerate that woman Jezebel, who calls herself a prophetess. By her teaching she misleads my servants into sexual immorality and the eating of food sacrificed to idols. I have given her time to repent of her immorality, but she is unwilling. So I will cast her on a bed of suffering, and I will make those who commit adultery with her suffer intensely, unless they repent her ways. I will strike her children dead. Then all the churches will know that I am he who searches hearts and minds, and I will repay each of you according to your deeds.[7]

The Latter-Days Saints, Pentecostal ministers, Jim Jones of the Peoples Temple two millennia ahead of themselves. As it is told, on this occasion by the "real" John, the disciple whom Jesus is said to have loved:

> When the day of Pentecost came, they were all together in one place. Suddenly a sound like the blowing of a violent wind came from heaven and filled the whole house where they were sitting. They saw what seemed to be tongues of fire that separated and came to rest on each of them. All of them were filled with the Holy Spirit and began to speak in other tongues as the Spirit had enabled them. . . . Amazed and perplexed, they asked one another, "What does this mean?" Some, however, made fun of them and said, "They have had too much wine."[8]

Be that as it may, for what to the outsider is a jumble of frightening stories is to the insider a key to revelation, repentance, salvation, divine grace, and self-made iconicity, nothing less than a road to Heaven chartered by the apostles. Most importantly, the converts somehow know that they have been blessed, the speaking in tongues the sign of a living icon, the holy communion embodied. Augustine's *Confessions* restaged, for to him the human being is no longer the perfect unity of body and soul that it once was, hence not the icon that he himself strove to become. And for that same reason the Catholic priests vow not to marry and the nuns to live in chastity.

But where did it come from, the heap of distorted implements the bats chased me into? From the Bar de Saussure, of course, an establishment equally famous for its enchanting views and its creative clientele, drinks and drugs for changing the minds, whips and guns for the bodies. So exciting is this exotic place that for their safety the guests are frequently frisked, their belongings confiscated and carried to the attic—knives for slashing the unbelievers' throats, LSD for making the converts see and hear what they never saw or heard before: God and God's language are one and the same. **Let there be me / and there I am**. "And let it also be known," says the icon, "that in the court of Peircean signs I am the *primus inter pares*, the symbolic index of an ever-changing and never-ending charade." Identities donned, identities cast off. Imagination running amok, the forces of socialization as well. Madness around the corner, psychologists at the couch munching on a *mille-feuille* of discarded masks.

Nietzsche was wrong: God is not dead merely the trademark of a perpetuum mobile, a noumenon always on the move, a power never resting content.

=

Dizziness overtakes me. Knowing neither up nor down, neither left nor right, I can still notice a bucket with what looks like slimy porridge, toxic gas welling up. No doubt the cause of my discomfort. And when I look more carefully, then I see a Peircean index disintegrating into its components, a **this is *that*** falling apart. To the scientist a disquieting revelation, to the experienced craftsman yet another illustration of how different materials require different connectives to tie them together. Hammer, nails, and screws for the carpenter; trowel, bricks and mortar for the mason; sickle probes, drills, and amalgam for the dentist; electricity, zeros, and ones for the code-breaker. Seemingly an issue of the *this* and *that*, in reality a question of the *is*, the copula with the magic power of turning indexes into multivariate probability distributions. The consequence is that the truth of **this is *that*** does not automatically lead to the truth of **that is *this***. On the contrary,

$$(a=b) \neq (b=a)$$

for even though two plus two always equals four, four may equal an infinite number of combinations, including two plus two. And so it is that the equals sign is best understood not as two parallel lines but as a finger-pointing arrow, causal inference by definition a one-way street, Euclid turned into Riemann.

The difference between the statistician's correlation and regression in a nutshell, the geographic inference problem as well. The Achilles heel of social engineering, the dream of a happy marriage between scientific knowledge and political action turned into a nightmare. Thus sounds nevertheless the power-wielder's call to the social sciences: "Capture the power of social relations in a net of scientific laws and you will possess the means not merely for understanding the world but for changing it as well. If the natural scientists know how to construct rockets that take them to the moon and the physicians how to save lives by transplanting hearts, then your duty as a social scientist is to build a better human. If not by eradicating poverty, then at least by eradicating my opponents, those damned deviants who are blocking the way to the Millennium. Exterminate the brutes, the good cause excusing the necessary violations of international law, no matter whether these are called 'genocide' (directed at population groups) or 'crimes against humanity' (directed at individuals). Politics Is The Will To Power!"

Heaven and Hell, the deep structure of Nazi Germany and the Swedish welfare state more closely related than what feels comfortable, every ideology and every critique a child of its own *Lebensraum*. Therefore, before you accept the calls to action you should ask yourself why we have accumulated knowledge in some areas and not in others. Why, for instance, do so many keep returning to Sophocles and Shakespeare for their insights into the human condition of hopes and fears, love and hate, while only historians of science read Plato for what he had to say about physics and medicine? Perhaps because the ontologies of the social and the physical sciences demand different epistemologies, speech acts and hard facts too different to be captured in the same reasoning net, Hitler's practice of equating the *is* of chemical physics and the *is* of social physics a category mistake on par with Stalin's use of Marx and bin Laden's of the Quran—the term "Gay Science" a legitimating misnomer.

Seen in that light it is clear why the majority of large-scale social engineering projects are better known for their failures than for their successes, the indexical = in reality the most complex, not the least ambiguous, of Peirce's signs. How otherwise could one understand German history between January 30, 1933, when Adolf Hitler was made *Reichskanzler*, and the Nuremberg convictions on October 1, 1946, when twelve of his closest collaborators were sentenced to death? How otherwise could one interpret the coordinated pogroms on the night between November 9 and 10, 1938 (*die Kristallnacht*), and the decision about the Final Solution (*die Endlösung der Judenfrage*) in January 1942?

Thirteen years, eight months, and one day. An eternity minutely planned, meticulously recorded. Silence the only possible answer to the screaming mattresses made of human hair and to the dimmed light from the Marsyan lampshades; the signals from the trains that carried no destination sign yet always arrived on time; the mass graves in the Ukrainian forests . . . . . everything an operationalization of *Mein Kampf*, the autobiography that changed the world. Little to say except that Hannah Arendt was right about the banality of evilness and that Primo Levi survived the camp because he was a chemist, eventually throwing himself to death no longer able to take it. Once marked, always marked, the forearm with the tattooed number a constant reminder. Guilt and punishment out of order, many survivors refusing to share their memories, some so ashamed of what they had witnessed that they keep blaming themselves for having been rescued, others so reconciled that even though they have not forgotten, they have chosen not to remember. Abysmal their fate, in everything reminiscent of Goya's *Saturn Devouring His Son*, an image too horrifying to reproduce.

*

Sophocles obviously knew what he did, when in the opening scene of *Oedipus Rex* he let the citizens beg the king to rescue them from the plague, just as he once had liberated the city from the terror of the flinty Sphinx. As their spokesman put it:

> Once, years ago, with happy augury,
> You brought us fortune; *be the same again!*[9]

The problem is, of course, that no one, not even a king, can ever be the same again. And therein lies the key to understanding Greek tragedy (social engineering its modernized version): a wonderful **this** in the beginning; a horrible **that** at the end; nothing to blame but a maltreated = in the middle.

Little wonder that Jocasta no longer could equate the name "Oedipus" with any of the alternative descriptions "my king," "my husband," or "father of my children." In desperation she cries out,

> Ah miserable!
> That is the only word I have for you now.
> That is the only word I can ever have.[10]

She runs to her apartment where a servant finds her with a twinned rope around her neck. When Oedipus learns what has happened he bursts into moaning, runs into the room, loosens the rope, lowers her body, rips the golden brooches from her gown, raises them and plunges them straight into his eyeballs. His mind groping for a different anchorage, he says about his daughters,

> Could I but touch them
> They would be mine again, as when I had my eyes.[11]

And yet he clearly understands that their identities will never be complete in the same sense that his own was once complete, his identity extending both into the past and into the future, theirs only into the past. The statement $(a=b) \neq (b=a)$ in its proper context.

But Creon, the uncle who later forbade Antigone to bury her brother, he lets the nephew know what he already knew:

> Think no longer
> That you are in command here, but rather think
> How, when you were, you served your own destruction.[12]

Penthouse

Earth shattering, these experiences *in* (not *at*) the upper limit of language, the Peircean signs that had served the arkotect so well suddenly turning ugly and despicable. Could he but rethink them, they might be his again, as when he had his wits.

And through a magic spell he finds himself moved from the Ball Room attic to the enchanting Penthouse, the creeping claustrophobia replaced by a splendor never experienced before. The sun rising in the Orient, an entire universe seen through the large windows, the Byzantium history of thought retold by the philosophers, bishops, monks, the emperor himself. And more important than anything else, the experience of seeing Peirce's signs mirroring themselves in the Nicaea debates, like the formative seminars on the Red River a variation on the same theme of identity formation, in both instances a drama of points, lines, and planes, time-bound takens-for-granted shaped in the process. Everything re-pre-figured in the political creation of Jesus Christ, history's most remarkable attempt to negotiate lasting peace between the humans and the utterly different. Eternal questions now brought to life again in the Crystal Palace.

But who was that revolutionary figure whose followers changed the world? Was he "begotten" and "divine by nature" or was he "created" and "divine by adoption"? How could the contradictory influences from Jewish monotheism and Greek polytheism be brought together in a coherent fashion? How were religious mysticism and logical precision to live with each other? Not so easy to tell, partly because our inherited preconceptions work so strongly against us.

As the situation was getting out of hand it fell on Constantine I, himself an unbaptized neophyte, to summon a general council of the whole Church, about 270 bishops, most of them from the eastern parts of the empire. The purpose of the meeting—held at his Nicaea summer residence between May 20 and June 19, 325—was to end the bishops' bitter wrangling and begin instead an era of harmony. A pivotal event in the history of Christendom, for here, as elsewhere, power and organization were one and the same.

As at other party conventions—the Socialist Internationals foremost among them—the arguments were strong and often invidious, perhaps because early Christianity, like other revolutionary movements, was set on creating a new type of human being, replacing one set of takens-for-granted with another. The common goal was nevertheless to reach a consensus, to determine once and for all the true nature of Christian faith, to establish a foundation of unquestionable solidity. And in that sense the meeting was certainly a great success, for, after small but significant revisions, the resulting document has remained the key codification of Christian dogma. Never a communion without it, the question of what it means to be human pushed to its limits. And so it is that Jesus Christ of Nicaea stands out as a most revolutionary invention, a triangulation of belief that in the same symbol brings together Moses's first stone tablet and Aristotle's Laws of Thought; not only does the first article of the Creed tie the faithful directly to the monotheism of the first commandment, but it states explicitly that here is a power so absolute that it knows nothing but its own identity. Thus,

We believe in one God, the Father Almighty, maker of heaven and earth, and of things visible and invisible.

From this beginning of beginnings the Creed swiftly moves to the second article, a most remarkable amendment to the censorship paragraph of the Ten Commandments, a drastic turnabout. For what this article projects is a desire totally alien to the Judaic tradition, a play of identity and difference in which Jesus Christ is actually made to occupy the same position as the LORD himself, both entities roaming the empty halls of Apsu's palace, both of them sharing the same penthouse at the top of the Plotinian house, both of them creatures of the excluded middle. A fix-point never fixed before, the tautological

$$A = A$$

begetting an informative

$$A = B$$

The wording is ingenious, a set of formulations well worthy of the emperor who stood behind them, a clear-cut case of how the mapmaker's scale determines what is what and who is who:

And [we believe] in one Lord Jesus Christ, the only-begotten
Son of God, begotten of the Father before all worlds, God of
God, Light of Light, Very God of Very God, begotten not made,
being of one substance with the Father by whom all things were
made; who for us men, and for or salvation, came down from heaven,
and was incarnate by the Holy Spirit of the Virgin Mary, and was
made man, and was crucified also for us under Pontius Pilate. He
suffered and was buried, and the third day he arose again according
to the Scriptures, and ascended into heaven, and sitteth on the right
hand of the Father. And he shall come again with glory to judge
both the quick and the dead, whose kingdom shall have no end.

Then, finally, the third article, in essence the *mappa* of Christian faith, a projection screen so carefully prepared that the messages of the previous articles will neither crack nor run off but forever stick to the taken-for-granted of the believers' thoughts-and-actions. And in this sense the emperor and the bishops were in agreement that just as every state must have its religion, so every religion must have its state. United we stand, divided we fall!

And thus it is that the Creed remains committed to the spirit, though not always to the letter, of the third paragraph of the Constitutional Law. Therefore, after an updating of the specific allegiances,

We believe in the Holy Spirit, the Lord and Giver of Life, who
proceedeth from the Father [and the Son], who with the Father and
the Son together is worshipped and glorified, who spoke by the
Prophets. And we believe in one holy catholic and apostolic Church.
We acknowledge one baptism for the remission of sins. And we
look for the resurrection of the dead, and life of the world to come.
Amen

Trinity created, triangulation at work. A codification of a belief system as power-filled as anything ever chiseled onto the first stone tablet, as logical as anything ever uttered in the Greek Academy. The parallels are astonishing and, as Plato foresaw at the end of *Timaeus*, composed half a millennium before Nicaea and for a long time the most popular of his dialogues:

> So the world received animals, mortal and immortal, and was fulfilled in them, and became a visible God, comprehending the visible, made in the image of the Intellectual, being the one perfect only-begotten heaven.[13]

*

And there it is, the outline of yet another map of power. Picture and story, truth and trust intricately interwoven in the borderline figure of Jesus Christ himself, the practice of proper names and definite descriptions long before Bertrand Russell imagined the theory; for whereas "Yeshua" is a Hebrew name, "Christos" is the Greek term for "anointed" or "consecrated." Make no mistake, though, for while one is Jewish by one's mother, one is Christian by baptism or communion, the former by biological necessity, the latter presumably by choice.

Now, on the Christian base map—as on the Platonic base map—there is a thin line that runs exactly midway between the two boundaries of the Territory of the Humans, the Mindscape of godly spirits placed on one side, the Rockscape of material monsters on the other. The name of that interesting line is "Jesus Christ," a denotation of the in-between whose (theo)logical meaning hinges on the Greek word *homoousios*—"of one substance"—a close relative to Plotinus's the One.

If the Nicene definition is to be believed, then this Lord Jesus Christ, the Son of one substance with the Father, was begotten not made. By decree a paradoxical figure in constant limbo; a slashy entity from the transition zone between ontological categories; the sole inhabitant of the no-man's land of Inter-Esse; the paradigmatic case of **Signifier** and **signified** inseparably merged together. Not, however, a Kantian phenomenon to be shared and understood but a noumenon imported from the lands beyond the beyond, an imagination which cannot be reached through common logic, only through an individual, Kierkegaardian leap of faith.

— ·— ·— ·— — — — — — — — ·— — —JESUS CHRIST

Base Map of the Christian
Homoousios.   ROCKSCAPE

The cartographic parallels are obvious, the rhetorical art of naming the fix-points, scales, and projection screens the church-fathers' modus vivendi. It follows that whenever I am asserting that a particular statement is true, then I am not saying that it is factually correct but that it is socially correct. A "true" statement is consequently true only if it is trustworthy, only if its truth-hood is shared by a sufficient number of others who for some reason know how to draw and mark the line between left and right, right and wrong, black and white, freeman and slave. And most tellingly, the term "propaganda" is the gerundive of the Latin *propagere*, where *pro* means "before" and *pag* is the root of *pangere*, "to fasten." And by no coincidence "Propaganda" is the name of the special committee of cardinals which since 1622 is in charge of the Vatican's foreign missions.

In this game of make-believe Constantine the Great was no amateur, perhaps because he was such an integral part of his own culture that he knew neither this nor that. Torn between the irreconcilable differences of Judaic monotheism and Greek polytheism his only hope of political survival was to reach some sort of conciliation between the opposing traditions. At issue was not only the interpretation of the Second Commandment but also the Aristotelian Laws of Thought, especially the principle of the excluded middle. The real challenge was to keep the warring factions at bay, to make sure that the people of the empire remained predictable and governable. And that is why the Penthouse visitor is stunned by a conversation he imagines between the emperor, the bishops, and Karl Marx, the two former focusing on the enigmas of Christ's being, the latter on the mixed values of a capitalist commodity. Hear here the travesty:

> The power of a belief system appears at first sight a very queer thing, abounding in metaphysical subtleties and theological niceties. Analysis shows, however, that it is, in reality a very inter-esting commodity located exactly in the taboo-ridden abyss of the excluded middle, the symbolic figure of Jesus Christ the most outstanding of all examples. Visible and invisible; touchable and untouchable; mind and matter— all powerholders being of one substance with the ontological transformations by which everything is made, the concept of nothingness included. Proper names and definite descriptions glued together by a concoction of guns and words. And that is why no organization is likely to survive as long as the holy catholic and apostolic Church already has, for prior to Facebook no other organization has ever had a spy in every village.[14]

*

A spy in every village, such is the wet dream of every politician—Marx, the bishops, and Constantine included. And as the sophisticated persons they were, they knew that in the long run it is more crucial to control the production of meaning than the making of things. Yet they also realized that the way to the mind always goes via the body, that the uncontrollable chains of metonymic meanings are set off by metaphoric detonators. In addition, they knew how to use ambiguous language for diffusing opposition; while belief may be a theological problem, coercion is an issue of politics. And that explains the explosive power of the holy icon: on the surface a question of idolatry, deeper down a question about the legitimation of power.

The major players in this game were naturally the church and the empire. However, neither church nor empire were monolithic organizations but powers which themselves were caught in the cross-fire between centripetal and centrifugal forces. Not only must the emperor at the center worry about uprisings in the peripheries but inside the church there were strong tensions between the clergy and the monks, the former via the bishops tied to the emperor, the latter bound to the local monasteries and therefore in immediate contact with the population at large.

Such was the setting of what eventually grew into a conflict about the right to control the symbols of veneration, the key metaphors no ruler can rule without. Who should have the last say, the venerated or the venerators, the idols or the idolaters? Who in these often deadly disputes should serve as supreme judge, who be appointed Director General of the Department of Truth? Not so easy, because whoever tries to mold the taken-for-granted is bound to learn that there is no institutional fact without a brute fact, no signified without a Signifier. Why else would the authors of the Constitutional Law have threatened the makers of graven images with such outrageous punishments? Why else would Jesus Christ of Nicaea ever have been invented?

But the forgers of the unconscious have also learned that different symbols belong to different congregations, that some minds are more conducive to abstract manipulation, others to brute facts. And the more volatile the situation, the more crucial the choice of metaphor; as John of Damascus noted, "*God spoke in many and various ways. A skillful doctor does not prescribe the same for all alike.*"[15] But how should that be done and by whom should the faithful be checked? By the governors or by the holy men, in the basilicas or in the monasteries? Through the participation in Eucharist or through the veneration of icons?

On one side in this quarrel stood the iconophiles ("the lovers of images") and on the other the more ardent iconodules ("the worshippers of images"), both groups believing that even though Christ, Mary, and the saints were in heaven, they could somehow be reached through their portraits. The connections with pagan practices from earlier times were obvious, especially since it was in the monasteries, not in the churches, that they were produced. It was in fact the decentralized network of monks and holy men that made the iconodules into such a serious threat to the central authorities. The real problem was that it is literally impossible to determine to whom a person in front of an icon is actually praying—kissing an icon is something entirely different from sharing the bread and wine of a last supper, the former a private act, the latter a public and communal performance. It was in the home, away from the clergy, that the Christian cult came closest to the pagan. As recalled, the complement of the third commandment is that you must never be alone, for left alone the cohesive powers cannot reach you.

Standing on the other side in this controversy were the iconoclasts ("image smashers"), to whom icons were not holy at all, merely a form of graven images that opened the way to idolatry and competing rulers. Hence these people argued that all pictures should be banned from religious services and that the Eucharist, the church building, and the cross should be used as the only intermediaries between the worshipper and the worshipped; the Eucharist because it was given by Christ himself; the basilicas because they were consecrated by the bishops, the cross because it had been given by God to Constantine before the battle at the Ponte Milvio in 312: *In hoc signo vinces*, "By this sign thou shalt conquer." In contrast, the icon was blessed by no one.

What a wonderful illustration of the third and second commandments intertwined, the certainties of collective unity overruling the ambiguities of individual freedom, the Eucharist shared in public, the icon addressed in private. No wonder the bishops and the governors preferred the cross, the monks and laypersons the icon. For whereas the cross is a geometric figure without a name, the icon is a face with two eyes to sink into. It was said that in his lifetime Jesus never closed them.

Beware, though, for the iconoclastic controversy was not only a struggle over political supremacy. In addition, and equally much, it spoke directly to the issue of incarnation, that most spectacular of all ontological transformations, the concept without which Eucharist itself loses its meaning. The lasting voice in that attempt to formulate a valid theory of human action belonged to John of Damascus (ca. 665–ca. 749), whose most revolutionary idea was that the possibility, nay the necessity, of materially representing the holy follows directly from Jesus's presence on earth; not only did he claim that the veneration of icons is a logical consequence of the incarnation, but he also argued that images have the same ability to represent the unseen as do the liturgy and the sacraments. To the accusations that the veneration of icons led to idolatry, he boldly answered that even though the fallacy of reification once had presented a real threat to social cohesion, it no longer did. In his own words:

> These commandments [the prohibition against graven images] were given to the Jews because of their proneness to idolatry. But to us it is given . . . to avoid superstitious error and to come to God in the knowledge of the truth; to adore God alone, to enjoy the fullness of divine knowledge, to attain to mature manhood, that we may no longer be children, tossed to and fro and carried about with every wind of doctrine. We are no longer under custodians, but we have received from God the ability to discern what may be represented and what is uncircumscript. "You cannot see My form," the Scripture says. What wisdom the Lawgiver has! How can one draw what is limitless, immeasurable, infinite? How can a form be given to the formless? How does one paint the bodiless? How can you describe what a mystery is? . . . [But] when the invisible One becomes visible to flesh, you may then draw his likeness. . . . [Thus] in former times God, who is without form or body, could never be depicted. But now when God is seen in the flesh conversing with men, I make an image of the God whom I see. I do not worship matter; I worship the Creator of matter who became matter for my sake, who willed to take His abode in matter. . . . I honor it, but not as God.[16]

What a remarkable rendering of the abracadabra of ontological transformations, the icon serving as the magic wand by which God's nature ($/$) is first transformed into the person of Jesus Christ ($-$), then into the flesh of his followers ($=$)! The connections to the Divided Line of Plato and the hypostases of the Plotinian house are immediate, not least because John

Damascene was so carefully distinguishing between six different categories of images, the Son as the consubstantial image of Father Almighty at the top, the conventional icons at the bottom.

To top it off—and as a connection between the ark of Exodus and the articles of Nicaea—the arkotect (here turned arkosopher) once again eavesdrops on the Damascene:

> We all use our senses to produce worthy images of Him, and we sanctify the noblest of senses, which is that of sight. For just as words edify the [Jewish] ear, so also the image stimulates the [Greek] eye. What the book is to the literate, the image is to the illiterate. Just as words speak to the ear, so the image speaks to the sight; it brings us understanding. For this reason God ordered the ark to be constructed of wood which would not decay, and to be guilded outside and in, and for the tablets to be placed inside, with Aaron's staff and the golden urn containing the manna in order to provide a remembrance of the past and an image of the future.[17]

* * *

Awestruck I am standing in the middle of the tetrahedron-shaped penthouse, the most beautiful of all geometric forms. Close by is a replica of the altar from the Island Chapel, the *Mappa Mundi* sculpture and catechesis symmetrically arranged on the marble top, the portable ark of acacia wood modernized into a glass tetrahedron, the Ten Commandments replaced by one difference and three identities. And farther away is a computer screen with moving pictures of the Crystal Palace itself, each level clearly marked:

> (0) the Basement with the blood-filled well at its center and the Peircean signs in the corners;
> (1) the Prophets' Hall, the pub of the Sharing Cross Station on the floor, the paintings in the ceiling;

(2) the Ball Room crowded with people circling the throne of Power, all in search of their proper pronouns and prepositions;

(3) the horrifying Attic, a madhouse of mistranslations;

(4) the Penthouse with the new altar, the place where everything comes together.

A paradigmatic case of artificial intelligence and three-dimensional computer graphics moved into the arkotect's mind, the Crystal Palace spinning around the invisible pillar that holds the construction together, Pallas Athene stringing the ruby, gold, finger, throne, and altar into a rosary never seen before. A whirlwind tour recording an outsider's view of the inside.

Whirlwind Tour of the Crystal Palace.
Computer graphics by Mathias Ruø Jensen.

True, yet not true enough. For as I now find myself standing inside Fabian Svensson's laser-built tetrahedron, I see with my own eyes that viewing the Palace from the outside and sensing it from the inside are two very different experiences. Most remarkably, the pinnacle—originally labeled **A = A** or **I AM WHO I AM**—now appears as a combination of "you are you" and "I am I," the fix-point of fix-points no longer a tautological LORD, but none less than I myself. A case of pre-positions begetting pro-nouns, theoretical philosophy a brainchild of practical geography, the arkotect a late-coming descendant. And sunk into myself I feel like a *topos* inside Timaeus's *chora*, a fetus in the womb of the taken-for-granted, a reminder that whoever approaches these questions is bound to hit his head against the ceiling of language.

Experiencing the Inside.
Photo by Fabian
Svensson.

*

A secular communion, old wine in a new chalice. A novel confession as well, the taken-for-granted stripped bare and adorned with new clothes, the Palace cornerstones turning into the fix-points of human thought-and-action, a minimalist condensation of what the explorer found along the way:

A

Damned be chaotic difference,
blessed the identities of cosmic order.

ERGO

a

We believe in the religious slash (/), the dialectical symbol of internal relations. No individual apart from society, no master without a slave, no slave without a master. Unbreakable is the world-wide-web of I and Thou, every definition an integral part of its own context.

$$\frac{a}{a}$$

We believe also in the semiotic fraction-line (—), the venerated icon whose equal we are striving to become. Desire is our lot, the Bar de Saussure our permanent residence.

a = b
Likewise, we believe in the scientific equal-sign (=), the magic
index of ontological transformations. Let there be, and there is.

*

And as imagination bodies forth, the poet's pen gives to
airy nothing a local habitation and a name.
FILIOQUE, SIMSALABIM

✶ ✶ ✶ ✶ ✶

Immediately following these ceremonies, a great party is arranged, Pallas
Athene the given guest of honor. A speech to celebrate the occasion:

I sing to you Pallas Athene, glorious goddess, courageous virgin,
bright-eyed, unbending of heart. Sprung from the head of Zeus, just
as millennia later you sprang from my own. For him a godly headache,
for me shear and painless joy. Grateful I am to have met you. Proud
as well, for I know that long ago you treated great Odysseus with the
same benevolence as you have been treating me.

Poseidon reeled horribly at both him and me, tossing us around
on the dark waves. But through your crafty wisdom and steady heart
you saved us both. In Odysseus's case by leading him back to his son,
wife, and father, in mine by letting me loose, sending me off first on
a visit to the Bar de Saussure, then to the Athenian's Republic and
the Königsberger's Island of Truth. And when in my excitement I
crashed into the sea you were there to pick me up and carry me into
the Crystal Palace, the place of my dreams, an edifice no mortal had
ever entered before. Everything with the godly purpose of helping
me grasp the taken-for-granted of my own time and place. Here—as
always—a power-filled play of identity and difference, a game of dice
in which the pronouns are the gamblers, the prepositions the croupier.

Polytropos—"much traveled"—such is our family name. Many personalities in one, fabulous Odysseus a man of twists and turns, I myself

first an arko-grapher, then an arko-logist *cum* arko-naut, finally an arko-tect (almost an arko-sopher). Throughout you led me to those sacred containers of rules that we follow blindly, invariably a blend of symbols, icons, and indexes, a fusion of the Peircean signs. Bouncing I am between the walls of science, religion, and the arts.

Some go crazy for less. Not I, though, but that, of course, is for others to judge. In the meantime I am praying that you will continue to keep a vigilant eye on your protégé. And rest assured that just as wise Zeus was glad to have you at his side, so am I.

Hail to you, owl-eyed beauty, you who taught me the signs of what it means to be human, blessed magician of ontological transformations. Dom Perignon, please!

*

And as the party proceeds, the sun sets over the Hesperidian Gardens, its golden apples promising eternal life to whomever consumes them. Busy is Idun replenishing her basket, Adam and Eve strictly forbidden to enter.

IV

Archives

Travelogue

The end is near, Godot once again returning to *Krapp's Last Tape*. So, here I end this reel. Box 4, spool 1. Perhaps my best years are gone. But who knows? With the fire in me now, there may still be a chance of happiness.

Yet, what is woven at dawn is undone at dusk, for even though creativity has neither beginning nor end, every show must sometimes open and sometimes it must close, the given texts turned into a drama of truth and verification, four acts opening with a suggestive epigram, closing with a summarizing emblem. And while the former are combining in the same figure the theater's writer, scenographer, and director, the lat-

ter serve as ark-like containers of whatever has been found, taboo-laden instances of the taken-for-granted. James Joyce's H. C. Earwicker (also known as "Here Comes Everybody" and "Haveth Children Everywhere") in search of himself. A man in constant motion.

I

The **Möbius** band forms the epigram of Act I, a surface with only one side and one boundary, mathematically uncontrollable. To make it, take a paper strip, give it a half-twist, join the ends, form a loop, and there it is. Magical it seems, its most striking feature that if one moves the full length of the strip one will return to the starting point without having crossed an edge, impossible to tell whether one is on the inside or the outside. A vivid description of the creation epics that were told and retold during the journey down the Red River Valley, self-referential stories at the same time closed and open. Already in antiquity the Möbius band was a symbol for eternity, a practice still in use.

And where is that drama taking us? Initially to the ark of the tabernacle, the beautifully designed chest that within it holds the prototype of all constitutional laws, *the* deification of the relations between the RULER and his subjects, detailed instructions for making the believers pliable, the enemies killable. Eventually to the **reliquary** of *Erik Translatus* and the truth that there is no power struggle without reification. Yet, such is the nature of *homo sacer* that even though he may be murdered, he must not be sacrificed.

II

Janus is the bard, scenographer and director of Act II, the pivoting symbol of gatekeeping. From his watchtower on the roof of Ea's palace it is he who keeps both sides of the apsu under constant surveillance, in the same glance catching a glimpse of those pasts that once were and of those futures that have yet to come.

Given the Greeks' fear of the void, Janus was invented in Rome, not in Athens. But in the lands around the Mare Nostrum he was everywhere to be seen, for not only was his image stamped on practically every coin, but in religious prayers this janitor was the first to be mentioned and in cultural rituals this son of January was the beginning of all beginnings. Diana was his godly consort and that explains why the doors of his temple stayed open in times of war and why they were shut in times of peace. Like ordinary lovers, gods need their privacy too.

Janus's main concerns were shared also by Saussure, Plato, and Kant, the mind-surveyors who spent their lives measuring in and marking out the limits of imagination, an adventure condensed into the emblematic **Map of the Human Territory**, you and I depicted as permanent residents of the Bar de Saussure. Everything sanctified by the sculpted catechesis of the *Mappa Mundi Universalis*, which so excited the arkologist in the island chapel. Nothing less than an up-to-date rendering of the philosopher's republic and the prophet's tabernacle.

III

Another deity—**Pallas Athene**—is the leading figure of Act III. No goddess like her, no teacher better equipped for opening the arkotect's eyes to the rules we follow blindly, her personality well described in the Penthouse speech given in her honor, her achievements beyond what any mortal could imagine, much less achieve. And that explains why her version of the ark is one with her own **self-portrait**, like Kazimir Malevich's *Black Square* a holy icon, the Peircean signs functioning as her eyes, nose, and mouth. Those of the present author as well.

Requiescat in pace. Répondez s'il vous plaît.

IV

Finally this closing Act IV, **Marcel Duchamp** its guiding spirit, here portrayed as his best known ready-made—the porcelain urinal which in the spring of 1917 was bought in a New York hardware store, carried to the exhibition hall of the Society of Independent Artists, laid on its back, turned around, signed "R. Mutt" and baptized *Fountain*. The scandal was immediate, the thing itself first hidden behind a screen, then officially rejected and eventually lost. Its non-existence notwithstanding, the piece was projected into eternity through a photographic image made by the trend-setting Alfred Stieglitz. Sacrificed in the process was the material object, resurrected the untouchable thought. The sensible buried in the rubble, the intelligible elevated to heaven, where it is often venerated as the most important artwork of the twentieth century.

It is hard to imagine an epigram more fitting to this grand tour as a whole, an archive of hidden quotations, a shameless reuse of readymade originals.

A collection of classic tunes lifted from the book *Abysmal: A Critique of Cartographic Reason* (handsomely produced by the University of Chicago Press). No container better suited to hold the concoction than the Sèvres **potpourri vase** made in 1763 and owned by Madame de Pompadour, its lid pierced with small holes to let the fragrance out. Breathe normally. And your mind will be changed.

* * * * *

And so it is that while the projections of Acts I–III are bouncing between the tetrahedron's glass walls, Act IV is etched into the square of its rock-bottom foundation—no *catharsis* without Gunnael Jensson's *Mappa Mundi Universalis*. Many insights glimpsed in the process, including the affinities between the five floors of the Crystal Palace and the thousand plateaus of Gilles Deleuze and Félix Guattari.

Thus encouraged, I am now carried back to the beginning of this grand tour, the signed Preface with the epigram of Marcel Duchamp's **Etant donnés**, the door which is not a door but a wall with two holes drilled at eye level, seven centimeters apart. Nose poking the slit in-between, there bound to realize that whatever I see is for me alone, an unexpected echo of Abraham's "Here I am," the French expression *étant donnés* a distant relative of the English "Let there be!" And by a commodious vicus of recirculation there it is, the untouchable simulacrum on the other side. Anamorphic is the perspective, chiastic the Möbius band, Anna Livia Plurabelle the given companion:

> So. Avelaval. My leaves have drifted from me. All. But one clings still. I'll bear it on me. To remind me of. Lff! So soft this morning, ours. Yes. Carry me along, taddy, like you done through the toy fair! If I see him bearing down on me now under widespread wings like he'd come from Arkangels, I sink I'd die down over his feet, humbly dumbly, only to washup. Yes, tid. There's where. First. We pass through grass behush the bush to. Whish! A gull. Gulls. Far calls. Coming, far! End here. Us then. Finn, again! Take. Bussoftlhee, mememormee!

Till thousendsthee. Lps. The keys too. Given! A way a lone a last a love a long the[1]

Rekindled is the fire in me now, perhaps there is still a chance of happiness. GO ON, GO ON. Krapp frowning, Athene twinkling her approval.

NOTES

I

1. *Enuma elish*, tablet 1, 1–8, in Heidel, *Babylonian Genesis*.
2. Mitchell, *Gilgamesh*, 69–70.
3. Gen. 3:22 (NIV).
4. Gen. 6:7, 6:13 (NIV).
5. Gen. 1:2–5 (NIV).
6. Gen. 17:2 (RSV).
7. Gen. 22 (NIV).
8. Gen. 27:18–27 (RSV), emphasis added
9. Gen. 32:24–32 (RSV), emphasis added.
10. Exod. 23:27–33 (NIV).
11. Exod. 24:12–18 (NIV).
12. Exod. 32:27–29 (NIV).
13. Deut. 10:16 (RSV).
14. Deut. 34:10–12 (RSV).
15. Job 38:2–5 (NIV), emphases added.
16. Job 40:4–5, 42:2–69 (NIV).

II

1. Homer, *Odyssey*, trans. Green, bk. 13, lines 290–303.
2. Shakespeare, *Midsummer Night's Dream*, 5.1.5–9, 5.1.15–18. References are to act, scene, and line.
3. Homer, *Iliad*, trans. Lattimore, bk. 19, lines 86–90.
4. Beckett, *Beckett Trilogy*, 352.
5. Plato, *Republic*, 511c–d, *Collected Dialogues*, 746.
6. Aristotle, *Nicomachean Ethics*, in *Basic Works of Aristotle*, 1094b–1095a.
7. Kant, *Critique of Pure Reason*, B 151, B 152, B 156, trans. Müller.
8. Wittgenstein, *Tractatus Logico-Philosophicus*, 4, 414.
9. Plato, *Republic*, 509, trans. Cornford, 224.
10. Plato, *Republic*, 507b, trans. Cornford, 217f.

11. Plato, *Republic*, 508d–511e, trans. Cornford, 219.

12. Plato, *Republic*, 511b, trans. Lee, 239.

13. Aristotle, *Metaphysics*, in *Basic Works of Aristotle*, 1078b.

14. Wittgenstein, *Tractatus Logico-Philosophicus*, 6.54.

15. Plato, *Republic*, 511d, trans. Cornford, 226.

16. Plotinus, *Enneads*, 5:2, emphasis added.

17. Plato, *Republic*, 514a–517c, trans. Cornford, 227–31, emphasis added.

18. Wittgenstein, *Zettel*, 393.

19. Plato, *Republic*, 517a, trans. Cornford, 231.

20. Plato, *Republic*, 517b, trans. Cornford, 231.

21. Plato, *Republic*, 533c–533d, trans. Cornford, 253–54, emphasis added.

22. *Oxford English Dictionary*, compact ed. (1971), s.v. "tissue."

23. Kant, *Critique of Pure Reason*, trans. Müller, A 236 / B 295.

24. Kant, *Critique of Practical Reason*, 5:162. References are to section and page.

25. Kant, *Critique of Pure Reason*, trans. Smith, A 51 / B 75.

26. Kant, *Critique of Pure Reason*, A 758 / B 786.

27. Casey, *Fate of Place*, 63.

28. Malpas and Thiel, "Kant's Geography of Reason," 199.

29. Wittgenstein, *Tractatus Logico-Philosophicus*, Preface and 7.

30. Kant, *Critique of Pure Reason*, trans. Müller, B 157, B 158.

31. Shakespeare, *Julius Cæsar*, 3.1.58–70.

32. Quoted in Düchting, *Paul Cézanne*, 214.

33. Rothko, *Artist's Reality*, 22.

34. Quoted in Sylvester, *Looking Back*, 166.

35. Hobbes, *Leviathan*, 82–83.

36. Job 41:24, 41:33 (NIV).

III

1. Ulven, *Replacement*, 20.

2. Carroll, *Through the Looking Glass*, ch. 6, quote slightly adjusted.

3. Joyce, *Ulysses*, 783

4. Blake, *Complete Illuminated Books*, 114–15.

5. Barthes, *Lover's Discourse*, 73.

6. Revelation 1:3, 1:9, 1:12, 1:17–18 (NIV).

7. Revelation 2:20–23 (NIV).

8. Acts 2:1–4, 2:12–13 (NIV).

9. Sophocles, *Oedipus Cycle*, 5.

10. Sophocles, *Oedipus Cycle*, 56.

11. Sophocles, *Oedipus Cycle*, 75.

12. Sophocles, *Oedipus Cycle*, 77.

13. Plato, *Collected Dialogues*, Timaeus, 92c.

14. Marx, *Capital*, 1:71–72, manipulated.

15. John of Damascus, *On the Divine Images*, 2:7, 2:54.

16. John of Damascus, *On the Divine Images*, 1:8, 1:18 and 1:16, 1:23.

17. John of Damascus, *On the Divine Images*, 1:17, 1:25.

IV

1. Joyce, *Finnegans Wake*, 628.

HIDDEN REFERENCES

Abel, Ulf. *Ikonen—bilden av det heliga*. Hedemora: Gidlunds Bokförlag, 1988.

Abrahamsson, Christian. *Topoi/Graphein: Mapping the Middle in Spatial Thought*. Foreword by Gunnar Olsson. Lincoln: University of Nebraska Press, 2018.

Abrahamsson, Christian, and Martin Gren, eds. *GO: On the Geographies of Gunnar Olsson*. Farnham, UK: Ashgate, 2012.

Ades, Dawn. *Dada and Surrealism Reviewed*. Introduction by David Sylvester. Supplementary essay by Elizabet Cowling. London: Arts Council of Great Britain, 1978.

Adorno, Theodore W. *Negative Dialectics*. Translated by E. B. Ashton. New York: Seabury Press, 1973.

Agamben, Giorgio. *Homo Sacer: Sovereign Power and Bare Life*. Translated by Daniel Heller-Roazen. Stanford: Stanford University Press, 1998.

Albrektsson, Bertil. *History and the Gods: An Essay on the Idea of Historical Events as Divine Manifestations in the Ancient Near East and in Israel*. Lund: Gleerup, 1967.

Albrektsson, Bertil, and Helmer Ringgren. *En bok om Gamla Testamentet*. 5e omarbetade upplagan. Malmö: Gleerup, 1992.

Alexievich, Svetlana. *Second-Hand Time: The Last of the Soviets*. Translated by Bela Shayevich. New York: Random House, 2016.

Andersen Troels. *Kazimir Malevic. The Artist, Infinity, Suprematism. Unpublished Writings 1913-33*. Translated by Xenia Hoffman. København: Borgen, 1978.

———, ed. *K. Malevic: Om nye systemer i kunsten. Skrifter 1915–1922*. København: Kunst og Kultur, 1963.

———. *K.S. Malevich: Essays on Art, 1915–1933*. Translated by Xenia Glowacki-Prus. New York: Wittenborn, 1968.

Annas, Julia. *An Introduction to Plato's "Republic."* Oxford: Clarendon Press, 1981.

Arendt, Hannah. *Eichmann in Jerusalem: A Report on the Banality of Evil*. New York: Viking, 1967.

Aristotle. *The Basic Works of Aristotle*. Edited by Richard McKeon. New York: Random House, 1941.

Armstrong, Karen. *Fields of Blood: Religion and the History of Violence*. New York: Vintage, 2014.

———. *A History of God: The 4000-Year Quest of Judaism, Christianity and Islam*. New York: Knopf, 1993.

Ashton, Dore. *About Rothko*. New York: Oxford University Press, 1983.

Asplund, Johan. *Det sociala livets elementära former*. Göteborg: Korpen, 1987.

———. *Rivaler och syndabockar*. Göteborg: Korpen, 1989.

———. *Tid, rum, individ och kollektiv*. Stockholm: Liber, 1983.

Assmann, Jan. *Of God and Gods: Egypt, Israel, and the Rise of Monotheism*. Madison: University of Wisconsin Press, 2008.

———. *The Invention of Religion: Faith and Covenant in the Book of Exodus*. Translated by Robert Savage. Princeton NJ: Princeton University Press, 2018.

Auerbach, Erich. *Mimesis: The Representation of Reality in Western Literature*. Translated by Willard R. Tusk. Princeton NJ: Princeton University Press, 1953.

Augustine of Hippo. *Confessions*. Translated by Garry Wills. New York: Penguin Books, 2006.

Austin, J. L. *How to Do Things with Words*. London: Oxford University Press, 1962.

Ayer, A. J., ed. *Logical Positivism*. New York. The Free Press, 1959.

Bachelard, Gaston. *The Poetics of Space*. Translated by Maria Jolas. Boston: Beacon Press, 1969.

Badiou, Alain. *Plato's "Republic": A Dialogue in Sixteen Chapters, with a Prologue and an Epilogue*. Translated by Susan Spitzer. Cambridge: Polity Press, 2012.

Baltrušatis, Jurgis. *Anamorphic Art*. Translated by W. J. Strachan. Cambridge: Chadwick-Healey, 1977.

Barasch, Moshe. *Icon: Studies in the History of an Idea*. New York: New York University Press, 1992.

Barnes, Julian. *The Noise of Time*. London: Jonathan Cape, 2016.

Barthes, Roland. *A Lover's Discourse: Fragments*. Translated by Richard Howard. New York: Hill and Wong, 1978.

———. *Mythologies*. Translated by Anette Lavers. London: Paladin, 1972.

———. *The Pleasure of the Text*. Translated by Richard Miller. New York: Hill and Wang, 1975.

Batailles, Georges. *The Story of the Eye*. Translated by Joachim Neugroschal. New York: Press, 1978.

Bateson, Gregory. *Mind and Nature: A Necessary Unity*. London: Wildwood House, 1979.

Baudelaire, Charles-Pierre. "L'Albatros/The Albatross." In *Baudelaire*, translated by Joanna Richardson, 38–39. Harmondsworth: Penguin, 1975.

Baudrillard, Jean. *Symbolic Exchange and Death*. Translated by Ian Grant. New York: Sage, 1993.

Bauer, Thomas. *Die Vereindeutigung der Welt. Über den Verlust an Mehrdeutigkeit und Vielfalt*. Stuttgart: Reclam, 2018.

Beckett, Samuel. *The Beckett Trilogy: Molloy, Malone Dies, The Unnamable*. London: Picador, 1979.

———. *Krapp's Last Tape*. New York: Grove, 1960.

———. *Waiting for Godot*. London: Faber and Faber, 1956.

———. *Whoroscope*. Paris: Hours Press, 1930.

Beckett, Samuel, et al. *Our Exagmination Round His Factification for Incamination of Work in Progress*. Paris: Shakespeare and Company, 1929.

Bely, Andrei. *Petersburg*. Translated by Robert A. Maguire and John E. Malmstad. Bloomington: Indiana University Press, 1978.

Benjamin, Walter. *The Arcades Project*. Translated by Howard Eiland and Kevin McLaughlin. London: Belknap Press, 1999.

———. *One-Way Street and Other Writings*. Introduction by Susan Sontag. Translated by Edmund Jephcott and Kingsley Shorter. London: Verso, 1985.

Benner, Erica. *Be Like a Fox: Machiavelli's Lifelong Quest for Freedom*. London: Allen Lane, 2017.

Bergson, Henri. *Matter and Memory*. Translated by Nancy Margaret Paul and W. Scott Paul. New York: Zone Books, 1991.

Berman, Marshall. *All That Is Solid Melts into Air*. New York: Simon & Schuster, 1982.

Bernstein, Richard. *Praxis and Action*. Philadelphia: University of Pennsylvania Press, 1971.

Besançon, Alain. *The Forbidden Image: An Intellectual History of Iconoclasm*. Translated by Jean Marie Todd. Chicago: University of Chicago Press, 2000.

Bibeln. Statens Offentliga Utredningar, SOU 1999:100. Stockholm: Bibelkommissionens utgåva, 1999.

Blake, William. *The Complete Illuminated Books*. London: Thames & Hudson, 2000.

Blanchot, Maurice. *Death Sentence*. Translated by Lydia Davis. Barrytown NY: Station Hill Press, 1978.

————. *The Space of Literature.* Translated by Ann Smock. Lincoln: University of Nebraska Press, 1982.

Bloom, Harold. *Shakespeare: The Invention of the Human.* New York: Riverhead Books, 1998.

Bodin, Per-Arne. *Den oväntade glädjen: Sju studier i den rysk-ortodoxa andliga traditionen.* Skellefteå: Artos, 1991.

The Book of Genesis. Illustrated by R. Crumb. New York: Norton, 2009.

The Book of J. Translated by David Rosenberg. Interpreted by Harold Bloom. New York: Faber and Faber, 1990.

Borch-Jacobsen. *Lacan: The Absolute Master.* Translated by Douglas Brick. Stanford CA: Stanford University Press, 1991.

Bostrom, Nick. *Superintelligence.* Oxford: Oxford University Press, 2016.

Bourdieu, Pierre. *Outline of a Theory of Practice.* Translated by Richard Nice. Cambridge: Cambridge University Press, 1977.

Bowie, Malcolm. *Lacan.* London: Fontana Press, 1991.

————. *Proust Among the Stars.* New York: Columbia University Press, 1998.

Breslin, James E. B. *Mark Rothko: A Biography.* Chicago: University of Chicago Press, 1993.

Breton, André. *Manifestoes of Surrealism.* Translated by Richard Seaver and Helen R. Lane. Ann Arbor: University of Michigan Press, 1969.

————. *Nadja.* Translated by Richard Howard. New York: Grove Press, 1960.

Brodsky, Joseph. *Collected Poems in English, 1972–1999.* Edited by Ann Kjellberg. New York: Farrar, Strauss and Giroux, 2000.

————. *Less Than One: Selected Essays.* New York: Farrar, Strauss and Giroux, 2000.

Brøndal, Viggo. *Præpositionernes theori: Inledning til en rationel betydningslære.* København: Ejnar Munksgaard, 1940.

Brown, Jonathan. *Francisco de Zurbarán.* New York: Harry N. Abrams, 1991.

Brown, Norman O. *Closing Time.* New York: Vintage Books, 1974.

————. *Life Against Death.* Middletown CN: Wesleyan University Press, 1959.

————. *Love's Body.* New York: Random House, 1966.

Brown, Peter. *The Body and Society: Men, Women, and Sexual Renunciation in Early Christianity.* New York: Columbia University Press, 1988.

————. *The Rise of Western Christendom: Triumph and Diversity, A.D. 200–1000.* 2nd ed. Oxford: Basil Blackwell, 2003.

Buber, Martin. *I and Thou.* New York: Scribner's, 1970.

Buck-Morss, Susan. *The Dialectics of Seeing: Walter Benjamin and the Arcades Project.* Cambridge MA: MIT Press, 1989.

Burkert, Walter. *Babylon, Memphis, Persepolis: Eastern Contexts of Greek Culture*. Cambridge MA: Harvard University Press, 2004.

———. *Creation of the Sacred: Tracks of Biology in Early Religions*. Cambridge MA: Harvard University Press, 1996.

Burton, Nina. *Gutenberggalaxens nova: En reseberättelse om Erasmus av Rotterdam, humanismen och 1500-talets medierevolution*. Stockholm: Albert Bonnier, 2016.

Buskirk, Martha, and Mignon Nixon, eds. *The Duchamp Effect: Essays, Interviews, Round Table*. Cambridge MA: MIT Press, 1996.

Butler, Judith. *Antigone's Claim: Kinship Between Life and Death*. New York: Columbia University Press, 2000.

———. *Bodies that Matter: On the Discursive Limits of "Sex."* New York: Routledge, 1993.

———. *Giving an Accord of Oneself*. New York: Fordham University Press, 2005.

———. *The Psychic Life of Power: Theories in Subjection*. Stanford CA: Stanford University Press, 1997.

Cabanne, Pierre. *Duchamp & Co.* Translated by Peter Snowdon. Paris: Editions Pierre Terrail, 1997.

Calvino, Italo. *Invisible Cities*. Translated by William Weaver. New York: Harcourt Brace Jovanovich, 1974.

Camfield, William A. *Marcel Duchamp, Fountain*. Introduction by Walter Hopps. Houston: Menil Foundation, 1989.

Campbell, Joseph, and Henry Morton Robinson. *A Skeleton Key to Finnegans Wake*. New York: Viking Press, 1961.

Campbell, Joseph, with Bill Moyers. *The Power of Myth*. New York: Anchor Books, 1991.

Canetti, Elias. *Auto-da-Fé*. Translated by C. V. Wedgwood. New York: Viking Press, 1963.

———. *Crowds and Power*. Translated by Carol Stewart. New York: Viking Press, 1966.

Carroll, Lewis. *Alice's Adventures in Wonderland*. London: Macmillan, 1865.

———. *Through the Looking Glass, and What Alice Found There*. London: Macmillan, 1872.

Casey, Edward S. *The Fate of Place: A Philosophical History*. Berkeley: University of California Press, 1997.

Cassirer, Ernst. *The Philosophy of Symbolic Forms*. Translated by Ralph Manheim. New Haven CT: Yale University Press, 1953–57.

Caunguilhem, Georges. *The Normal and the Pathological*. Translated by Carolyn Fawcett in collaboration with Robert S. Cohen. Introduction by Michel Foucault. New York: Zone Books, 1991.

Caygill, Howard. *A Kant Dictionary*. Oxford: Basil Blackwell, 1995.

———. *Walter Benjamin: The Colour of Experience*. London: Routledge, 1998.

Certeau, Michel de. *The Practice of Everyday Life*. Translated by Steven F. Rendall. Berkeley: University of California Press, 1984.

Cervantes, Miguel de. *Den snillrike riddaren Don Quijote av la Mancha. Första och andra delen*. Översatt av Jens Nordenhök. Stehag: Symposion, 2001.

Christensen, Inger. *Alfabet*. København: Gyldendal, 1981.

———. *Det*. København: Gyldendal, 1969.

———. *Verden ønsker at se sig selv*. Digte, prosa, udkast redigert af Peter Borum og Marie Silkeberg. København: Gyldendal, 2018.

Cioran. E. M. *The Trouble with Being Born*. Translated by Richard Howard. New York: Viking Press, 1976.

Cixous, Hélène. "The Laugh of the Medusa." Translated by Keith Cohen and Paula Cohen. *Signs* 1, no. 4 (Summer 1976): 875–93.

———. *The Newly Born Woman*. Translated by Betsy Wing. Minneapolis: University of Minnesota Press, 1986.

Clair, Jean, dir. *L'âme au corps: Arts et sciences 1793–1993*. Paris: Réunion des musées nationaux, 1994.

———. *Méduse: Contribution à une anthropologie des arts du visuel*. Paris: Gallimard, 1989.

Clark, Ronald W. *Einstein: The Life and Times*. New York: World Publishing, 1971.

Clark, T. J. *Farewell to an Idea: Episodes from a History of Modernism*. New Haven CT: Yale University Press, 1999.

Clay, Jenny Strauss. *The Wrath of Athena: Gods and Men in the Odyssey*. Princeton NJ: Princeton University Press, 1983.

Conrad, Peter. *Modern Times, Modern Places: Life and Art in the 20th Century*. London: Thames and Hudson, 1998.

Crone, Rainer, and David Moos. *Kazimir Malevich: The Climax of Disclosure*. London: Reaktion Books, 1991.

Culler, Jonathan. *Saussure*. London: Fontana Press, 1976.

Dalley, Stephanie. *Myths from Mesopotamia: Creation, the Flood, Gilgamesh, and Others*. Oxford: Oxford University Press, 1989.

Damisch, Hubert: *The Origin of Perspective*. Cambridge MA: MIT Press, 1994.

———. *A Theory of /Cloud/: Toward a History of Painting*. Translated by Janet Lloyd. Stanford CA: Stanford University Press, 2002.

D'Andrea, Jeanne, ed. *Kazimir Malevich, 1878–1935*. Los Angeles: Armand Hammer Museum of Art and Cultural Center, 1990.

Danielsson, Ulf. *Den bästa av världar: Skapelse, slump, apokalyps, död*. Stockholm: Bonniers, 2008.

Dante Alighieri. *The Divine Comedy*. Translated by C. H. Sisson. Introduction and notes by David H. Higgins. Oxford: Oxford University Press, 2008.

Debray, Cécile, dir. *Marcel Duchamp la peinture, même*. Paris: Centre Pompidou, 2014.

Deleuze, Gilles. *The Fold: Leibniz and the Baroque*. Translated by Tom Conley. Minneapolis: University of Minnesota Press, 1993.

———. *Francis Bacon: The Logic of Sensation*. Translated by Daniel W. Smith. Afterword by Tom Conley. Minneapolis: University of Minnesota Press, 2004.

———. *Kant's Critical Philosophy*. Translated by Hugh Thomlinson and Barbara Haberjam. Minneapolis: University of Minnesota Press, 1984.

Deleuze, Gilles, and Félix Guattari. *Anti-Oedipus*. Translated by Robert Hurley, Mark Seem, and Helen R. Lane. Minneapolis: University of Minnesota Press, 1983.

———. *A Thousand Plateaus: Capitalism and Schizophrenia*. Translated by Brian Massumi. Minneapolis: University of Minnesota Press, 1987.

———. *What is Philosophy?* Translated by Hugh Tomlinson and Graham Burchell. New York: Columbia University Press, 1994.

de Man, Paul. *Allegories of Reading: Figural Language in Rousseau, Nietsche, Rilke, and Proust*. New Haven CT: Yale University Press, 1979.

Derrida, Jacques. *Dissemination*. Translated by Barbara Johnson. London: Athlone Press, 1981.

———. *Edmund Husserl's Origin of Geometry: An Introduction*. Translated by John P. Leavey Jr. Lincoln: University of Nebraska Press, 1989.

———. *Of Grammatology*. Translated by Gayatri Charavorty Spivak. Baltimore: Johns Hopkins University Press, 1974.

———. *Margins of Philosophy*. Translated by Alan Bass. Chicago: University of Chicago Press, 1982.

Descharnes, Robert, and Gilles Néret. *Salvador Dalí 1904–1989: The Paintings, Part I, 1904–1946*. Köln: Taschen, 2006.

Detienne, Marcel. *The Masters of Truth in Archaic Greece*. Translated by J. Lloyd. New York: Zone Books, 1996.

Dewey, John. *Art as Experience*. New York: Penguin, 1980.

D'Harnoncourt, Anne, and Kynaston McShine, eds. *Marcel Duchamp*. New York: The Museum of Modern Art, 1973.

Doel, Marcus A. "Gunnar Olsson's Transformers: The Art and Politics of Rendering the Co-Relation of Society and Space in Monochrome and Technicolor." *Antipode* 35 (2003): 140–67.

———. *Poststructuralist Geographies: The Diabolical Art of Spatial Science*. Edinburgh: Edinburgh University Press, 1999.

Dostoyevsky, Fyodor. *The Brothers Karamazov*. Translated by Richard Pevear and Larissa Volokhousky. New York: Farrar, Strauss and Giroux, 1990.

Drake, James. *Constantine and the Bishops: The Politics of Intolerance*. Baltimore: Johns Hopkins University Press, 2000.

Drndić, Daša. *Belladonna*. Translated by Celia Hawkesworth. London: MacLehose Press, 2017.

Duchamp, Marcel. *Duchamp du signe: Ecrits*. Réunis et présentés par Michel Sanouillet. Paris: Flammarion, 1975.

————. *In the Infinitive: A Typotranslation by Richard Hamilton and Ecke Bonk of Marcel Duchamp's "White Box."* N.p.: The Typographic Society, 1999. (European distribution, Buchhandlung Walther König, Köln).

————. *La boite verte. La Mariée mise à nu par ses célibataires, même*. Paris: Éditions Rrose Sélavy, 1934. Translated by George Heard Hamilton as *The Bride Stripped Bare by Her Bachelors, Even: A Typographic Version by Richard Hamilton of Marcel Duchamp's "Green Box."* New York: Wittenborn, 1960.

————. *Manual of Instructions for Étant donnés: 1° la chute d'eau, 2°le gaz d'éclairage*. Philadelphia: Philadelphia Museum of Art, 1978.

Düchting, Hajo. *Paul Cézanne, 1839–1906: Nature into Art*. Translated by Michael Hulse. Köln: Taschen, 1991.

Dummett, Michael. *Frege: Philosophy of Language*. New York: Harper & Row, 1973.

Duve, Thierry de, ed. *The Definitely Unfinished Marcel Duchamp*. Cambridge MA: MIT Press, 1991.

————. *Kant after Duchamp*. Cambridge MA: MIT Press, 1996.

Eco, Umberto. *Art and Beauty in the Middle Ages*. New Haven CT: Yale University Press, 1986.

Edgerton, Samuel Y., Jr. *The Renaissance Rediscovery of Linear Perspective*. New York: Basic Books, 1975.

Elden, Stuart, ed. *Sloterdijk Now*. Cambridge: Polity Press, 2012.

————. *Terror and Territory: The Spatial Extent of Sovereignty*. Minneapolis: University of Minnesota Press, 2009.

Elden, Stuart, and Eduardo Mendieta, eds. *Reading Kant's Geography*. Albany: State University of New York Press, 2011.

Elensky, Torbjörn. *Gränser*. Stockholm: Fri Tanke, 2017.

Eliade, Mircea. *The Sacred and the Profane*. Translated by Willard R. Task. New York: Harcourt, Brace, 1959.

Elias, Norbert. *The Civilizing Process: State Formation and Civilization*. Translated by Edmund Jephcott. Oxford: Basil Blackwell, 1982.

———. *The Civilizing Process: The Development of Manners; Changes in the Code of Conduct and Feeling in Early Modern Times.* Translated by Edmund Jephcott. New York: Urizen Books, 1978.

Eliot, T. S. *The Waste Land.* Edited by C. B. Cox and Arnold P. Hinchliffe. London: Macmillan, 1968.

Elkins, James. *Pictures of the Body: Pain and Metamorphosis.* Stanford CA: Stanford University Press, 1999.

Ellman, Richard. *James Joyce.* New York: Oxford University Press, 1959.

Enuma elish: Det babyloniska skapelseeposet. Översatt med en kommentar av Ola Wikander. Stockholm: Wahlström och Widstrand, 2005.

The Epic of Gilgamesh: The Babylonian Epic Poem and Other Texts in Akkadian and Sumerian. Translated and edited by Andrew George. London: Penguin, 1999. In addition see the translations of *Enuma elish* and *Gilgamesh* listed under Heidel and Mitchell.

Espmark, Kjell. *Kvällens frihet.* Stockholm: Norstedts, 2019.

Evans, Helen C. *Byzantium: Faith and Power (1261–1557).* New York: Metropolitan Museum of Art, 2004.

Farinelli, Franco. *Blinding Polyphemus: Geography and the Models of the World.* Translated by Christina Chalmers. London: Seagull Books, 2018.

———. "De Nobis Ipsis Silemus." In Abrahamsson and Gren, *GO,* 375–83.

———. *I segni del mondo. Immagine cartografica e discorso geografico in età moderna.* Firenze: La nuova Italia, 1992.

Farinelli, Franco, Gunnar Olsson, and Dagmar Reichert, eds. *Limits of Representation.* München: Accedo, 1994.

Ferlin, Nils. *Dikter.* Stockholm: Albert Bonnier, 1951.

Filipovic, Elena. *The Apparently Marginal Activities of Marcel Duchamp.* Cambridge MA: MIT Press, 2016.

Fisher, Sally. *The Square Halo and Other Mysteries of Western Art: Images and the Stories That Inspired Them.* New York: Harry N. Abrams, 1995.

Focillon, Henri. *The Life of Forms in Art.* Translated by Charles B. Hogan and George Kubler. New York: Zone Books, 1989.

Foucault, Michel. *Discipline and Punish: The Birth of the Prison.* Translated by Alan Sheridan. Harmondsworth, UK: Penguin, 1979.

———. *The History of Sexuality: An Introduction.* Translated by Robert Hurley. Harmondsworth, UK: Penguin, 1981.

———. *The Order of Things: An Archeology of the Human Sciences.* Translated by Alan Sheridan. New York: Pantheon, 1970.

———. *Power/Knowledge: Selected Interviews and Other Writings 1972–1977*. Edited by Colin Gordon. New York: Random House, 1981.

French, Marilyn. *The Book as World: James Joyce's "Ulysses."* Cambridge MA: Harvard University Press, 1976.

Freud, Sigmund. *Drei Abhandlungen zur Sexualtheorie*. Studienausgabe 5. Frankfurt: Fischer, 1972.

———. *Moses and Monotheism*. Translated by Katherine Jones. New York: Knopf, 1939.

———. *Totem and Taboo*. Translated by Abraham Brill and James Strachey. London: Routledge and Kegan Paul, 1950.

Fröding, Gustaf. *Dikter*. Stockholm: Albert Bonnier, 1948.

Frostensson, Katarina. *K*. Stockholm: Polaris, 2019.

———. *Tre vägar*. Stockholm: Wahlström och Widstrand, 2013.

Frye, Northrop. *The Great Code: The Bible and Literature*. New York: Harcourt Brace Jovanovich, 1982.

———. *Words with Power: Being a Second Study of "The Bible and Literature."* New York: Harcourt Brace Jovanovich, 1990.

Gale, Stephen, and Gunnar Olsson, eds. *Philosophy in Geography*. Dordrecht: Reidel, 1979.

Gasché, Rodolphe. *Geophilosophy: On Gilles Deleuze and Félix Guattari's "What is Philosophy?"* Evanston IL: Northwestern University Press, 2014.

———. *The Tain of the Mirror: Derrida and the Philosophy of Reflection*. Cambridge MA: Harvard University Press, 1986.

Gass, William. *On Being Blue: A Philosophical Inquiry*. Boston: David R. Godine, 1976.

———. *Reading Rilke: Reflections on the Problems of Translation*. New York: Knopf, 1999.

———. *Willie Master's Lonesome Wife*. Designed by Lawrence Levy. Photography by Burton L. Rudman. New York: Knopf, 1971.

Georgescu-Roegen, Nicholas. *Analytical Economics*. Cambridge MA: Harvard University Press, 1966.

Giacometti, Massimo, ed. *The Sistine Chapel: The Art, the History, and the Restoration*. New York: Harmony Books, 1986.

Gilgamesheposet: Han som såg Djupet. Nytolkning av Lennart Warring och Taina Kantola. Stockholm: Natur och Kultur, 2001.

Girard, René. *Job: The Victim of His People*. Translated by Yvonne Freccero. Stanford CA: Stanford University Press, 1987.

———. *The Scapegoat*. Translated by Yvonne Freccero. Baltimore: Johns Hopkins University Press, 1986.

———. *A Theater of Envy: William Shakespeare*. Oxford: Oxford University Press, 1991.

————. *Things Hidden Since the Foundation of the World*. Translated by Stephen Bann and Michael Metteer. Stanford MA: Stanford University Press, 1987.

Glacken, Clarence J. *Traces on the Rhodian Shore: Nature and Culture in Western Thought from Ancient Times to the End of the Eighteenth Century*. Berkeley: University of California Press, 1967.

Goethe, John Wolfgang von. *Faust. A Tragedy in Two Parts with the Unpublished Scenarios for the Walpurgis Night and the Urfaust*. Translated by John R. Williams. Ware, UK: Wordsworth Editions, 2007.

Golding, John. *Duchamp: The Bride Stripped Bare by Her Bachelors, Even*. London: Allen Lane, 1973.

Golding, William. *Lord of the Flies*. London: Faber and Faber, 1954.

Gombrowicz, Witold. *Ferdydurke*. Translation by Macgibbon and Kee. New York: Harcourt, Brace, 1961.

Good, Edwin M. *In Turns of Tempest: A Reading of Job with a Translation*. Stanford CA: Stanford University Press, 1990.

Gough-Cooper, Jennifer, and Jacques Caumont. *Ephemerides on and about Marcel Duchamp and Rrose Sélavy, 1887–1968*. Exhibition Catalogue, Palazzo Grassi, Venezia. Milano: Pompiani, 1993.

Gould, Peter, and Gunnar Olsson, eds. *A Search for Common Ground*. London: Pion, 1982.

Graeber, David, and Marshall Sahlins. *On Kings*. Chicago: University of Chicago Press, 2018.

Grafton, Anthony. *Leon Battista Alberti: Master Builder of the Italian Renaissance*. London: Penguin Books, 2002.

Graham-Dixon, Andrew. *Michelangelo and the Sistine Chapel*. London: Weidenfeld & Nicholson, 2008.

————. *Renaissance*. London: BBC Worldwide, 1999.

Granström, Erik. *Vanderland: Fjärde delen av krönikan om den femte konfluxen*. Stockholm: Coltso, 2016.

Greenblatt, Stephen. *The Rise and Fall of Adam and Eve*. New York: Vintage, 2017.

————. *Tyrant: Shakespeare on Politics*. New York: Norton, 2018.

Gren, Martin. *Earth Writing: Exploring Representation and Social Geography In-Between Meaning/Matter*. Gothenburg: Department of Human and Economic Geography, University of Gothenburg, 1994.

Grossmann, Reinhardt. *Reflections on Frege's Philosophy*. Evanston IL: Northwestern University Press, 1969.

Grootenboer, Hanneke. *The Rhetoric of Perspective: Realism and Illusionism in Seventeeth-Century Dutch Still-Painting.* Chicago: University of Chicago Press, 2005.

Habermas, Jürgen. *The Theory of Communicative Action.* Translated by Thomas McCarthy London: Heinemann, 1984.

Hansen-Møller, Jette. "Chiasm/Rubric." In Abrahamsson and Gren, *GO*, 204–25.

——— . *Den skjulte diagonal: En landskabsfortelling i ord og billeder.* København: Christian Ejlers' Forlag, 1995.

Haralambidou, Penelope. *Marcel Duchamp and the Architecture of Desire.* Farnham, UK: Ashgate, 2013.

Harari, Yuval Noah. *Homo Deus: A Brief History of Tomorrow.* London: Harvill Secker, 2015.

——— . *Sapiens: A Brief History of Humankind.* London: Harvill Secker, 2014.

Hare, R. M. *The Language of Morals.* New York: Oxford University Press, 1964.

Harries, Karsten. *Infinity and Perspective.* Cambridge MA: MIT Press, 2001.

Harvey, David. *The Condition of Postmodernity.* Oxford: Basil Blackwell, 1989.

——— . *Explanation in Geography.* London: Edward Arnold, 1969.

——— . *The Limits to Capital.* Oxford: Basil Blackwell, 1982.

——— . *Marx, Capital and the Madness of Economic Reason.* London: Profile Books, 2017.

——— . *Social Justice and the City.* Baltimore: Johns Hopkins University Press, 1973.

Hassan, Ihab. *The Dismemberment of Orpheus: Toward a Postmodern Literature.* New York: Oxford University Press, 1971.

——— . *The Right Promethean Fire: Imagination, Science, and Cultural Change.* Urbana: University of Illinois Press, 1980.

Haven, Cynthia L. *Evolution of Desire: A Life of René Girard.* East Lansing: Michigan State University Press, 2018.

Hegel, G. W. F. *The Phenomenology of Mind.* Translated by J. B. Baille. New York: Harper Torchbooks, 1967.

Heidegger, Martin. *Being and Time.* Translated by John Macquarrie and Edward S. Robinson. New York: Harper & Row, 1962.

Heidel, Alexander. *The Babylonian Genesis: The Story of Creation.* 2nd. ed. Chicago: University of Chicago Press, 1951.

——— . *The Gilgamesh Epic and Old Testament Parallels: A Translation and Interpretation of the Gilgamesh Epic and Related Babylonian and Assyrian Documents.* Chicago: University of Chicago Press, 1949.

Held, George F. "Parallels between the *Gilgamesh Epic* and Plato's *Symposium.*" *Journal of Near Eastern Studies* 42 (1983): 133–41.

Heller-Roazen, Daniel. *Dark Tongues: The Art of Rouges and Riddlers*. New York: Zone Books, 2013.

———. *Echolalias: On the Forgetting of Language*. New York: Zone Books, 2005.

Hellström, Hans. *Erik den helige: Sveriges skyddshelgon*. Stockholm: Veritas, 2011.

Hemingway, Ernest. *Across the River and into the Trees*. London: Jonathan Cape, 1950.

———. *The Old Man and the Sea*. London: Jonathan Cape, 1952.

Hess, Thomas B. *Barnett Newman*. New York: The Museum of Modern Art, 1971.

Hobbes, Thomas. *Leviathan*. Edited by C. M. Macpherson. London: Penguin, 1968.

Hodges, Andrew. *Alan Turing: The Enigma*. New York: Simon & Schuster, 1983.

Hofstadter, Douglas R. *Gödel, Escher, Bach: An Eternal Golden Braid*. New York: Basic Books, 1979.

The Holy Bible. New International Version. Grand Rapids MI: Zondervan Publishing House, 1972.

———. Revised Standard Version. New York: Thomas Nelson & Sons, 1959.

Homer. *The Iliad*. Translated by Peter Green. Berkeley: University of California Press, 2015.

———. *The Iliad*. Translated by Richmond Lattimore. Drawings by Leonard Baskin. Chicago: University of Chicago Press, 1962.

———. *The Odyssey*. Translated by E. V. Rieu. Harmondsworth: Penguin Books, 1946.

———. *The Odyssey*. Translated by Robert Fitzgerald. Drawings by Hans Erni. Garden City NY: Doubleday, 1963.

———. *The Odyssey*. Translated by Peter Green. Berkeley: University of California Press, 2018.

Homeros. *Odysséen*. Från grekiskan av Erland Lagerlöf. Lund: Gleerups, 1957.

Horkheimer, Max, and Theodor W. Adorno. *Dialectic of Enlightenment*. Translated by John Cumming. New Seabury Press, 1972.

Høy, Pia. *Det dekonstruerede maleri: Marcel Duchamps Étant donnés*. København: Ræevens Sorte Bibliotek, 2001.

Husserl, Edmund. *Cartesian Meditations: An Introduction to Phenomenology*. Translated by Dorion Cairns. The Hague: Martinus Nijhoff, 1973.

———. *The Crisis of European Science and Transcendental Phenomenology*. Translated by David Carr. Evanston IL: Northwestern University Press, 1970.

Hyppolite, Jean. *Genesis and Structure of Hegel's Phenomenology of Spirit*. Translated by Samuel Cherniak and John Heckman. Evanston IL: Northwestern University Press, 1974.

Irigaray, Luce. *This Sex Which Is Not One*. Translated by Catherine Porter with Carolyne Burke. Ithaca NY: Cornell University Press, 1985.

Jangfeldt, Bengt. *Språket är gud: Anteckningar om Joseph Brodsky*. Stockholm: Wahlström och Widstrand, 2010.

———. *Mayakovsky: A Biography*. Translated by Harry D. Watson. Chicago: University of Chicago Press, 2015.

Jensen, Ole Michael. "Red River Valley: Geo-Graphical Studies in the Landscape of Language." *Environment and Planning D: Society and Space* 11 (1993): 295–301.

———. "To be Human (the Secret of the Pyramid)." In Abrahamsson and Gren, *GO*, 349–63.

———. *Vægge Kundskabens projektioner / Walls: Projections of Knowledge*. Copenhagen: Scandinavian University Press, 1995.

Jensson, Gunnael. "Mappa Mundi Universalis: A Commentary on the Power of Carto-graphical Reason." Reprinted in Abrahamsson and Gren, *GO*, 315–33. (First exhibited in the Uppsala Cathedral, 2000, presently in the art collections of the Uppsala University.)

John of Damascus. *On the Divine Images: Three Apologies against Those Who Attack the Divine Images*. Translated by David Anderson. Crestwood NY: St. Vladimir Seminary Press, 1980.

Johnson, Eyvind. *Strändernas svall*. Stockholm: Albert Bonniers, 1946.

Joselit, David. *Infinite Regress: Marcel Duchamp 1910–1941*. Cambridge MA: MIT Press, 1998.

Joyce, James. *Finnegans Wake*. New York: Viking Press, 1939.

———. *Ulysses*. New York: Random House, 1934.

Kafka, Franz. *The Trial*. Translated by Illa and Edwin Muir. New York: Knopf, 1956.

Kandinsky, Wassily. *Concerning the Spiritual in Art*. Translated by M. T. H. Stadler. New York: Dover, 1977.

———. *Point and Line to Plane*. Translated by Howard Dearstyne and Hilla Rebay. Preface by Hilla Rebay. New York: Dover, 1979.

Kant, Immanuel. *Critique of Judgment*. Translated by James Creed Meredith. Oxford: Clarendon Press, 1952.

———. *Critique of Practical Reason*. Translated by Mary Gregor. Cambridge: Cambridge University Press, 1997.

———. *Critique of Pure Reason*. Translated by F. Max Müller. Garden City NY: Doubleday, 1966.

———. *Critique of Pure Reason*. Translated by Norman Kemp Smith with an introduction by Howard Caygill. New York: Palgrave Macmillan, 2003.

Karatani, Kojin. *Architecture as Metaphor: Language, Number, Money*. Translated by Sabu Kohso. Edited by Michael Speaks. Cambridge MA: MIT Press, 1995.

Kaufmann, Walter. *Nietzsche: Philosopher, Psychologist, Antichrist*. Princeton NJ: Princeton University Press, 1974.

———. *Tragedy and Philosophy*. Garden City NY: Doubleday, 1968.

Kazantzakis, Nikos. *The Odyssey: A Modern Sequel*. Translations into English verse, introduction, synopsis, and notes by Kimon Friar. New York: Simon & Schuster, 1958.

Kellner, Douglas. *Jean Baudrillard: From Marxism to Postmodernism and Beyond*. London: Polity Press, 1989.

Kierkegaard, Søren. *Fear and Trembling: A Dialectical Lyric*. Translated by D. F. Swenson and Walter Lowrie. Princeton NJ: Princeton University Press, 1941.

King, Ross. *Michelangelo and the Pope's Ceiling*. New York: Vintage, 2003.

Klemke, E. D., ed. *Essays on Frege*. Urbana: University of Illinois Press, 1968.

Knausgård, Karl Ove. *Min kamp 6*. Oslo: Oktober, 2011.

———. *Towards the Forest—Knausgård on Munch*. Oslo: Munch Museum, 2017.

Koerner, Joseph Leo. *The Moment of Self-Portraiture in German Renaissance Art*. Chicago: University of Chicago Press, 1993.

Koestler, Arthur. *Janus: A Summing Up*. New York: Random House, 1978.

Kojève, Alexandre. *Introduction to the Reading of Hegel: Lectures on "The Phenomenology of Spirit."* Translated by James H. Nichols Jr. Ithaca NY: Cornell University Press, 1980.

Kolakowski, Leszek. *A Leszek Kolakowski Reader*. *TriQuarterly* 22 (Fall 1971).

———. *Main Currents of Marxism*. Translated by P. S. Falla. Oxford: Oxford University Press, 1978.

Körner, Stephan. *Categorial Frameworks*. Oxford: Oxford University Press, 1970.

———. *Kant*. Harmondsworth, UK: Penguin, 1955.

Kripke, Saul. *Wittgenstein on Rules and Private Language*. Oxford: Basil Blackwell, 1982.

Kristensson Uggla, Bengt. *Kommunikation på bristningsgränsen: En studie i Paul Ricoeurs projekt*. Stehag: Brutus Östlings Bokförlag, 1994.

Kristeva, Julia. *Desire in Language: A Semiotic Approach to Literature and Art*. Edited by Leon S. Roudiez. Translated by Thomas Gora, Alice Jardine, and Leon S. Roudiez. Oxford: Basil Blackwell, 1980.

———. *Polylogue*. Paris: Éditions du Seuil, 1977.

Kronholm, Tryggve. *De tio orden*. Stockholm: Verbum, 1992.

Kuehn, Manfred. *Kant: A Biography*. Cambridge: Cambridge University Press, 2001.

Kuenzli, Robert E., and Francis M. Naumann, eds. *Marcel Duchamp: Artist of the Century*. Cambridge MA: MIT Press, 1989.

Kuhn, Thomas S. *The Structure of Scientific Revolutions*. Chicago: University of Chicago Press, 1962.

Kuryluk, Ewa. *Veronica and Her Cloth: History, Symbolism, and the Structure of a "True" Image*. Oxford: Basil Blackwell, 1991.

Lacan, Jacques. *Écrits: A Selection*. Translated by Alan Sheridan. London: Tavistock, 1977.

————. *The Four Fundamental Concepts of Psycho-Analysis.* Edited by Jacques-Alain Miller. Translated by Alan Sheridan. New York: Norton, 1981.

Lachterman, David Rapport. *The Ethics of Geometry: A Genealogy of Modernity.* New York: Routledge, 1989.

Lacroix, Alexandre, and Martin Legros. "Espèce d'espace." *Philosophie Magazine* 77 (2014): 30–37.

Lagerlöf, Selma. *Gösta Berlings saga.* Stockholm: Hellberg, 1891.

————. *Nils Holgerssons underbara resa genom Sverige. Del 1–2.* Stockholm: Bonnier (Läseböcker för Sveriges barndomsskolor), 1906–7.

Lakoff, George. *Women, Fire, and Dangerous Things: What Categories Reveal about the Mind.* Chicago: University of Chicago Press, 1987.

Lakoff, George, and Mark Johnson. *Philosophy in the Flesh: The Embodied Mind and Its Challenge to Western Thought.* New York: Basic Books, 1999.

Lang, Uwe Michael. *John Philoponus and the Controversies over Chalcedon in the Sixth Century: A Study and Translation of the "Arbiter."* Sterling VA: Peeters, 2001.

Larsen, Svend Erik. *Sprogets geometri: En analyse af sammenhæng og perspektiv i grundbegreberne i Viggo Brøndals sprogfilosofi.* Odense: Odense Universitets Forlag, 1986.

Latour, Bruno. *Facing Gaia: Eight Lectures on the New Climatic Regime.* London: Polity Press, 2017.

Latour, Bruno, and Peter Weibel, eds. *Iconoclash: Beyond the Image Wars in Science, Religion, and Art.* Karlsruhe: ZKM | Center for Art and Media, 2002.

Levi, Primo. *Is This a Man.* Translated by Stuart Woolf. New York: Abacus, 1979.

————. *The Periodic Table.* Translated by Raymond Rosenthal. New York: Abacus, 1986.

Lévinas, Emmanuel. *Collected Philosophical Papers.* Translated by Alphonso Lingis. Dordrecht: Martinus Nijhoff, 1987.

————. *The Levinas Reader.* Edited by Seán Hand. Oxford: Basil Blackwell, 1989.

————. *Proper Names.* Translated by Michael B. Smith. London: Athalone, 1996.

————. *Totality and Infinity: An Essay on Exteriority.* Translated by Alphonso Lingis. Pittsburgh: Duquesne University Press, 1969.

Lévi-Strauss, Claude. *The Raw and the Cooked.* Translated by John and Doreen Weightman. New York: Harper & Row, 1969.

Linde, Ulf. *De ou par Marcel Duchamp par Ulf Linde.* Stockholm: Konstakademien, 2011.

————. *Marcel Duchamp.* Stockholm. Rabén och Sjögren, 1986.

Łukasiewicz, Jan. *Elements of Mathematical Logic.* Translated by Olgierd Wojtasiewicz. New York: Macmillan, 1964.

Lyotard, Jean-François. *Les transformateurs Duchamp.* Paris: Editions Galilée, 1977.

Machado, Antonio. *Times Alone: Selected Poems of Antonio Machado*. Chosen and translated by Robert Bly. Middletown CT: Wesleyan University Press, 1983.

Magee, Bryan. *Confessions of a Philosopher: A Journey through Western Philosophy*. New York: Random House, 1997.

Mallarmé, Stephane. *A Tomb for Anatole*. A bilingual edition, translated and with an introduction by Paul Auster. San Francisco: North Point Press, 1983.

———. "Un coup de dés." In *Mallarmé*, translated and introduced by Anthony Hartley, 204–33. Baltimore: Penguin Books, 1965.

Malmberg, Carl-Johan. *Stjärnan i foten: Dikt och bild, bok och tanke hos William Blake*. Stockholm: Wahlström och Widstrand, 2013.

Malpass, Jeff. *Heidegger's Topology: Being, Place, World*. Cambridge MA: MIT Press, 2008.

Malpas, Jeff, and Karsten Thiel. "Kant's Geography of Reason." In *Reading Kant's Geography*, edited by Stuart Elden and Eduardo Mendieta, 195–214. Albany: State University of New York Press, 2011.

Mann, Thomas. *Doctor Faustus: The Life of the German Composer Adrian Leverkühn as Told by a Friend*. Translated by H. T. Lowe-Porter. New York: Knopf, 1948.

Marcuse, Herbert. *One-Dimensional Man*. Boston: Beacon Press, 1964.

Martinsson, Harry. *Aniara: En revy om människan i tid och rum*. Stockholm: Albert Bonnier, 1956.

Marquez, Gabriel Garcia. *One Hundred Years of Solitude*. Translated by Gregory Rabassa. New York: Avon Books, 1971.

Marx, Karl. *Capital*. Translated by Samuel Moore and Edward Aveling. New York: International Publishers, 1967.

Marx, Karl, and Friedrich Engels. *The Communist Manifesto*. Translated by Samuel Moore with an introduction by Stefan T. Possony. Chicago: Henry Regnery, 1954.

———. *The German Ideology*. Edited with an introduction by C. J. Arthur. New York: International Publishers, 1970.

Matsson, Olle. *Allt är gift: Om dödliga ämnen och deras roll i historien*. Stockholm Natur & Kultur, 2018.

Maturana, Humberto R., and Francisco J. Varela. *Autopoesis and Cognition: The Realization of the Living*. With a preface to "Autopoesis" by Sir Stafford Beer. Dordrecht: Reidel, 1980.

Mauss, Marcel. *The Gift: Forms and Functions of Exchange in Archaic Societies*. Translated by Ian Gunnison. Introduction by E. Evan-Pritchard. London: Cohen & West, 1966.

May, J. A. *Kant's Concept of Geography and its Relation to Recent Geographical Thought*. Toronto: University of Toronto Press, 1970.

McGinn, Colin. *Philosophy of Language.* Cambridge MA: MIT Press, 2015.

Megill, Allan. *Prophets of Extremity: Nietzsche, Heidegger, Foucault, Derrida.* Berkeley: University of California Press, 1985.

Melberg, Arne. *Försök att läsa Montaigne.* Stehag: Brutus Östlings Bokförlag, 2000.

Melville, Herman. *Moby-Dick: or, the Whale.* San Francisco: Arion Press, 1979.

Melzer, Arthur M. *Philosophy between the Lines: The Lost History of Esoteric Writing.* Chicago: University of Chicago Press, 2014.

Mendelsohn, Daniel. *An Odyssey: A Father, a Son, and an Epic.* New York: Knopf, 2017.

Merleau-Ponty, Maurice. *Sense and Non-Sense.* Translated by Herbert L. Dreyfus and Patricia Dreyfus. Evanston IL: Northwestern University Press, 1964.

———. *The Visible and the Invisible.* Translated by Alphonso Lingis. Evanston IL: Northwestern University Press, 1968.

Miles, Jack. *Christ: A Crisis in the Life of God.* London: William Heinemann, 2001.

———. *God: A Biography.* New York: Simon & Schuster, 1995.

———. *God in the Qur'an.* New York: Knopf, 2018.

Milner, John. *Kazimir Malevich and the Art of Geometry.* New Haven CT: Yale University Press, 1996.

Mitchell, Stephen. *The Book of Job.* Berkeley: North Point Press, 1987.

———. *Gilgamesh: A New English Version.* Simon & Schuster, 2004.

Mitrovic, Branko. *Philosophy for Architects.* New York: Princeton Architectural Press, 2011.

Moberg, Ulf Thomas. *Gunnar Ekelöf framför bilden.* Stockholm: Cinclus Förlag, 1999.

Moi, Toril, ed. *French Feminist Thought: A Reader.* London: Basil Blackwell, 1987.

Morris, Errol. *The Ashtray (Or the Man Who Denied Reality).* Chicago: University of Chicago Press, 2018.

Musil, Robert. *The Man without Qualities.* Translated and with a foreword by Eithne Wilkins and Ernst Kaiserby. London: Picador, 1979.

Nagel, Ernest, and James R. Newman. *Gödel's Proof.* New York: New York University Press, 1968.

Nancy, Jean-Luc. *The Ground of the Image.* Translated by Jeff Fort. New York: Fordham University Press, 2005.

Nehamas, Alexander. *The Art of Living: Socratic Reflections from Plato to Foucault.* Berkeley: University of California Press, 1998.

Netz, Reviel. *Barbed Wire: An Ecology of Modernity.* Middletown CN: Wesleyan University Press, 2004.

———. *The Shaping of Deduction in Greek Mathematics.* Cambridge: Cambridge University Press, 1999.

Netz, Reviel, and William Noel. *The Archimedes Codex: Revealing the Secrets of the World's Greatest Palimpsest*. London: Weidenfeld & Nicolson, 2007.

Newman, Barnett. *Selected Writings and Interviews*. Edited by P. O'Neill. Text notes and commentary by Mollie McNickle. Introduction by Richard Still. New York: Knopf, 1990.

Nietzsche, Friedrich. *The Birth of Tragedy*. Translated by Walter Kaufmann. New York: Vintage Books, 1967.

———. *Gay Science: With a Prelude in Rhymes and an Appendix of Songs*. Translated with a commentary by Walter Kaufmann. New York: Vintage Books, 1974.

———. *Thus Spoke Zarathustra*. Translated by Walter Kaufmann. Harmondsworth, UK: Penguin, 1978.

———. *The Will to Power*. Translated by Walter Kaufmann and R. J. Hollingdale. New York: Vintage Books, 1968.

Nilsson, Martin P:n. *Olympen*. Stockholm: Hugo Geber, 1919.

Norris, Christopher. *Derrida*. London: Fontana Books, 1987.

———. *Paul de Man. Deconstruction and the Critique of Aesthetic Ideology*. London: Routledge, 1988.

Oliva, Achille Bonito. *Figurabile Francis Bacon*. Milano: Electa, 1993.

Ollman, Bertell. *Alienation: Marx's Conception of Man in Capitalist Society*. Cambridge: Cambridge University Press, 1971.

Olsson, Gunnar. *Abysmal: A Critique of Cartographic Reason*. Chicago: University of Chicago Press, 2007.

———. *Antipasti*. Göteborg: Korpen, 1990.

———. *Birds in Egg / Eggs in Bird*. London: Pion, 1980.

———. "Chiasm of Thought-and-Action." *Environment and Planning D: Society and Space* 11, (1993), 279–94.

———. "Finding the Way." *The Arab World Geographer* 19 (2016), 105–11.

———. "Glimpses." In *Geographical Voices: Fourteen Autobiographical Essays*, edited by Peter Gould and Forrest R. Pitts, 237–68. Syracuse: Syracuse University Press, 2002.

———. *Lines of Power / Limits of Language*. Minneapolis: University of Minnesota Press, 1991.

———. "Skinning the Skinning." In *Spaces of Danger: Culture and Power in the Everyday*, edited by Heather Miller and Lisa M. Hoffman, 38–50. Athens: University of Georgia Press, 2015.

———. "Thought-in-Action / Action-in-Thought." In *Knowledge and Action*, edited by Peter Meusburger, Benno Werlen, and Laura Suarsana. Heidelberg: Springer, 2017, 67–88.

———. "Translation is Everything (including the art of making new boots out of the old ones)." *Historical Social Research* 42 (2018): 113–23.

———. "Untitled." *Environment and Planning D: Society and Space* 26 (2008): 752–57.

Ondaatje, Michael. *The Cat's Table*. London: John Cape, 2011.

Orwell, George. *Animal Farm*. New York: Harcourt, Brace, 1946.

———. *Nineteen Eighty-Four. A Novel*. London: Secker and Warburg, 1949.

Päbo, Svante. *Neanderthal Man: In Search of Lost Genomes*. New York: Basic Books, 2014.

Padovan, Richard. *Proportion: Science, Philosophy, Architecture*. London: E. & F.N. Spon, 1999.

Panofsky, Erwin. *Perspective as Symbolic Form*. Translated by Christopher S. Wood. New York: Zone Books, 1991.

Papafava, Francesco, ed. *The Sistine Chapel*. Florence: Scala, 1986.

Partouche, Marc. *Marcel Duchamp*. Marseille: Images en Maneuvres Editions, 1992.

Paz, Octavio: *Marcel Duchamp: Appearance Stripped Bare*. Translated by Rachel Phillips and Donald Gardiner. New York: Viking Press, 1978.

Peirce, Charles Sanders. "Logic as Semiotic: The Theory of Signs." In *Philosophical Writings of Peirce*, edited by Justus Buchler, 98–120. New York: Dover, 1955.

———. *Peirce on Signs: Writings on Semiotics*. Edited by James Hoopes. Chapel Hill: North Carolina Press, 1991.

———. *Reasoning and the Logic of Things: The Cambridge Conferences Lectures of 1898*. Edited by Kenneth Laine Ketner. Cambridge MA: Harvard University Press, 1992.

Pepiatt, Michael. *Francis Bacon: Anatomy of an Enigma*. London: Weidenfeld & Nicolson, 1996.

Perec, George. *Life a User's Manual*. Translated by David Bellos. London: Vintage, 2003.

———. *A Void*. Translated by Gilbert Adair. London: Harvill Press, 1994.

Pesoa, Fernando. *The Book of Disquiet*. Edited and translated by Richard Zenith. London: Penguin Classics, 2002.

Peterson, Jordan B. *Maps of Meaning: The Architecture of Belief*. New York: Routledge, 1999.

Phillips, Tom. *A Humument: A Treated Victorian Novel*. Fiftieth anniversary edition. London: Thames & Hudson, 2016.

Philo, Chris. "Escaping Flatland: A Book Review Essay Inspired by Gunnar Olsson's *Lines of Power / Limits of Language*." *Environment and Planning D: Society and Space* 2 (1994): 229–52.

———. "Gunnar Olsson, Figures of 'Madness' and a Form of Schizologie." In Abrahamsson and Gren, *GO*, 281–309.

———. "Reflections on Gunnar Olsson's Discourse in Contemporary Human Geography." *Environment and Planning D: Society and Space* 12 (1984): 217–40.

Pickles, John. *A History of Spaces: Cartographic Reason, Mapping and the Geo-Coded World*. London: Routledge, 2004.

Pirsig, Robert M. *Lila: An Inquiry into Morals*. New York: Bantam Press, 1991.

——. *Zen and the Art of Motorcycle Maintenance: An Inquiry into Values*. New York: Bantam Books, 1974.

Plato. *Collected Dialogues of Plato*. Edited by Edith Hamilton and Huntington Cairns. Bollingen Series 71. Princeton NJ: Princeton University Press, 1961. (Especially *Republic, Symposium, Timaeus*.)

——. *The Republic*. Translated with introduction and notes by Francis MacDonald Cornford. Oxford: Oxford University Press, 1941.

Platon. *Staten*. Översättning, förord och noter av Jan Stolpe. Stockholm: Atlantis, 2003.

Plotinus. *Enneads*. Translated by A. H. Armstrong. Cambridge MA: Harvard University Press, 1985.

Popper, Karl. *The Open Society and Its Enemies*. London: Routledge and Kegan Paul, 1945.

Potolsky, Matthew. *Mimesis*. New York: Routledge, 2006.

Pred, Allan. *Even in Sweden: Racisms, Racialized Spaces, and the Popular Geographical Imagination*. Berkeley: University of California Press, 2000.

Proust, Marcel. *Remembrance of Things Past*. Translated by C. K. Scott Moncrieff and Terence Kilmartin. 3 vols. Harmondsworth, UK: Penguin Books, 1983.

Pynchon, Thomas. *The Crying of Lot 49*. London: Jonathan Cape, 1967.

——. *Gravity's Rainbow*. New York: Viking, 1973.

——. *Mason & Dixon*. New York: Henry Holt, 1997.

Quine, W. V. *Word and Object*. Cambridge MA: MIT Press, 1960.

Railing, Patricia. *On Suprematism: 34 Drawings*. Forest Row, UK: Artists Bookworks, 1990.

Ramírez, José L. *Skapande mening—en begreppsgenealogisk studie av rationalitet, vetenskap och planering*. Stockholm: Nordplan, 1995.

Ramírez, Juan Antonio. *Duchamp: Love and Death, Even*. Translated by Alexander Tull- och. London: Reaktion Books, 1998.

Rayor, Diane J. *The Homeric Hymns: A Translation with Introduction and Notes*. Berkeley: University of California Press, 2014.

Reichert, Dagmar, Hrsg. *Räumliches Denken*. Zürich: vdf Hochschulverlag AG an der ETH Zürich, 1996.

Rewald, John. *The Paintings of Paul Cézanne: A Catalogue Raisonné*. Vol. 1, *The Texts*. Vol 2, *The Plates*. New York: Harry N. Abrams. 1996.

Ricoeur, Paul. *Memory, History, Forgetting*. Translated by Kathleen Blamey and David Pellauer. Chicago: University of Chicago Press, 2004.

Rojas, Carlos. *The Valley of the Fallen*. Translated by Edith Grossman. New Haven CN: Yale University Press, 2019.

Rorty, Richard. *Philosophy and the Mirror of Nature*. Princeton NJ: Princeton University Press, 1979.

Rothko, Mark. *The Artist's Reality: Philosophies of Art*. New Haven CN: Yale University Press, 2004.

Rotman, Brian. *Signifying Nothing: The Semiotics of Zero*. London: Macmillan, 1987.

Roudinesco, Elisabeth. *Jacques Lacan: Esquisse d'une vie, histoire d'un système de pensée*. Paris: Libraire Arthème Fayard, 1993.

Rushdie, Salman. *The Satanic Verses*. New York: Viking Penguin, 1989.

Russell, Bertrand. *A History of Western Philosophy; And Its Connection with Political and Social Circumstances from the Earliest Times to the Present Day*. New York: Simon & Schuster, 1945.

Ruthrof, Horst. *The Body in Language*. London: Cassell, 2000.

Sacks, Oliver. *The Man Who Mistook His Wife for His Hat and Other Clinical Tales*. New York: Summit Books, 1985.

———. *Seeing Voices: A Journey into the World of the Deaf*. Berkeley: University of California Press, 1990.

Sallis, John. *Being and Logos: The Way of Platonic Dialogue*. Atlantic Highlands NJ: Humanities Press, 1986.

Sands, Philippe. *East West Street: On the Origins of "Genocide" and "Crimes against Humanity."* New York: Knopf, 2016.

Sartre, Jean-Paul. *Baudelaire*. Translated by Martin Turnell. New York: New Directions, 1950.

———. *Being and Nothingness*. Translated by H. E. Barnes. New York: Washington Square Press, 1988.

———. *Mallarmé or The Poet of Nothingness*. Translated and introduced by Ernest Sturm. University Park: Pennsylvania State University Press, 1988.

Saussure, Ferdinand de. *Course in General Linguistics*. Translated and annotated by Roy Harris. London: Duckworth, 1983.

Schildt, Göran. *Cézanne*. Stockholm: Wahlström och Widstrand, 1946.

Schmidt, Lisa. *Radera: Tippex, tusch, tråd och andra poetiska tekniker*. Göteborg: Glänta Produktion, 2018.

Schopenhauer, Arthur. *The World as Will and Representation*. Translated by E. F. J. Payne. New York: Dover, 1966.

Schroeder, Frederic. *Form and Transformation in the Philosophy of Plotinus*. Montreal: McGill-Queen's University Press, 1992.

Schüssler Fiorenza, Elisabeth. *The Book of Revelation: Justice and Judgment*. Philadelphia: Fortress Press, 1985.

Searle, John R. *Speech Acts*. Cambridge: Cambridge University Press, 1969.

Sebald, W. G. *After Nature*. Translated by Michael Hamburger. New York: Random House, 2002.

———. *Austerlitz*. Translated by Anthea Bell. New York: Random House, 2001.

———. *Campo Santo*. Translated by Anthea Bell. New York: Random House, 2005.

Seife, Charles. *Zero: The Biography of a Dangerous Idea*. New York: Penguin, 2000.

Seigel, Jerold. *The Private Worlds of Marcel Duchamp: Desire, Liberation, and the Self in Modern Culture*. Berkeley: University of California Press, 1995.

Serres, Michel. *Angels: A Modern Myth*. Translated by Francis Cowper. Paris: Flammarion, 1993.

———. *Genesis*. Translated by Geneviève James and James Nielson. Ann Arbor: University of Michigan Press, 1995.

———. *Les origines de la géométrie*. Paris: Flammarion, 1993.

———. *Mapping*. Edited by Niran Abbas. Ann Arbor: University of Michigan Press, 2005.

———. *The Troubadour of Knowledge*. Translated by Sheila Glaser with the assistance of William Paulson. Ann Arbor: University of Michigan Press, 1997.

Shakespeare, William. *Julius Cæsar*. In *The Complete Works of William Shakespeare*, edited by Hardin Craig and David Benington, 719–43. Glenville IL: Scott, Foresman, 1973.

———. *A Midsummer Night's Dream*. In *The Complete Works of William Shakespeare*, edited by Hardin Craig and David Benington, 139–58. Glenville IL: Scott, Foresman, 1973.

Shattuck, Roger. *Marcel Proust*. New York: Viking Press, 1974.

Sheridan, Alan. *Michel Foucault: The Will to Truth*. London: Tavistock Publications, 1980.

Simmons, W. Sherwin. *Kazimir Malevich's Black Square and the Genesis of Suprematism 1907–1915*. New York: Garland Publishing, 1981.

Sloterdijk, Peter. *Bubbles: Spheres Volume I: Microspherology*. Translated by Wieland Hoban. Los Angeles: Semiotext(e), 2011.

———. *Critique of Cynical Reason*. Translated by Michael Eldred. Foreword by Andreas Huyssen. Minneapolis: University of Minnesota Press, 1987.

———. *God's Zeal: The Battle of the Three Monotheisms*. Translated by Wieland Hoban. Cambridge: Polity Press, 2009.

Sollers, Philippe. *Les passions de Francis Bacon*. Paris: Gallimard, 1996.

Solzhenitzyn, Alexandr I. *The Gulag Archipelago, 1918–1956: An Experiment in Literary Investigation, I-II*. Translated by Thomas P. Whitney. New York: Harper & Row, 1974.

Sophocles. *The Oedipus Cycle*. Harvest ed. Translated by Dudley Fitts and Robert Fitzgerald. New York: Harcourt, Brace, 1949.

Spencer Brown, G. *Laws of Form*. London: George Allen and Unwin, 1969.

Starobinski, Jean. *Montaigne in Motion*. Translated by Arthur Goldhammer. Chicago: University of Chicago Press, 2009.

Statten, Henry. *Wittgenstein and Derrida*. Oxford: Basil Blackwell, 1985.

Stein, Gertrude. *The Autobiography of Alice B. Toklas*. New York: Harcourt, Brace, 1933.

———. *Tender Buttons*. New York: Dover Publications, 1997.

Steiner, George. *After Babel: Aspects of Language and Translation*. New York: Oxford University Press, 1975.

Stella, Frank. *Working Space*. Cambridge MA: Harvard University Press, 1986.

Stevens, Wallace. *Collected Poems*. New York: Vintage, 1990.

Strawson, P. F. *The Bounds of Sense: An Essay on Kant's "Critique of Pure Reason."* London: Methuen, 1966.

Sussman, Henry. *Franz Kafka: Geometrician of Metaphor*. Madison WI: Coda Press, 1979.

Sylvester, David. *Looking Back at Francis Bacon*. London: Thames & Hudson, 2000.

Tarasov, Oleg. *Icon and Devotion: Sacred Spaces in Imperial Russia*. London: Reaktion Books, 2002.

Tate Gallery Trustees, et al. *Mark Rothko*. New York: Stewart, Rabori and Chang, 1996.

Taylor, Charles. *Hegel*. Cambridge: Cambridge University Press, 1975.

Taylor, Mark C. *Abiding Grace: Time, Memory, Death*. Chicago: University of Chicago Press, 2018.

Tegmark, Max. *Life 3.0: Being Human in the Age of Artificial Intelligence*. New York: Knopf, 2017.

Temkin, Ann, ed. *Barnett Newman*. Catalogue of an exhibition held at the Philadelphia Museum of Art. New Haven CT: Yale University Press, 2005.

Temple, Richard. *Icons: Divine Beauty*. London: Saqi Books, 2004.

Thordeman, Bengt, ed. *Erik den helige: Historia, kult, reliker*. Stockholm: Nordisk rotogravyr, 1954.

Tomkins, Calvin. *Duchamp: A Biography*. London: Pimlico, 1996.

Trotzig, Birgitta. *Dykungens dotter: En barnhistoria*. Stockholm: Bonniers, 1985.

Tyner, James. *From Rice Fields to Killing Fields: Nature, Life, and Labor under the Khmer Rouge*. Syracuse NY: Syracuse University Press, 2018.

Ulmer, Gregory L. *Applied Grammatology: Post(e)-Pedagogy from Jacques Lacan to Joseph Beuys*. Baltimore: Johns Hopkins University Press, 1985.

Ulven, Tor. *Replacement*. Translated by Kerri A. Pierce. Afterword by Stig Sæterbakken. Champaign: Dalkey Archive Press, 2012.

Vaihinger, Hans. *The Philosophy of "As-If": A System of the Theoretical, Practical and Religious Fictions of Mankind*. Translated by C. K. Ogden. London: Routledge and Kegan Paul, 1924.

Valéry, Paul. *Selected Writings*. Numerous translators. New York: New Directions, 1950.

van Alphen, Ernst. *Francis Bacon and the Loss of Self*. London: Reaktion Books, 1992.

Varela, Francisco J., Evan T. Thompson, and Eleanor Rosch. *The Embodied Mind: Cognitive Science and Human Experience*. Cambridge MA: MIT Press, 1991.

Vergil. *The Aeneid*. Translated by Sarah Ruden. New Haven CN: Yale University Press, 2009.

Vergilius. *Aeneiden*. Tolkad och kommenterad av Ingvar Börjeson. Stockholm: Natur och Kultur, 1988.

Vernant, Jean-Pierre, and Pierre Vidal-Naquet. *Myth and Tragedy in Ancient Greece*. Translated by Janet Lloyd. New York: Zone Books, 1988.

Verene, Donald Phillip. *Knowledge of Things Human and Divine: Vico's New Science and Finnegans Wake*. New Haven CT: Yale University Press, 2003.

Vico, Giambattista. *The New Science of Giambattista Vico*. Translated by Thomas Goddard Bergin and Max Harold Fish. Ithaca NY: Cornell University Press, 1984.

Vitruvius. *The Ten Books on Architecture*. Translated by M. H. Morgan. New York: Dover, 1960.

von Wright, Georg Henrik. *An Essay in Deontic Logic and the General Theory of Action*. Acta Philosophica Fennica, Fasc. 21. Amsterdam: North-Holland, 1968.

———. *Explanation and Understanding*. Ithaca NY: Cornell University Press, 1971.

Wakeman, Mary K. *Gods Battle with the Monster: A Study in Biblical Imagery*. Leiden: E. J. Brill, 1973.

Walcott, Derek. *Omeros*. New York: Farrar, Strauss and Giroux, 1990.

Watson, James D. *The Double Helix: A Personal Account of the Discovery of the Structure of DNA*. New York: Atheneum, 1968.

Watts, Michael J. "Of Bats, Birds and Mice." In Abrahamsson and Gren, *GO*, 143–54. Farnham, UK: Ashgate, 2012.

———. *Silent Violence*. Athens: University of Georgia Press, 1983.

Weber, Max. *The Protestant Ethic and the Spirit of Capitalism*. Translated by Talcott Parsons with a foreword by R. H. Tawney. New York: Scribner's, 1958.

Weiss, Jeffrey. *Mark Rothko*. Washington DC: Yale/National Gallery of Art, 1998.

Wellisch, Erich. *Isaac and Oedipus: Study in Biblical Psychology of the Sacrifice of Isaac— The Akedah*. London: Routledge and Kegan Paul, 1954.

Westin, Sara. *The Paradoxes of Planning: A Psycho-Analytical Perspective*. Farnham, UK: Ashgate, 2014.

Wheatley, Paul. *The Pivot of the Four Quarters: A Preliminary Enquiry into the Origins and Character of the Ancient Chinese City*. Chicago: Aldine, 1971.

Whitehead, Alfred North, and Bertrand Russell. *Principia Mathematica*. 2nd ed. London: Cambridge University Press, 1925.

Whitman, Walt. *Leaves of Grass*. "Death-Bed Edition" of 1881. New York: New American Library, Signet Classic, 1955.

Wikander, Ola. *Gud är ett verb: Tankar om Gamla Testamentet och dess idéhistoria*. Stockholm: Norstedts, 2014.

Wilden, Anthony. *System and Structure: Essays in Communication and Exchange*. 2nd. ed. London: Tavistock Publications, 1980.

Wittgenstein, Ludwig. *Philosophical Investigations*. Translated by G. E. M. Anscombe. Oxford: Basil Blackwell, 1953.

———. *Tractatus Logico-Philosophicus*. Translated by D. F. Pears and B. F. McGuiness. Routledge and Kegan Paul, 1961.

———. *Zettel*. 2nd. ed. Edited by G. E. M. Anscombe and G. H. von Wright. Oxford: Basil Blackwell, 1981.

Wittkower, Rudolf. *Architectural Principles in the Age of Humanism*. London: Alec Tiranti, 1967.

Wright, Robert. *The Evolution of God*. New York: Little, Brown, 2009.

Yates, Frances A. *The Art of Memory*. Chicago: University of Chicago Press, 1978.

Zeruneith, Keld. *Træhesten: Fra Odysseus til Sokrates; En bevidshedshistorie*. København: Gyldendal, 2002.

Zornberg, Avivah Gottlieb. *The Beginning of Desire: Reflections on Genesis*. New York: Doubleday, 1995.

Alpha and Omega

FRONT COVER

Théodore Géricault: *The Raft of the Medusa*. 1818–19. Oil on canvas. 491 × 716 cm. (cropped). Musée du Louvre, Paris.

PREFACE

Epigram: Marcel Duchamp: *Etant donnés: 1° la chute d'eau, 2° le gaz d'éclarage*. 1946–66. Exterior view. Philadelphia Museum of Art. Gift of the Cassandra Foundation 1969. © Succession Marcel Duchamp/BUS 2019.

PART I: RED RIVER WAKE

Epigram: *Möbius Band*. Bing images, www.videoblocks.com.

Emblem: *Erik den heliges relikskrin*. Reliquary in gilded silver, made by Hans Rosenfälth, 1574–79. 100 × 45 × 113 cm. Uppsala domkyrka. Photo by Olle Norling/ Upplandsmuseet.

PART II: NAVIGARE NECESSE EST

Epigram: *Janus*. Sculpture. Vatican Museums, Museo Chiaramonti. © Vatican Museums, all rights reserved.

Emblem: *Base Map of the Human Territory*.

PART III: CRYSTAL PALACE

Epigram: Teophil Hansen: *Pallas Athene Brunnen*. Statue in gold and ivory conceived in 1870, erected by Carl Kundmann, 1898–1902. At the entrance of the Austrian Parlamentsgebäude, Vienna. Bing images (cropped), www.videoblocks.com.

Emblem: *Self-Portrait*. Photomontage by Idun Wahlgren.

PART IV: ARCHIVES

Epigram: Marcel Duchamp: *Fontän*. 1917. Porcelain, 33 × 42 × 52 cm. Replica of ready-made executed by Ulf Linde, 1963. Signed by Marcel Duchamp in Milan, 1964. Moderna Museet, Stockholm. © Succession Marcel Duchamp/BUS 2019.

Emblem: *Sèvres Potpourri Vase in the Shape of a Ship*. 1764. The Walters Art Museum, Baltimore.

Given

Life is like a summer break that never ends, a throw of loaded dice, a game of ontological transformations, April the ideal time for friendly meetings. And just as bright-eyed Athene came in many shades, so do Christian Abrahamsson, Martin Gren, Fabian Svensson, Torbjörn Elensky, Sara Westin, Alf Ekström, Johannes Møllgaard, Eric Cullhed, all of them loyal squires, certified analysts of the professor's windmills. None comparable to Ole Michael Jensen, though, co-creator of the *Mappa Mundi Universalis*, the other half of the pseudonym Gunnael Jensson. And without Ole Michael there would never have been his son Mathias, expert helper with the computerized pictures. In addition, of course, there are the stories of *Enuma elish*, Gilgamesh, Genesis, and Exodus; the taboo-laden limits of Saussure, Plato, and Kant; the various floors of the Crystal Palace; the secret code to the non-public library. The giants stripped bare by the midget, even, nothing more sacred than the divider between sensible things and intelligible ideas.

Thus blessed—gratefully acknowledging Elizabeth Zaleski's editorial care and a grant from Riksbankens Jubileumsfond—may I now rest in peace content with whatever I have learned over the years, most of it given in foreign languages and faraway lands. Rich is the experience, hopefully never to leave me. Yet such is the art of memory that what was the last to be learned is the first to be forgotten, the metonymic associations as lively as ever, the names of the metaphoric detonators not always at hand. Therefore, when the curtain is finally closing, I am led back home not by the stellar constellation of Homer, Job, Plato, Kant, Joyce, Beckett, and Duchamp, but by the two poets Gustaf Fröding (1860–1911) and Nils Ferlin (1898–1961), the arkotect's house-tour a version of the latter's midnight whim:

> *Man dansar däruppe—klarvaket*
> *är huset fast klockan är tolv.*
> *Då slår det mig plötsligt att taket*
> *mitt tak, är en annans golv.**

And in the futile search for proper expressions I have often felt like his bootless boy:

> *Du har tappat ditt ord och din papperslapp,*
> *du barfotabarn i livet.*
> *Så sitter du åter på handlarns trapp,*
> *och gråter så övergivet.*

---

* They're dancing upstairs—sleepless / is the house between dusk and dawn. / Then it strikes me, alas / that the ceiling—my ceiling / is someone else's floor.

Vad var det för ord—var det långt eller kort,
var det väl eller illa skrivet?
Tänk efter nu—förrn vi föser dig bort,
du barfotabarn i livet.*

As to Fröding, the English fails me, the music of the Swedish taken-for-granted impossible to transcribe, no way of eradicating the distance between the powers I am writing *about* and the language I am catching them *in*, *homophrosynê* the Greek term for the perfect fit, the soul-searching monk a memento for future reviewers:

Den gode han är väl ej så god,
som själv han tror i sitt övermod.
[Och] den onde han är ej så ond ändå,
som själv han tror när kvalen slå.
Thy skall du ej mycket berömma,
ej mycket häckla och döma.†

Av jord är du kommen, ord skall du åter varda.‡

[Och de] satte fram bålar med vin, till bräddarna fyllda,
göto så dryckesoffer åt de eviga gudar,
främst av alla likväl åt Zeus' strålblickande dotter.
Natten gick hän, och det grydde till dag, och de seglade ständigt.§

---

* You've lost your word and your mem'ry-slip / you barefoot child in life. / Sitting once more on the grocer's steps / torn and inconsolably weeping. // What was the word— was it long or short / was it well or poorly written? / Quick now—before we chase you away / you barefoot child in life.

† Fröding, "En fattig munk från Skara," in *Dikter*, 93.

‡ From dust you came, to words you shall return.

§ And setting out the winebowls all a-brim / they made libations to the gods, the undying, the ever-new / most of all to the grey-eyed daughter of Zeus. / And the prow sheared through the night into the dawn. Homer, *Odyssey*, trans. Fitzgerald, bk. 2, lines 431–34.

Index

A = A, 75, 90, 92, 95, 96, 101, 102, 103, 106, 129, 146, 155

a = a, 77, 96, 98, 103, 118, 119, 121

Aaron, 30, 33, 34, 154; Moses and, 31

a = b, 75, 90, 95, 98, 101, 102, 103, 106, 118, 119, 124, 141, 144, 146, 157

Abraham (Abram), viii, 16, 37, 81, 166; God and, 17, 19–20; Isaac and, 17–18, 20

Abrahamsson, Christian, 195

the Absolute, 5, 95, 101, 103, 115

Abysmal: A Critique of Cartographic Reason (Olsson), viii, 82, 166

acheiropoieton, 121

Achilleus, 43

action: knowledge and, 116; thought and, 84

action-in-thought, 116

Adam, 13, 17, 125, 126, 158

administrative map, 56 (fig.)

adverbs, 132

Aeschylus, 43

affections in the soul, realm of, 49 (fig.)

Agamemnon, 42, 137

agora, 60, 82

Ahab, Captain, 84

Akedah, 17, 20

Alexander the Great, 51

Alexievich, Svetlana, 138

Almighty, 13, 17, 23, 26, 84, 92, 95, 126, 146, 154; categorization and, 96; image of, 101; laws and, 94; name of, 96

Anaximander, 67, 111

Angelico, Fra, 98, 104

Annunciation (Fra Angelico), 98

Anoikumene, 68

Antigone, 144

Anu, 8

Apocalypse, 139

Apollo, 119, 133, 134, 135

Apsu, 4, 9, 16, 29, 35; Enlil and, 13

apsu, 5, 164

Archimedean fix-point, 48, 51

Archimedes, deductions of, 111

architecture, 32, 48, 67, 112, 129

Arcimboldo, 83

Arendt, Hannah, 143

Aristotle, 44, 51, 59, 98, 112, 146; dialectics and, 58; difference/identity and, 115; Laws of Thought of, 53; Plato and, 48

ark, viii, 41, 126, 154

arkographers, ix, 29, 37, 44, 54, 113, 120, 158

Arkography: A Grand Tour through the Taken-for-Granted (Olsson), 82

arkologists, ix, 44, 54, 85, 112, 113, 158, 165

arkonauts, x, 113, 117, 120, 158

arkosophers, 154, 158
arkotects, 125, 158, 165, 196
the arts, 99, 100 (fig.), 119, 120, 125, 127
Athene, 47, 67, 82, 112, 113, 115, 119, 125,
    167, 195. *See also* Pallas Athene
Attic, 135–44, 155
Augustine, 140
aulos, 133, 134
Auschwitz, 20, 111, 131, 138

b = a, 141, 144
Babylon, 5, 104
Babylonian Captivity, 11
Babylonians, 14, 104; naming and, 5–6
Bacon, Francis, 79, 80, 81, 112; work of,
    79 (fig.)
Ball Room, 128–29, 131, 135–36, 145, 155
baptism, 99, 147, 148
Bar de Saussure, 44–46, 47, 48, 53, 67, 78,
    79, 85, 96, 118, 135, 140, 156, 157, 165;
    Plato and, 55
Bar-in-Between, 45, 47
Barthes, Roland: on language, 134
Basement, 61, 115–17, 154
Basement Corners: fix-points of, 118
    (fig.); signs of, 118 (fig.)
Beauty, 57
Beckett, Samuel, 46, 56, 78, 134, 196
Being: concept of, 59; God and, 92;
    modes of, 116
beliefs, 58, 62, 150; alternative, 116
Bible, 11, 24–25
Big Data, 124
Bin Laden, Osama, 142
Black Square (Malevich), 121, 122 (fig.), 165
Blake, William: on prisons/brothels, 131

Blindland, 54, 55, 56
Bloom, Harold: biblical authors and, 11
Bloom, Molly, 70, 130
body, stone and, 90
Boudin à la Méseopotamie, 5, 79
boundaries, 47, 53, 54, 55, 60, 71, 72, 78,
    82, 117, 148, 163
Brodsky, Joseph, 137
Buddha, 16
Bull of Heaven, 8
Byzantium, 145

Caesar, 75–76
Cain, 22
Canaan, 16, 34
canvas of canvases, 104
cartographical reason, 105, 108
cartography, 72, 84
Casey, Edward, 71
categorization, socialization and, 95
Cave, 63; allegory of, 50, 51, 60, 62, 65, 119
cave-dwellers, 64, 77–78
Cedar Forest, 7–8
Cézanne, Paul, 78–79, 81, 120
Chamber of Destinies, 4
"Chanting the Square Deific" (Whit-
    man), 121
Charon, 10
chora, 71, 155
Christianity, 145, 146; base map of, 148;
    function of, 103
Christians, 24, 152; *Akedah* and, 17
circumcision, 17, 28, 34, 47, 76
Citizen K, 25
civil law, 24, 29
Codex, 85

cognition, 73, 78; objects of, 57
commandments, viii, 23, 24, 26, 29, 31,
    112, 127, 146, 149, 153, 154
commonwealth, Hobbesian, 83
communion, 33, 99, 140, 146, 148, 156
The Communist Manifesto (Marx and
    Engels), 138
compass, 106 (fig.)
computer graphics, 155
Confession (Twenty-first century),
    156–57
Confessions (Augustine), 140
conjunctions, numbers and, 132
consciousness, 69, 82, 84; flow of, 70;
    unity of, 78
Constantine the Great, 145, 149, 150, 152
Constitutional Law, viii, 24, 25, 29, 33, 75,
    76, 78, 82, 99, 104, 122, 147, 151; formu-
    lation of, 94
Cornered Points of Distinction, 107 (fig.)
cosmic order, identities of, 156
Council of Babylonian Gods, 10, 13
Court of Power, 6
covenant, 11, 14, 17, 31
creation, 145; self-referential, 113, 128;
    stories, 3, 128
Creation of Adam (Michelangelo), 125,
    126 (fig.), 127 (fig.)
Creator, 153
Creon, 144
crimes against humanity, 142
criminal law, 24
critique, 26, 27, 76, 84, 142
Critique of Pure Reason (Kant), 68
Crystal Palace, viii, x, 85, 92, 93 (fig.), 94,
    95, 96, 98, 99, 101, 103, 104, 111, 112, 113,

115, 119, 127, 128, 134, 145, 154, 155, 156,
    157, 166, 196
Cullhed, Eric, 195
culture, 45, 92, 115, 130
Cyrus Cylinder, 15
Cyrus II, 14, 32

D (compiler), 11, 23
Damisch, Hubert, 49
Damkina, 4
Das Kapital (Marx), 136
Deafland, 54, 55, 56
death, 6, 9, 133, 139, 143
Dedalus, Stephen: on universe, 114
Deleuze, Gilles, 166
Derrida, Jacques, 119
desire, 16, 61, 66, 75, 83, 101, 112, 116, 135,
    146, 156; mimetic, 15, 45, 47, 114, 115;
    short-/long-term, 138
Destiny, 4, 42, 137
Deuteronomy, 24, 28; composer of, 11
dialectics, 13, 26, 50, 52, 58, 59, 65, 66, 118,
    130, 132, 134, 136, 137
Diana, 164
dianoia, 20, 57
difference, 53; identity and, 13, 23, 73, 75,
    90, 92, 115, 123–24, 154
Difference Formation, 10
Dionysos, 135
Divided Line, 55, 60, 62, 82, 104, 153
doctrine, 83, 103, 125, 153
Double Helix of the DNA Molecule, 124
    (fig.)
Duchamp, Marcel, xi, 46, 85, 98, 104, 120,
    165, 166, 196
Dyer, George, 81

E (Elohist), 11, 12, 19
Ea (storm-god), 4, 5, 14, 164
Eanna Temple, 6
Earwicker, H. C., 163
Ebstorfer Weltkarte, 54
Eden, 72
edging, 67–70
Egypt, 16, 25, 28, 30, 35; Israelites in, 29
eikasia, 56, 58
Einstein, Albert, 120, 123
Ekström, Alf, 195
Elements (Euclid), speech elements of, 104
Elensky, Torbjörn, 196
Elohim, 11
Endlösung der Judenfrage, 143
Enkidu, 7, 8, 9, 35
Enlil, 9, 13
Enuma elish, viii, 3–5, 16, 28, 35, 128, 196
Epic of Gilgamesh, 6–10, 35
Epimenides, 123
epistemology, 29, 49, 53, 55, 71, 142
Erasmus, 124
Erik, King, ix
Erik Translatus, 164
Esau, 21–22
étant donnés, 85, 166
Étant donnés (Duchamp), viii, 166
Ethics (Aristotle), 112
Eucharist, 101, 125, 151, 152
Euclid, 44, 104, 111, 141
Euripides, 43
Eve, 17, 125, 126, 158
Exodus, 23–35, 126, 128, 196; ark of, 154;
    composer of, 11
Experiencing the Inside, 156 (fig.)

Far-Away, 9

Father, 101, 121, 147, 148
Ferlin, Nils, 117, 196
Fifth Book of Moses, composer of, 11
Final Solution, 132, 143
Fingering Fingers (Michelangelo), 127,
    127 (fig.)
First Sacrifice, traces of, 114 (fig.)
fix-points, 98, 134, 155; Archimedean,
    48, 51
The Flaying of Marsyas (Titian), x, 80,
    133, 133 (fig.), 134, 135
Flood, 6, 14, 125
Fontana, Lucio, 122
Form, 59, 65; non-changeable, 61; objects
    of thought and, 58; pure, 57
Form of Forms, 59
Form of Goodness, 65
Form of the Good, 59
Fountain (Duchamp), xi, 165
Francis, Pope, 120, 122
Fröding, Gustaf, 196, 197

Garden of Eden, 13, 125
Gay Science, 142
Genesis, 10–23, 35, 90, 104, 124, 128, 196;
    composer of, 11; creation epic of, 14;
    historical setting of, 15; Lord of, 12
geography, 67, 68, 71; imagination and, ix,
    112; knowing, 111–12
geometry, ix, 50, 51, 119; Euclidean, 99;
    knowing, 111; post-Euclidean, 123;
    rhetoric and, 112
Gilgamesh, viii, 6–10, 196; Shamhat and, 7
Glaucon, 49, 50, 52, 59, 65; Socrates and, 58
God, 11, 22, 23, 24, 30, 44, 71, 101, 104, 147,
    148; Abraham and, 17, 19–20; ark and,
    154; Being and, 92; Constantine and,

152; dwelling place of, 26–27; finger of, 126, 127 (fig.); Greekjew and, 51; image of, 123–24, 154; imitation of, 13, 103; Job and, 36, 37; language of, 140; Man and, 35; mercy/compassion of, 126; Moses and, 25, 33, 34, 41; name of, 115; path of, 138; power of, 25–26; promises of, 16; stone tablets and, 33, 146; transformation of, 153; worshipping, 14–15. *See also* Lord; Lord God

goddess, 7, 67, 74, 85, 96, 113, 118, 157

Gödel, Kurt, 112, 123, 124

good, 12, 50, 51, 57, 59, 132

Goodness, 57, 58, 65

Goya, Francisco, 143

Grand Palais, 81

Greek Academy, 147

Greek House of Representatives, 49

Greeks, 44, 51, 197

Green Box (Duchamp), 85

Gren, Martin, 195

Grenzen, 71, 72

Guattari, Félix, 166

guilt, punishment and, 10

Gulag, 20, 131, 138

Hades, 139

Hall of Mirrors, 129

Heaven, 65, 138, 140, 142, 151; Earth and, 5

Hegel, G. W. F., 77, 137

Hell, 72, 142

Heraclitean, 59

Here Comes Everybody (HCE), 10, 163

"Here I am," 19

Hesperidian Gardens, 73, 158

Highest Court, 101

history, story and, 11

Hitler, Adolf, 94, 142

Hittites, 31

Hivites, 31

Hobbes, Thomas, 82, 83; Immanuel Kant and, 84; work of, 83 (fig.)

Holy Place, 32

Holy Spirit, 101, 121, 140, 147

Homer, 42, 112, 116, 196, 197

homo ad quadratum, 129, 135–36

homoousios, 101, 148; base map of, 149 (fig.)

homophrosynê, 197

homo sacer, 16

Houston Chapel, 123

human relations, 5–6

human rights, 15

Human Territory, ix, 55, 85

Humbaba, 8

Hutus, 32

I AM WHO I AM, 155

Icaros, ix, 113

icon (—), x, 100, 103, 133, 152, 153, 154, 156

iconoclasts, 152

iconodules, 151

iconophiles, 151

iconostasis, 139

identity, 46, 53, 81, 113, 127, 144; collective, vii, communicable, 114; difference and, vii, 13, 23, 73, 75, 90, 92, 115, 123–24, 154; existence and, 43; formulation, 116; imagined, 115; original, 116

idolatry, 11, 27, 33, 150, 152, 153

Idun, 158

image, 62, 63; mind and, 60

imagination, ix, 62, 63, 125, 141, 157; geography and, 112; individual, 56; synthesis of, 53 *imitatio dei*, 15, 103

impossibility theorem, 112

incarnation, 30, 114, 152, 153

index (=), x, 43, 98, 101, 103, 119, 125, 127, 134, 140, 141, 142, 157, 158

the Intellect, the Soul and, 62

Intellectual, image of, 148

intelligence, 42, 62, 65, 73, 81, 82; artificial, 155; possession of, 58

Intelligibility Region, 55, 57

intelligible, visible and, 57

Intelligible Region, 55

Inter-Esse, 148

invisible, 19, 29, 33, 51, 52, 55, 58, 67, 69, 70, 92, 95, 98, 101, 104, 125; visible and, 27, 79, 82, 146, 150

Isaac, x, 16, 19, 22, 68; Abraham and, 17–18, 20; Jacob and, 21

Ishmael, 84

Isis, 16

Island of Chapel, 111, 154

Island of Truth, ix, 74 (fig.), 75–78, 112, 157

Island of Truth-and-Power, 83

J (Yahwist), 11, 12, 23, 27

Jacob, 16, 37, 104; Isaac and, 21; power and, 22

Janus, 16, 116, 164

Jensen, Harald, 117

Jensen, Mathias Ruø, 155, 195–96; work of, 127 (fig.)

Jensen, Ole Michael, 87, 117, 195

Jensson, Gunnael, 85, 117, 166, 195; work of, 117 (fig.), 127 (fig.)

Jesus Christ, 101, 121, 139, 145, 146, 147, 148, 149, 150, 151, 154; imitation of, 103; John and, 140; presence of, 153

Jews, 24, 32, 104, 132, 148; *Akedah* and, 17; deportation of, 14

Jezebel, 139

jihad, 138

Job, 35–37, 104, 135, 196; God and, 36, 37

Jocasta, 144

John of Damascus, 152–54

John of Patmos, 139, 140

Jones, Jim, 140

Joshua, 34

Joyce, James, 56, 115, 163, 196; perfect writing and, 70

Kant, Immanuel, 53, 54, 67, 68, 72, 73, 77, 148, 164, 196; geography and, 71; original suggestion of, 75; philosophy of, 69; Thomas Hobbes and, 84; thought-and-action and, 84; work of, 69–70

Kierkegaard, Søren, 138, 148

Kik, Gitte, 117

Kim Jong-un, 30

King James Bible, 24–25

Kingu, 4, 5

knock-down argument, 130

knowledge, 53, 119; action and, 116; desire for, 61; gaining, 48, 61; modes of, 99; planes, 99; *a priori*, 70; scientific, 141; truth and, 58

Königsberger, 82–83, 157

Krapp, 167

Krapp's Last Tape (Beckett), 163

Kristallnacht, 143

Lacan, Jacques, 15–16, 44–45, 46, 48, 74

Lacanian Real, 47

Lakoff & Associates, Inc., 77

Lakoff Beach, 78

Lakoff Cape, 77
*La mariée mis à nu par ses célibataires,
meme* (Duchamp), 85, 98
language, viii, 129; power and, 94, 97; as
skin, 134
laws, 94–97
Laws of Thought (Aristotle), 53, 146, 149
Leader, 94, 95, 96
Lebensraum, 142
Lenin, Vladimir, 25, 137
Le Penseur (Rodin), 134
Let there be, 15, 22, 92, 103–4, 126, 140,
157, 166
Levi, Primo, 143
Leviathan, 84
Leviathan (Hobbes), 83 (fig.)
Library of Invisible Maps, 104
line, 50, 52; allegory of, 50; Ptolemaic, 51
Line of Trinity, 107 (fig.)
Lines of Power, 107 (fig.)
Lines of Projection, 107 (fig.)
Lord, 11, 12, 18, 19, 20, 22, 27, 29, 30, 35, 37,
94, 112, 124, 146, 147, 155; dwelling of, 32;
as Human, 127; identity of, 81; loving/
fearing, 96; machinery of, 26; Moses
and, 32, 126; power of, 25; Sabbath and,
28; slave-drivers and, 31. *See also* God
Lord God, 12–13, 16, 21, 27, 29, 33, 34, 81;
jealousy of, 26; Noah and, 14; Sabbath
and, 28; worshipping, 32. *See also* God
Luther, Martin, 94, 99, 124

Machiavellian Prince, 24
Mafioso, 9
Magritte, René, 114
Malevich, Kazimir, 121, 122, 165; works of,
122 (fig.)

Man, God and, 35
Mao Zedong, 25, 94, 136
Map of the Human Territory, 165
mappa, 51, 66, 67, 78, 82, 84, 85, 134, 147
Mappa Europœa Mundi, 103
mappa mundi, 72, 106 (fig.), 114
Mappa Mundi Universalis (Jensson), viii, ix,
54, 85, 87–108, 112, 117, 154, 165, 166, 195
mapping, 103–4; cartographical reason
and, 108; triangulation and, 108
map-room, 48, 53, 82, 85, 112
maps, 67, 74
Marduk, 4, 5, 12, 15, 16, 27, 35, 51, 119, 128
Mare Nostrum, 164
Marsyas, 133, 134, 135
martyrdom operations, 139
Marx, Karl, 77, 120, 122, 136, 137, 142, 150
mathematics, 57, 65, 119
Mecca, 94, 128
Mein Kampf (Hitler), 143
Melville, Herman, 84–85
Metamorphoses (Ovid), 133
metaphor-blindness, 125
metaphors, 26, 27, 75, 76, 85, 125, 130, 151;
casual, 45; likeness of, 95; visual, 58
metonymies, 75, 76, 150
Michelangelo Buonarroti, 120, 124–27;
work of, 126 (fig.), 127 (fig.)
Midas, King, 133, 134, 135
Mindscape, 3, 54, 56, 86, 148, 149
Möbius band, 105, 163–64, 166
Moby-Dick, 84
Mohammed, 94
Møllgaard, Johannes, 117, 195
monolatry, 26
monotheism, 12, 92, 115, 149
Mosaic law, 75

Moses, viii, 23, 24, 29–30, 42, 85, 104;
   Aaron and, 31; God and, 25, 32, 33, 34,
   41, 126; Israel and, 35; Levites and, 34;
   stone tablets and, 146; tabernacle of, 128
Most Holy Place, 32
Mount Ararat, 14, 125
Mount Moriah, 17, 37
Mount Olympos, 113, 116
Mount Sinai, 31, 32, 33
Müller, Max, translation by, 68–69
Munch, Edvard, 45, 80
Museum of Collective Memory, 85
Muslims, 24; *Akedah* and, 17
Mutt, R., 165

naming, 5–6, 23
Narcissus, 16, 47, 101
nature, 79; enlightened/unenlightened, 63
Nazi Germany, 32, 132, 137, 142
New Testament, 25, 98, 139
Nicaea, 62, 101, 145, 146, 148, 154
Nicene Creed, 146–47
Nietzsche, Friedrich, 71, 137, 141
Nile, 30, 35
Nineveh, 6
Noah, 9, 14, 125
noiesis, 58
North Pole, 51, 72, 104
North Star, 72
noumena, 69, 73, 77, 78, 79
nouns, 43, 105; abstract/concrete, 131
nous, 69
Nowhere, 25, 90
Numbers: composer of, 11; conjunctions
   and, 132

objects, realm of, 49 (fig.)

objects of thought, Forms and, 58
Odysseus, ix, 42, 81, 113, 157
Odyssey (Homer), 112
Oedipus, 43, 144
Oedipus Rex (Sophocles), 112, 143
Oikumene, 68
Old Testament, 25, 98, 125
Olsson, Gunnar, 87, 117
Olympians, 44
The One, 62, 63, 148
One and Only, 17
"On the Ground of Distinction of All
   Objects in General into Phenomena
   and Noumena" (Kant), 68
ontological transformations, 14, 16, 45, 49,
   131, 136, 150, 152, 153, 157, 158, 195; Archi-
   medean point of, 51; rhetorical art of,
   95; ruler over, 103–4; story of, 101
ontology, 49, 101, 142
Orthodox church, 32, 139
Orwell, George, 27, 139
Osiris, 16
Other, 137
Ovid, 133

pagans, 12, 151, 152
Paintings of the Prophets' Ceiling (Jensson
   and Jensen), 127 (fig.)
Pallas Athene, ix, x, 42, 43, 46, 85, 155,
   157–58, 165. *See also* Athene
Pan, 135
Paradise, 72
Pareto, Vilfredo, 136
Passions, 51, 52, 83
P code (priestly code), 11, 12, 14
Peirce, Charles Sanders, x, 98, 119–20,
   133, 142, 145

Peircean signs, 115, 119, 140, 141, 144, 154, 158

Peniel, 22

Pentecost, 140

Penthouse, 61, 136, 144–50, 154, 155, 165

Peoples Temple, 140

perspectiva artificialis/perspectiva naturalis, 49

Pharaoh, 30, 35

phenomena, 68, 69, 73, 77, 78

philosophers, 60, 61, 137, 145

philosophy, 23, 69

Pietà (Michelangelo), 121

Pinocchio, 51

pistis, 20, 56, 58

plane, 50, 52; Ptolemaic, 51

Planes of Knowledge, 107 (fig.)

Plato, 27, 44, 46, 49, 51, 52, 54, 56, 58, 59, 60, 61, 67, 68, 71, 73, 98, 142, 164, 196; Aristotle and, 48; base map of, 148; boundary of, 82; Cave and, 63, 119; Divided Line of, 104, 153; logos of, 116; Saussurean Bar and, 55; Sun and, 104; visible/intelligible and, 57

Platonic Form, 59

Platopolis, ix, 35–37, 47

Plato's Academy, 53, 111

Plotinian House, 62, 146, 153

Plotinus, 148; Cave and, 63; Neoplatonic blueprint of, 60; Saussurean rendering of, 62

Plurabelle, Anna Livia (ALP), 166

point, 50, 52

pointer of pointers, 104

Points of Distinction, 91 (fig.), 107 (fig.)

Points of Signs, 107 (fig.)

politics, 73, 97, 116, 141, 142, 150

Pol Pot, 94, 136

polytheism, 14, 16, 92, 115, 145, 149

Polytropos, 157

Pompadour, Madame de, xi, 166

Ponte Milvio, 151

Pontius Pilate, 147

Poseidon, x, 113, 157

power, 25, 150, 155; absolute, 92; adverb/adjective, 132; concept of, 60; geometry of, 108; language and, 94, 97; politics of, 51; as pronoun, 132; vision of, 84

Power of Identity, 10

prepositions, 132–33

projections, 98–99, 115, 116, 119, 127, 166

pronouns, 132

propaganda, 23, 129, 149

proper names, theory of, 96

Prophets' Ceiling, plan of, 120 (fig.)

Prophets' Hall, 117–19, 154

Province A, 56

Province B, 56, 57

Province C, 57, 58

Province D, 57, 58, 59

Ptolemy, 51

punishment, guilt and, 10

pyramid on granite base, 89 (fig.)

Pythagoras, theorem of, 123

Quod Moses velat Christi doctrina revelat, 125

Quran, 138, 142

R (Redactor), 11

Rainbow, 14, 16, 90

Raphael, 48; painting by, 48 (fig.)

reality, 64; truth and, 62

The Realm of *Kinds* of Cognition, 54–55
The Realm of *Objects* of Cognition, 54
Realm of Psychosis, 47
Realms of Cognition, 54–55, 60
reason, 57; cohesion of, 116
Rebekah, 21
Red River, 3, 6, 35, 73, 145, 164
religion, 100 (fig.), 116, 119, 120, 125, 127;
    ethics of, 99
remember/remind, 60
Renaissance, 72, 125
Republic (Plato), ix, 48–60, 98, 104;
    administrative map of, 56 (fig.);
    base map of, 54 (fig.); categories
    of, 49 (fig.); Divided Line of, 82;
    mapping of, 53–54; socioeconomic
    map of, 61 (fig.)
revelation, 44, 69, 79, 105, 122, 139, 140, 141
rhetoric, 26, 50, 58, 67, 95; geometry and, 112
Riemann, Bernhard, 141
Riksbankens Jubileumsfond, 196
Rockscape, 54, 55, 56, 85, 149
Rodin, Auguste, 134
Rothko, Mark, 79, 81, 112, 123; on paint-
    ing, 80; works of, 80 (fig.), 123 (fig.)
Royal Map Room, 82
Rudbeck, Olof, 73
Ruler, 5, 24, 51, 76, 78, 82, 129, 164
Russell, Bertrand, 96, 148
Rwandans, 32, 132

Sabbath, 28, 92
sacraments, 99, 153
Sarah (Sarai), 17, 20
Satan, 35, 121
Saturn Devouring His Son (Goya), 143
Saussure, Ferdinand de, 44, 48, 78, 164, 196

Saussurean Bar, ix, 44–46, 47, 48, 53, 67,
    78, 79, 85, 96, 118, 135, 140, 156, 157, 165;
    Plato and, 55
scale, 106 (fig.)
scale of scales, 103–4
The School of Athens (Raphael), 48, 48 (fig.)
Schranken, 71, 72
science, 99, 100 (fig.), 119, 120, 125, 127
Scream (Munch), 80
scripture, 126, 147, 153
Second Commandment, 149
Sensibility Region, 55, 56
Shakespeare, William, 42, 75–76, 142
Shamhat, Gilgamesh and, 7
Sharing Cross Station, 119, 154
The Sharing Cross Station and the Space of
    the Prophets' Hall (Jensson), 117 (fig.)
signified, 44, 45, 46, 48, 64, 67, 98, 114,
    116, 148, 151; ontology of, 115
Signifier, 44, 45, 46, 48, 64, 67, 98, 114,
    116, 148, 151; ontology of, 115
silence, physical/spiritual land of, 90
Simsalabim, 16, 157
Sîn-lēqi-unninni, 6
Sistine Chapel, 119, 125, 128
slaves, 5, 8, 31, 76
social engineering, 141, 142, 143
Socialist Internationals, 145
socialization, 97; categorization and, 95
social relations, 76, 142
social sciences, 96, 132, 142
Society of Independent Artists, 165
socioeconomic map, 61 (fig.)
Socrates, 49, 50, 51, 52, 59, 62, 65; Glau-
    con and, 58; mind/images and, 60
Sodom and Gomorrah, 16
Solomon, King, 12, 125

Son of God, 101, 121, 147, 148, 154
Sophocles, 42, 43, 112, 142, 143; religion
   and, 116
the Soul, 58; Intellect and, 62
Sphinx, 143
Spirit of God, 15
Stalin, Joseph, 27, 51, 94, 136, 142
Stieglitz, Alfred, 165
stone, body and, 90
story, history and, 11
suicide bombers, 138, 139
Sun, 58, 65, 104; analogy of, 50; Greekjew
   and, 51
*Suprematist Composition: White on
   White* (Malevich), 122, 122 (fig.)
Svensson, Fabian, 155, 195
symbol (/), x, 98, 100, 119, 133, 151, 156

tabernacle, 32, 85, 128, 165; ark of, 164
taken-for-granted, viii, 59
Ten Commandments, 23, 24, 31, 112, 127,
   146, 149, 154
terra incognitae, 53, 67
Territory of the Humans, 54, 148
terrorist bombers, 138
Testimony, 32
tetrahedrons, 85, 98, 112, 115, 127, 129, 154,
   155, 166
Thales, 67
that, 125, 144
that is *this*, 141
Theory of Form, 58
THIS, 114
this, 114, 118, 125, 128, 133, 136, 143–44
this is *that*, 114, 118, 128, 141
this is *this*, 114, 118, 128, 133, 138
Thoth, 119

thought, 58, 62; abstract, 78; action and,
   84; perceptual, 56; scientific, 57
thought-and-action, 147, 156
thought-in-action, 116
Three Studies for a Crucifixion (Bacon),
   79 (fig.)
Thyatira, 139
Tiamat, 4, 16, 29, 35
Timaeus, 148; *chora* of, 155
Titian, x, 80, 133, 134, 135; work of, 133 (fig.)
Tivoli, 129
topos, 3, 19, 49, 71, 155
totalitarianism, 27, 76
Travelogue, 35, 163
tree of the knowledge of good and evil,
   12, 125
triangles, 84, 92, 114, 115
triangulation, 103; geometry of, 51, 108;
   mapping and, 108
Trinity, 101, 147; line of, 102 (fig.)
Trojan War, 137
Trotsky, Leon, 137
Trump, Donald, 25, 30
truth, 95, 130; conception of, 84; knowl-
   edge and, 58; reality and, 62
Turing, Alan, 120, 123, 124
Tutsis, 32, 132
Tympanum, 45, 46, 78

United Nations, 15, 32
universe, 5, 60, 67, 83, 92, 103, 105, 114,
   115, 145
Unnamable (Beckett), 46
Untitled (Rothko), 80 (fig.), 81, 123, 123 (fig.)
Uppsala Cathedral, ix, 117
Ur, 16
Ur-shananbi, 10

Uruk, viii, 6, 7, 8, 10
Uta-napishti, 9, 10, 14
Uz, 104

Vatican, 120, 149
Veil of Veronica (Zurbarán), 121
veneration, symbols of, 151, 153
Venus, 96
verbs, 131
Versailles, 129
Vico, Giambattista, 15
Virgin Mary, 147, 151
visible, 55, 60, 65, 67, 95, 135, 148, 153;
    intelligible and, 57; invisible and, 27,
    79, 82, 146, 150
Vitruvius, 129, 132, 135

Washington, George, 45
Westin, Sara, 195

"What Is Orientation in Thinking?"
    (Kant), 72
Whirlwind Tour of the Crystal Palace,
    155 (fig.)
White Box (Duchamp), 85
Whitman, Walt, 21
witch-hunter, 23
Wittgenstein, Ludwig, 46, 54, 64, 68, 70,
    71–72, 75
Wittkower, Rudolf, 129
woman, creation of, 13
World Center, 75
worshippers, worshipped and, 152

Yahweh, 11, 12, 26, 104

Zeus, ix, 42, 157, 158, 197
Zurbarán, Francisco de, 121; work of,
    121 (fig.)

In the Cultural Geographies + Rewriting the Earth series

Topoi/Graphein: Mapping the Middle in Spatial Thought
Christian Abrahamsson
Foreword by Gunnar Olsson

Mapping Beyond Measure: Art, Cartography, and the Space of Global Modernity
Simon Ferdinand

Psychoanalysis and the GlObal
Edited and with an introduction by Ilan Kapoor

Arkography: A Grand Tour through the Taken-for-Granted
Gunnar Olsson

To order or obtain more information on these or other University of Nebraska Press titles, visit nebraskapress.unl.edu.

CPSIA information can be obtained
at www.ICGtesting.com
Printed in the USA
LVHW020910200221
679493LV00002B/2